# The Waterdrinkers

*By the same Author*

KING CHOLERA

*Manchester Public Librari*

TEMPERANCE ORATORS URGE THEIR AUDIENCE TO 'CLENCH THE NAILS' AND RENOUNCE DRINK

# The Waterdrinkers

*A HISTORY OF TEMPERANCE*

BY

NORMAN LONGMATE

*Illustrated*

HAMISH HAMILTON
LONDON

*First published in Great Britain, 1968*
*by Hamish Hamilton Ltd*
*90 Great Russell Street London WC1*


SBN: 241 01510 3

*Printed in Great Britain by*
*Western Printing Services Ltd, Bristol*

Good ale, the true and proper drink of Englishmen. He is not deserving of the name of Englishman who speaketh against ale.

—George Borrow, *Lavengro*, 1851

Lastly (and this is, perhaps, the golden rule), no woman should marry a teetotaller.

—Robert Louis Stevenson, *Virginibus Puerisque*, 1880

## Contents

*Foreword* xi
1. Jolly Good Ale and Old 1
2. A Moral Species of Beverage 13
3. Singing and Sprawling 23
4. Signing the Pledge 33
5. Jerusalem, Lancs 42
6. Throwing off the Shackles 52
7. Firing Bombshells 64
8. Going on Gloriously 76
9. The Drunken Committee 89
10. Mischief at St. Ives 98
11. The Greatest Man in Ireland 107
12. The Band of Hope 121
13. The Accursed Trade 134
14. The High Priest of the Water Pump 144
15. Flat Beer on Sunday 158
16. Prescribing Poison 172
17. Wine for thy Stomach's Sake 182
18. The Temperance Industry 192
19. Coffee at the Pub 203
20. Better Free than Sober 214
21. A Licence to do Harm 228
22. A Fight to the Death 242
23. The Greatest Enemy 257
24. Ten Minutes More 275

*A Note on Sources* 293
*Index* 313

## *List of Illustrations*


Temperance speakers in action *Frontispiece*

*facing page*

The signing of the first pledge 18
Church Street, Preston 18
The Cockpit, Preston 19
The first teetotal procession 19
The arrival of the Preston missionaries at Blackburn 50
An open-air meeting broken up by a bear 50
James Teare attacked in Somerset 51
A temperance meeting stormed in Essex 51
A London beer-shop, by Cruikshank 82
A London gin-palace, by Cruikshank 82
John Finch 83
James Silk Buckingham 83
James Teare 83
Thomas Whittaker 83
Father Mathew's medal 114
Father Mathew 114
The departure of Father Mathew for America 114
Father Mathew's birthplace 115
The Friary, Cork 115
Anne Jane Carlile 146
The Rev. Jabez Tunnicliff 146
A Band of Hope Procession 146
A Band of Hope meeting in Exeter Hall 147
The entrance to Exeter Hall 147
John B. Gough 178

Dr. Frederick Lees 178
Gough's meeting at Sadler's Wells 178
Gough's birthplace 179
Gough's home in Massachusetts 179
Joseph Malins 242
Sir Wilfrid Lawson 242
Nathaniel Card 242
George Cruikshank 242
A temperance rally near Chester 243
Cardinal Manning administering the pledge 243
The coffee room at Dorking 274
The temperance hall, Leicester 274
The Liberals versus Lansdowne 275

# Foreword

THIS BOOK is a history of the British temperance movement from its origins early in the nineteenth century until the present day. It is not a survey of drinking customs, nor an account of the licensing laws, though both subjects are at various times involved in the story.

Despite the importance of the temperance movement in British social life and politics during the nineteenth century this is, to the best of my knowledge, the first full-scale study of the movement to be published for many years. Two major propagandist histories were published during the 1890s and the first volume of a third, far more satisfactory, work appeared in 1933. Unfortunately this dealt only with the period up to 1899 and, according to private information given to me, because the author was critical of one section of the movement, pressure was successfully put upon him to abandon the book.

All these previous histories, and many minor works on similar lines, have been written by teetotallers who were concerned to further the cause they supported, though there are also a number of hostile contemporary studies, probably in some cases financed by the licensed trade. This book is, I believe, the first to be written strictly from the point of view of a historian who is not concerned either to advance or discredit teetotalism. I have not sought help at any point from the licensed trade, apart from the two untypical organisations of Trust Houses Ltd., and the Carlisle State Management Scheme, and though various members of the temperance movement have given me considerable assistance, they made no attempt to press their point of view upon me. As, however, previous historians of the movement have invariably explained their relationship to it, I should add that I come neither from a nonconformist nor from a drunken family, but belong to that category of moderate drinkers so despised by many teetotallers.

Within the temperance movement, although they would not, I am sure, wish to be associated with my conclusions, I am particularly grateful for the help of Mr. T. Garth Waite, Secretary of the United Kingdom Alliance, Mr. G. Thompson Brake, General Secretary of the National Temperance Federation, Mr. Edward Winkless, Secretary of the Western Temperance League, and Mr. Mark H. C. Hayler, Secretary of the World Prohibition Federation, still, in his eighties, a most vigorous advertisement for waterdrinking. For providing information, my thanks are also due to Mr. James T. Dick, General Secretary of the North of England Temperance League, Mr. William H. Jaffray, Secretary of the British National Temperance League, Mr. Christopher G. Peet, Grand Superintendent, Public Relations, of the Grand Lodge of England of the International Order of Good Templars, and Mr. Douglas Carr, High Secretary of the Independent Order of Rechabites. Mr. Meredith Whittaker of Scarborough went to great trouble to provide me with much unpublished material about his great-grandfather, Thomas Whittaker; Canon W. E. F. Walters of Wellesbourne kindly brought my knowledge of *The Boar's Head*, Hampton Lucy, up to date; Mrs. Ida Payne of Trust Houses Ltd. made available some details of the early history of the company; Mr. E. M. Kemp, Archivist of Thomas Cook and Son Ltd., supplied me with details of the first Thomas Cook's connection with the temperance movement; Mr. D. A. Daniels of Joseph Terry and Sons Ltd. sent me a set of temperance lozenges; Mr. J. N. Adams, its General Manager, gave me much information on the Carlisle and District State Management Scheme, as did Miss Tufnell of the Home Office; and Mrs. Lorna Callingham of the Liberal Party Information Department was also most helpful.

I am also in the debt of all those who loaned me, or borrowed for me, books or illustrations, or allowed me to make use of their copyright material. In addition to those already named, my thanks are due to Mr. G. E. Davidson; Mr. John D. Beasley, Office Secretary of the United Kingdom Band of Hope Union; Miss Jane A. Downton and the staff of the Harris Public Library, Preston; Mr. R. J. Smirk and the Record and Survey Committee of the Preston Scientific Society; Mr. Brian W. Preston, Deputy Curator of the Harris Museum and Art Gallery, Preston; Mr. T. Walsh, Local History Librarian of the Manchester Public Libraries; the Birmingham Central Reference Library; Miss Jane McBain; Blackie and Son Ltd.; the Wellcome Trustees; and the staff of the BBC Library. Mr. R. J. Roberts of the British Museum kindly obtained for me some pamphlets on Jonathan Turner not in the Museum, and I am grateful to all who helped in my, finally unsuccessful, search for a drawing of Turner, including the Rev. R. Hubert Luke of Truro, the Rev. Thomas Shaw of Redruth, and the Methodist Archives and Research Centre.

I have occasionally modernised the punctuation of extracts where the original was misleading and have adopted throughout the modern spelling of 'teetotaller', though in the early days the normal form was 'tee-totaler' and the single and double 'l' occur indiscriminately throughout the nineteenth century and were still both in use in *Hansard* in 1961. The word 'waterdrinker' also appeared in the past as 'water drinker' and 'water-drinker'; as it has dropped out of use I have adopted the form I prefer.

February 1968 N.R.L.

have [illegible] musical illustrations to those already many- [illegible] to Mr G. F. Davidson; Mr John R. [illegible] Officer Secretary of the United Kingdom Band of Hope Union [illegible] and the staff of the [illegible] Library [illegible] and the Portland [illegible] Committee of the [illegible] Temperance Society; Mr [illegible] [illegible] Library; Curator of the Laing Museum and Art Gallery [illegible] Librarian of the Manchester Public Libraries, the Birmingham Central Reference Library, the late William Jackson and [illegible] the [illegible] staff of the BBC Library; Mr [illegible] British Museum kindly [illegible] for me [illegible]

I have occasionally modernized the punctuation of extracts [illegible] original way of spelling [illegible] have altered through- [illegible]

February 1966

*Chapter One*

# JOLLY GOOD ALE AND OLD

'Though I go bare, take ye no care,
I am nothing acold:
I stuff my skin, so full within,
Of jolly good ale and old.'

— WILLIAM STEVENSON,
*Gammer Gurton's Needle*, *c.* 1551

ALCOHOL IS almost as old as man. Stone-age man may have discovered for himself that grapes left to ferment produced a beverage pleasant to the taste and intoxicating to the senses, and long before Biblical times, around 1000 B.C., it was a normal article of diet. 'A plea for the use of intoxicating liquors', complained a temperance historian in the nineteenth century, 'has sometimes been advanced on the grounds of its antiquity and prevalence. Historical evidence . . . does not stretch farther back than the days of Noah, who "drank of the wine and was drunken"—surely an ominous example of cause and consequence.' China, Assyria, Egypt and India were in turn said to have been addicted to drinking while, according to the same author, 'the overthrow of Babylon was the natural consequence of vinous licentiousness'.

Wine was probably introduced into the British Isles by the Romans, but the previous inhabitants had already discovered alcohol in another form. As a first-century writer commented: 'Their ordinary drink was water. Upon extraordinary occasions they drank a kind of fermented liquor, made of barley, honey or apples', clearly referring to ale, mead and cider.

In A.D. 81 the Emperor Domitian launched a massive attack on excessive drinking, ordering half the vineyards in the Roman Empire to be destroyed and forbidding the planting of any further vines without his permission, an edict not formally revoked until 200 years later, when vines became a common sight in England.

The most comprehensive histories of drinking in England were written in Victorian times by temperance reformers, to whom English history was a long series of disasters, all due to drink. These writers recalled with relish how the monster Grendel, in the poem 'Beowulf', written about A.D. 800, slew the warriors carousing in the 'great mead hall' and how the Britons were beaten by the Saxons after getting drunk the night before an important battle. Another poem described

> This hearth: no shout of heroes now adheres to it
> More usual on its floor
> Was the mead; and the inebriated warriors.

The monk Gildas, writing around the year 540, recorded how 'Not only the laity but Our Lord's own flock and its shepherds . . . slumbered away their time in drunkenness as if they had been dipped in wine . . . If any monk through drinking too freely gets thick of speech so that he cannot join in the psalms', he advised, 'he is to be deprived of his supper.' For centuries church festivals, such as the consecration of a cathedral, were often marred by scenes of drunkenness in which the clergy took the lead, although an eighth-century edict warned that drunken bishops would be deposed and forbade any priest to frequent a tavern. In fact the tavern was often kept by the parish priest, just as the monasteries, accommodating travellers, were the inns of the time.

King Sweyne of Denmark was said to have decided in A.D. 1000 to invade England after learning that King Ethelred was 'a driveller, wholly given up to wine', and drink was, of course, responsible for the Norman Conquest, for the English soldiers spent the night before the Battle of Hastings drinking, while the Normans devoted it to fasting and prayer.

After the Conquest, so temperance writers claimed, it was the drunkenness of the crew of *The White Ship* in 1120 which caused the death of the king's heir, Prince William, and thus civil war fifteen years later, over the disputed succession, and drink which undermined the health of Richard I so that he died in 1199 from a wound received in the Crusades. This in turn paved the way for the disastrous John—though his premature death in 1216, from a surfeit of new ale, should surely have been placed to alcohol's credit.

Before the Conquest, King Edgar, who died in 975, had tried to limit the number of ale-houses to one per village and had ordered that all drinking horns should contain a row of pegs or 'pins' and that no man should in one draught drink beyond the next mark—about a modern half-pint. Pin-drinking, however, soon became regarded as a challenge. Men competed to see who could uncover the most pins at a sitting, and expressions such as 'He is in a merry pin' or 'He is pin-drunk' passed into the language, until in 1102 the Archbishop of Canterbury ordered 'That priests go not to drinking bouts, nor drink to pegs.'

The celebration of Church wakes, a term derived from the 'watch' or vigil kept in Church before a major saint's day, was a frequent cause of complaint by the higher clergy. In the course of time those attending 'fell to letcherie and songs and daunses, with harping and piping and also to glotony and sinne' and the Church only succeeded in suppressing the wakes by substituting another festival like 'St. Bartholomew's Fair' or 'Michaelmas Fair'. Almost as troublesome was the 'ale' or 'merry gathering'. There were church-ales, at which every parishioner was expected to contribute a fixed sum to the church, bride-ales, at which, in return for gifts of money, a bride offered the beer she had brewed herself, tithe-ales, lamb-ales and leet-ales. At scot-ales the expenses were shared among all those participating, and, according to Archbishop Edmund in 1156, 'all . . . are obliged to drink equal draughts and he carries away the credit who hath made the most drunk'.

The taxation and regulation of the drink trade have a long history. King John imposed a primitive form of duty on imported wines around the year 1200, claiming one tun (about 250 gallons) of every cargo carried aft of the mast, and later in the century a duty varying from one penny to two shillings a tun was levied. Most early licensing legislation was, however, designed to protect the drinker rather than the public at large, ale-conners being appointed in the fifteenth century who swore an oath to check the quality of all beer sold. Signboards probably came into use at this time, the brewer being required to hoist a sign while brewing was in progress so the inspectors could call; later it became a permanent fixture. Control at this early stage was essentially local. Some justices suppressed surplus ale-houses, or demanded sureties of good behaviour from ale-house keepers, and in 1428 the Corporation of Hull forbade vintners or ale-house keepers to open on Sunday.

Although the chronicler Holinshed recorded around 1580 fifty-six 'small' or light wines in use in England, including 'theologicum' from the few surviving monastic vineyards, and thirty heavier ones, such as sack and malmsey, roughly resembling modern sherry, ale was by now the supreme English drink. The ales of the Middle Ages had been heavy and sweet, spices being added to give an edge to their taste, but ale with a sharper taste, known as beer and flavoured with hops, was introduced from the Low Countries during the fifteenth century. Hops were first grown here in Henry VIII's reign, according to the traditional rhyme:

Hops, Reformation, bays and beer
Came to England all in one year.

When in 1555 Philip of Spain married Mary I he tried to demonstrate that he was a true Englishman by drinking ale, instead of wine, at a public dinner. He could have chosen from one of many varieties: single-beer or 'small ale', double-beer, double-double-double-beer, dagger-ale, 'mad-dog', 'angel's food' and 'dragon's milk'. From this period, too, dates the first surviving English drinking song of any merit. Its somewhat dyspeptic opening

I cannot eat but little meat,
My stomach is not good . . .

and its defiant conclusion

Back and side go bare, go bare,
Both foot and hand go cold:
But belly God send thee good ale enough,
Whether it be new or old

led a Victorian temperance writer to comment sourly that it well illustrated 'the tippling propensity, with its evil consequences, moral and physical'.

The growing consumption of beer and the spread of ale-houses, often kept by clergy left destitute by the Reformation, led to the first major Licensing Act in 1552, followed two years later by a second. These laid down the principles of control of the liquor trade which have survived to the present day. To open a 'tippling-house' a licence from the justices was needed and it required annual renewal, which the justices could refuse at their discretion, often exercised when the house had been badly run or was surplus to local requirements. The justices could also impose any conditions they liked, concerning, for example, opening days or hours or a ban on games, music or dancing on the premises. There were no national rules. An ale-house might be open twenty-four hours a day, seven days a week, in one parish and close early in the evening on weekdays, and all day Sundays, in the next. One almost universal requirement, however, was that licensed premises should be in a spot open to observation, and consist of good-sized rooms where villains could not conspire unseen.

Ale-houses were often identified by red paint on the window frames and in 1632 Thomas Dekker wrote that 'a whole street was in some places but a continuous ale-house, not a shop to be seen between red lattice and red lattice'. Wine-shops were usually called 'taverns', an eighteenth-century writer explaining that a tavern was 'a degree . . . above an ale-house, where men are drunk with more credit and apology'. A new Act limited the number of taverns, from two in certain small places to forty in the City of London, and ordered all taverns to be suppressed except in boroughs and market towns. The legislation was not successful and in the eighteenth century the taverns, too, came under the control of the justices, who were kept up to the mark by orders from the Privy Council, by royal proclamations, and by the assize judges on circuit, who admonished lax magistrates and themselves suppressed particularly troublesome ale-houses.

During Queen Elizabeth's reign drunkenness became a national problem, being blamed, like the later introduction of spirits, on foreign influence. One writer explained that 'Superfluity of drink is a sin that, ever since we mixed ourselves with the Low Countries, is counted honourable, but before we knew their lingering wars, was held in the highest degree of hatred.'

The early reign of James I was marked by an incident which was still doing duty in a temperance textbook in the twentieth century, although it had occurred in 1606 when James entertained the King of Denmark:

> After dinner the representation of Solomon, his temple, and the coming of the Queen of Sheba, was made . . . The lady who did play the Queen's part did carry most precious gifts to both their majesties, but forgetting the steps arising to the canopy, overset her caskets in His Danish Majesty's lap and fell at his feet . . . Much was the hurry and confusion—cloths and napkins were at hand to make all clean. His Majesty then got up and would dance with the Queen of Sheba, but he fell down . . . and was carried to his inner chamber. The entertainment and show went forward and most of the presenters went backward or fell down, wine did so occupy their upper chambers . . . The gunpowder fright is out of all our heads and we are going hereabouts as if the devil were contriving every man should blow himself up by wild riot, excess and devastation of wine and intemperance.

A few years after the scene described above a contemporary observer was remarking, in *England's Bane, or the Description of Drunkenness*: 'There are in London drinking schools: so that drunkenness is professed with us a liberal art and science.' He recorded one of the customs of the time, 'drinking for a muzzle', which required the first man to drink one pint, the second two pints, the third three, and so on round the circle until seven was reached, when they started again. It was said that prodigious quantities of from twenty-one to thirty-six pints a head had been drunk at a sitting. *The Drunkard Opened*, published in 1635, listed some of the numerous euphemisms then in use to indicate intoxication: 'He is foxt, he is flustered, he is subtle, cupshot, he hath seene the French king, he hath swallowed ... a tavern-token, he hath whipt the cat, he hath been at the scriveners ... he ... is bit by a barne-weasell.'

For those who were bit by the barne-weasell too often or too publicly the penalty, under a law of 1604, was a fine of five shillings or six hours in the stocks. This was a good deal more lenient than the Elizabethan custom of making offenders parade through the streets in 'the drunkard's cloak', a barrel with the bottom knocked out and holes cut in its sides for the arms.

In the Civil War, which broke out in 1642, both sides contained a strong temperance element, for Charles I, unusually for an English king, was highly abstemious, while Oliver Cromwell enforced rigid rules against drunkenness in his New Model Army. Nevertheless heavy drinking continued and to this period belongs the Everlasting Club devoted to singing and drinking. The members were divided into shifts and as one shift staggered off duty another moved in to take its place, so that the work of celebration went on round the clock. In its brief existence the Club was said to have 'smoked fifty tons of tobacco, drank 30,000 bottles of ale, 1,000 hogsheads of red port and 200 barrels of brandy'. A Frenchman writing home during the Commonwealth recorded: 'Drinking is the afternoon diversion ... As for taverns, London is composed of them.'

The Restoration of Charles II in 1660 was celebrated with such hard drinking that the king himself issued a Proclamation complaining of those 'giving no other evidence of their affection to us but in drinking our health', and even the liberal-minded Pepys confided to his diary that so prevalent were 'the vices of drinking, swearing and loose amours that I know not what will be the end of it but confusion'.

From court a spirit of laxness in private behaviour spread into every section of society. Taverns multiplied in the towns and in the country licences were granted almost on demand. Spirits were now becoming more popular—one church, which in 1639 had given a visiting preacher a quart of sack, now in 1691 presented him with a pint of French brandy—while the first non-alcoholic stimulants also made their appearance. Coffee, tea and chocolate were all introduced into the British Isles between about 1650 and 1660—the year in which Pepys drank tea for the first time—and the coffee-house became an important feature of social life. Defoe, writing of Shrewsbury in 1714, noted that there were 'the most coffee-houses . . . that ever I saw in any town, but when you come into them they are but ale-houses, only they think that the name of coffee-house gives them a better air'. The coffee-house was not, however, subject to the licensing laws, although tea, coffee and chocolate were considered luxuries, qualifying for far heavier taxation than such necessities as beer.

The new drinks, later often recommended as sober alternatives to alcohol, did not escape vigorous criticism. Because of tea, wrote the philanthropist Jonas Hanway in 1757, already an object of public derision because he had pioneered the use of the umbrella, men were losing their stature, women their beauty, and

> the very chambermaids their bloom . . . Will the sons and daughters of this happy isle for ever submit to the bondage of so tyrannical a custom as drinking tea? . . . It is an epidemical disease . . . You may see labourers who are mending the roads drinking their tea . . . it is even . . . sold out of cups to haymakers . . . Were they the sons of tea-sippers who won the fields of Crécy and Agincourt or dyed the Danube's shores with Gallic blood?

So far drinking in England had almost exclusively involved fermented liquors, beverages such as wine, beer, mead and cider that were produced by relatively natural processes, from the basic fruits of the earth. At an early date, man discovered how to produce the other great category of alcoholic drinks, distilled liquors, or spirits. Distillation depends on the fact that if a liquid containing alcohol, such as wine, is heated and the resulting vapour condensed, a purer and more powerful form of alcohol is produced, though unpalatable until flavouring ingredients have been added. Thus, it was later suggested, spirits were 'unnatural', while beer and wine were not. Fermented liquors, it was argued, had been made by God; distilled spirits were the work of man.

The first spirits may have been produced in Ceylon and India as early as 800 B.C., but temperance historians usually credit the Arabs, around A.D. 800, with the discovery. Italy was turning wine into brandy by 1100 and the Irish ale into 'usquebaugh', later corrupted into 'whisky', which was first produced in Scotland around 1500. In the Middle Ages spirits were recommended as love potions or elixirs of life, and in Elizabeth's reign they were stocked by apothecaries, as aqua-vitae, 'the water of life'. A hard-selling advertisement for aqua-vitae claimed that 'It sloweth age; it strengtheneth youth; it helpeth digestion... it abandoneth melancholie; it relisheth the heart; it lighteneth the mind; it quickeneth the spirits;... it keepeth the hands from shivering, the sinews from shrinking, the veins from crumbling, the bones from aching.' Rum was being manufactured from sugar cane in the West Indies by 1647, where it was known as 'rumbullion' or 'kill-devil' and where English sailors acquired a taste for it. In 1740 Admiral Vernon, known as 'old grog' because of his grogram coat, ordered that the rum ration should be diluted with water, the mixture being labelled 'grog', but it was not till the nineteenth century that this became a common drink among civilians. Gin, so called from the Dutch 'genever', the juniper berries used to flavour it, was probably invented by a Dutch professor who died in 1672, and it was introduced into England by King William III in 1688 and by English soldiers who had served in the Low Countries. In the alcohol 'family' gin stands close to absinthe and aquavit, which use different flavouring agents, and not far removed from vodka, which is based on potatoes. Dutch gin was, however, far less potent than English gin which became disastrously popular after 1690, when, to create a market for low-grade corn unsuitable for brewing, the government heavily increased the duty on imported spirits, and threw open the distilling and spirit-selling industry to all comers, without any licence or control.

Seldom can any policy have succeeded so completely. Within a few years 7,000 dram-shops, or punch-shops, sprang up all over London, and as the brewers tried to protect their trade by competition, the number of ale-houses also multiplied with them. By 1740 more than 15,000 of the 96,000 houses in the capital sold drink for consumption on the premises, nearly 9,000 of them being gin-shops. The annual consumption of spirits in London was now fourteen gallons a head, but the average Londoner still drank ninety gallons of beer a year. *The Gentleman's Magazine* referred unsympathetically in 1762 to: 'Brewers pining at the hardships they labour under and rolling away in their coaches and six to their several villas to drown their grief in burgundy and champagne.'

The most often quoted testimony was given about 1760 by Tobias Smollett in his *History of England*:

> The retailers of this poisonous compound set up painted boards in public, inviting people to be drunk for the small expense of one penny, assuring them they might be dead drunk for twopence, and have straw for nothing. They accordingly provided cellars and places strewed with straw, to which they conveyed those wretches who were overwhelmed with intoxication.

A Dublin clergyman witnessed similar scenes:

> Sunday is especially devoted to the worship of this great spirit, Gin, and when the early sabbath bells announce the arrival of that day, then do the lower orders begin to shake off the beery slumbers of the midnight pay-table and wander forth in maudlin, unwashed multitudes to the temples of the great Gin; and there you may see them, the aged and the infant . . . old men and maidens . . . fathers and mothers . . . crawling and jostling and sucking in the portion of the spirit which the flaunting priestesses of the temple dole out to them in return for their copper offerings.

Despite all the evidence that the 'free gin' policy had failed, the government was slow to take action. New duties, on manufacturers and retailers, imposed in 1729, were widely evaded, the gin-shop proprietors selling their wares under fancy names such as 'Cuckold's Comfort', 'Ladies' Delight' and 'Knock-me-down', a mixture of hot spiced ale and punch. Some mockingly renamed the traditional drinks 'Parliament Gin' and 'Parliament Brandy'. In 1736 the government tried again with the famous Gin Act, which imposed a prohibitive duty of twenty shillings per gallon on the retailer and raised the cost of a spirit licence to £50 a year. This drastic measure led to riots in the streets and mock funerals for 'Madame Gin', suitably celebrated by getting drunk. One peer aptly commented that 'as the poor had run gin-mad, the rich had run anti-gin mad' and made 'such a law as could not be executed'. The gin trade simply went underground. As a bishop explained in the House of Lords:

> It is true we have not now those public and open scenes of wickedness and debauchery that appeared in every gin-shop before the making of the law . . . but the trade is carried on, though more privately, yet with as great excess as ever, and the reason we do not see more objects in streets is because most of them sleep out the dose in the private corner where they took it in.

In the next seven years only two of the new £50 licences were taken out but the volume of spirits manufactured rose enormously. Excessive strictness, too, having failed, in 1743 a new Bill, reducing the cost of a licence from £50 to £1, and abolishing the duty on retail sales altogether, was hurried into law, and in the following ten years, a series of other Acts was passed, which extended to the gin-shop the same rules that had for centuries applied to the ale-house.

By the end of the eighteenth century, spirit-drinking, though still a problem, was within bounds, legislation having been helped by temperance literature like *A Friendly Admonition to the Drinkers of Brandy* and Hogarth's drawings *Gin Lane* and *Beer Street*, which contrasted the dangers of spirit-drinking with the virtues of honest ale. Magistrates now enforced the law more strictly, imposing a rough and ready rule of one public house per village, insisting on 10 p.m. closing and suppressing surplus licences without compensation, a fact of great importance in the future.

Societies for the Reformation of Manners, active around 1700, became influential again in the 1780s, encouraged by a Royal Proclamation in 1787 against 'all manner of vice, profaneness and immorality'. Although the societies' real targets were 'loose and licentious prints', such as *The Rights of Man*, and 'profanation of the Lord's day', drunkenness, though only of the poor, also came under attack. In the eighteenth century excessive drinking had been one of the few things that rich and poor had in common. Now, as the Industrial Revolution undermined the old social structure, the gulf between the classes widened. Dr. Johnson recalled in 1773 a time 'when all the decent people in Lichfield got drunk every night and was not thought the worse of', but already drunkenness among the respectable classes was beginning to go out of fashion. If the future George IV, who at his wedding in 1795 could barely stand, was characteristic of the eighteenth century, the symbol of the new era was to be his high-principled and abstemious niece, Victoria.

*Chapter Two*

## A MORAL SPECIES OF BEVERAGE

'So long as it might be thought necessary... to afford to the people that species of exhilaration... so long... the lawgiver was best performing his duty by giving to them what under present circumstances might be called a moral species of beverage.'

— Henry Brougham, M.P., in the House of Commons, 4th May 1830

At the beginning of the nineteenth century, brandy, rum, and gin could be bought everywhere in England, though whisky was still mainly a Scottish drink. Ale and beer were, however, the main drinks, whether 'old', 'brown', 'pale', or 'three threads', a mixture of all three. Since about 1720 a near-black, heavily-hopped beer had also become popular, especially in Ireland, known as 'porter', from its popularity with market porters, or 'stout', to distinguish it from weaker drinks. Many names still familiar in the trade were well established by 1800, and the increase in the power of the breweries was causing some concern. The tied-house system began as a result of the justices demanding improvements in the premises before they would grant a licence, or heavy personal sureties from the would-be licensee. Many an ale-house keeper borrowed money for these purposes from the brewers, promising in return to buy all his beer and other supplies from them, or let them buy the house and install him as their tenant. This development was considered by everyone except the brewers to be against the public interest, but all attempts to halt it failed. By 1816 half the 'victualling houses' in London were already tied and in Reading only two out of 68 licensees were still free.

In the whole of England and Wales 14,200 ale-houses, excluding places selling spirits, already belonged to the brewers and only 10,800 to the occupiers, while a further 22,700 were the property of outsiders. Tied houses were criticised by a House of Commons Committee in the same year and by the Committee on Public Breweries two years later, largely on the grounds that the publican was forced to sell poor beer, but they continued to spread. The large firms possessed the capital and experience which the little man lacked, but free-traders and moral reformers united in distrusting them. In 1823 and 1824 Acts were passed to encourage home-brewing, while many justices also tried to open up the trade by granting licences to all who applied for them. From 1825, when the price of a spirit licence was reduced, there was also a widespread merging of gin-shops and ale-houses, so that by 1830 only 5,000 out of 51,000 ale-houses in England and Wales still sold nothing but beer.

Few people realised that the trend towards large-scale brewing was part of the general economic movement of the time. But for the wicked brewer, many reformers believed, the independent village ale-house keeper would again come into his own, and there would be no tied-house tenants pressing unwanted drinks upon their customers for fear of being turned out of job and home. It was often alleged, too, that 'tied' beer and spirits had been adulterated with drugs to make them more intoxicating. In 1824 an experienced beer-drinker complained:

> It has seldom been my fortune, in a great number of years, to taste unadulterated purchased ale... At present the chief articles of adulteration which my well-practised palate can discover, are seeds, sugar and salt... Cocculus indicus (Indian Berry), a most intoxicating and deleterious drug, the flavour of which I well know, was formerly much in use.

Many such charges were obviously exaggerated, for the average publican did not want to knock his customers out with the first glass but to keep them sober as long as possible. The stories persisted, however, of logwood (a harmless colouring agent) in the wine, turpentine in the whisky, and sulphuric acid in the beer or gin, usually under its more alarming name of vitriol. A doctor who later examined this last charge dismissed it as 'a complete fable'; in significant amounts the acid would make any drink unpalatable, while 'vitriol in such a dilute form as alone is swallowable . . . is a capital stomachic and general tonic'.

Although the drunkenness of the first thirty years of the nineteenth century was less alarming than that of a hundred years before it was still a serious problem. Possibly the worst of the three kingdoms was Ireland. A former Customs and Excise official, writing in 1824, quoted the opinion of an American visitor: 'the Irish people were the most drunken race on the face of the earth'. Every public holiday in Ireland was attended with drunkenness, particularly Donnybrook Fair, held in the last week of August on the outskirts of Dublin. By the end of the last day, Walking Sunday, 'one third part of the public lay, or rolled about drunk. Others . . . screamed, shouted and fought. The women rode about, sitting two and three upon an ass . . . smoked with great delight and coquetted with their sweethearts.' For days afterwards the hospitals were full of people suffering from exposure after sleeping out while in a drunken stupor, and the expression, 'a regular Donnybrook Fair', was a synonym for a brawl.

Scotland was almost equally drunken. An eyewitness at Arthur's Seat in Edinburgh described how 'on May Morning . . . the sun rises to shed its light on a scene of swearing and depravity . . . Nothing prevails but disorder and dissipation and shouts of laughter, caused by the floundering of someone more drunken than his fellows; and one would almost imagine the assembled crowd were there like a company of heathens, to worship the sun through drunkenness.' In Skye old people on their death-beds said 'they could not be happy unless men were drunk and fought at their funerals' and one saw 'the distressed widow . . . going without shoes or head-dress with six, seven or eight, ragged and starving children; while perhaps her only cow must be disposed of to procure whisky to make her neighbours drunk'.

A press report in the summer of 1830 described a typical rural debauch.

> A gentleman of large estates ... gave a large feast on his coming of age ... A large ox was roasted and placed in the middle of the square ... to which was added an unlimited supply of porter, strong ale and whisky ... The work of jollification went on briskly ... In a very short time hundreds were in a state of deep intoxication and hand-barrows and carts were ... put in requisition to convey them to their several habitations. On the roads ... in every direction people were found lying helpless. One man states that between Bannockburn and Stirling, he loosened the neckcloths of ... no less than eight individuals ... in danger of suffocation ... Around the table ... men, women and children, were to be seen staggering about in inimitable confusion, tumbling over each other ... and lying by scores in every direction ... On Sunday morning, parties were out in all directions looking for relations and friends and removing them from the highways that they might not be observed by people going to church.

England, too, had little to boast about, as one visitor discovered at Manchester on William IV's coronation day in 1830.

> We saw whole pitchers thrown indiscriminately among the crowd —men holding up their hats to receive drink; people quarrelling and fighting for the possession of a jug; the strong taking the liquor from the weak; boys and girls, men and women, in a condition of beastly drunkenness, staggering before the depositary of ale, or lying prostrate on the ground ... in every degree of exposure, swearing ... vomiting, but calling for more liquor ... when they could not stand, or even sit, to drink it.

General elections were another traditional occasion for free drinking, as at Horsham, Sussex, in 1844:

> Every public house and beershop in the parish was secured by one side or the other as an electioneering stronghold. At every one of them Pink or Blue flags were flying, the meaning of which could not be misunderstood ... If a voter wanted a drink he could go into any public house and obtain any kind of refreshment without ... being asked for payment ... The labourer whose taste was usually satisfied with small beer was now in a position to discover and indulge a palate capable of appreciating more aristocratic

beverages; and ... no niggardly rule was made as to kind or number of friends a voter might introduce ... It is not too much to say that most of the male population of Horsham were frequently drunk, many were continually drunk and some were continuously drunk for the whole six weeks preceding Election Day.

The most important cause of everyday drunkenness was the system of drinking usages which had grown up in many trades. John Dunlop, a Greenock magistrate, devoted ten years to a detailed survey of these customs, and his final report, *The Philosophy of Artificial and Compulsory Drinking Usages in Great Britain and Ireland*, published in 1839, described in detail 300 usages in 98 different trades. He exposed two widespread illusions, the 'usual but great mistake in the upper ranks ... that the forms of courtesy are less binding on the lower classes than on themselves' and the belief among many workmen that such customs were peculiar to their particular occupation. In fact they were almost universal.

In the country free drink was due 'at putting on the rims or tyres of cartwheels, at sharpening of plough-shares and of sickles ... at milling of grain ... at weighing of hay', while in the pits in Scotland miners were given a gallon of whisky when a workable seam of coal was discovered, and masons received a 'founding pint', of from a sovereign to ten guineas for drink, when a foundation stone was laid. Carpenters, too, collected 'joist money' for laying the first joist, and 'men are sometimes induced, after partaking of drink on this occasion, to attempt to walk a joist longitudinally and sustain injury by falling'.

Many tradesmen were subjected to extortion from their customers' employees. The supplier of putty and nails who failed to 'mug' with free drink the carpenters who used them knew that they would report that his materials were inferior. A coach-builder who ignored hints that 'the leather was dry' from the coachman who called to collect a new carriage, would soon hear from its new owner that it was badly scratched on arrival. In England brass merchants paid out 'brass money' to local foundry workers at Whitsun and iron and tin merchants made a similar gift on New Year's Day. The butchers of Dublin kept up on Easter Eve the tradition of 'Whipping the herring'. One man was dressed in a sheepskin and cocked hat, with a birchbroom in his hand, and mounted on a donkey. His escort, carrying herrings on sticks, then led him on a tour of the city, soliciting money for drink, while 'His Majesty' beat the herring with his broom, reciting:

> We come from Merrin
> To whip the herring
> And wish you a happy Easter.

Many usages related to an individual's private life. In some Liverpool workshops there was a shilling fine for drink after one's first 'pleasure sail round the black rock in the Mersey', and becoming a parent also attracted a fine, in Scotland the rule being 'a bottle of whisky for a daughter and two for a son'. In many places, noted Dunlop, 'when a wedding takes place in any trade a number of the lower orders surround the house with old pots, kettles, horns, etc., and keep up a continual noise until they receive "socket money" or are dispersed by the police'. Joining a new firm, or moving to a new workshop, was also an expensive business, for a man might have to buy the vacant place at a workbench or pay an entry fee. The 'footing' for admission to a skilled trade ranged from ten shillings in the cotton trade to seven pounds among calico-printers, and the charges were rigorously enforced. One destitute Irish apprentice sailmaker—ironically, the son of a drunkard—was given four months to pay and could be seen begging in the streets 'every evening in the twilight' to raise the cash.

Once admitted, the poor apprentice had to disburse more money every time he learned a new process. It cost a would-be plumber one to five shillings when he cast his first sheet of lead; a trainee printer paid a pound when he cut his first block and an apprentice hatter bought a 'plank pint', costing several shillings, the first time he moulded felt upon a plank. There were also fines for various misdemeanours; an apprentice carpenter paid sixpence when he failed to mend the fire, knocked

JOSEPH LIVESEY (*left*) AND JOHN KING SIGN THE PLEDGE

*Harris Public Library, Preston*

HURCH STREET, PRESTON, SHOWING LIVESEY'S CHEESE SHOP AND TEMPERANCE HOTEL

*Harris Public Library, Preston*

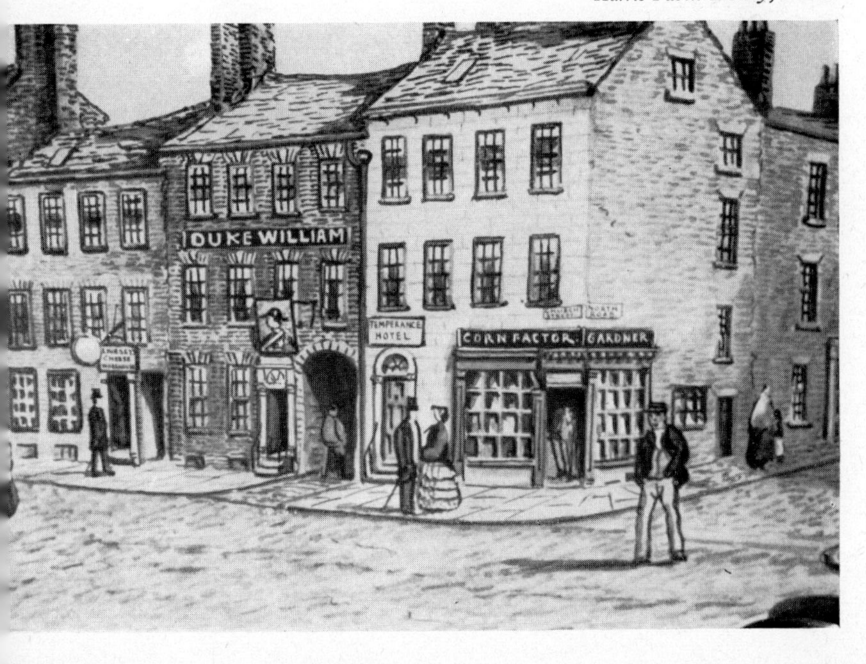

*Harris Public Library, Pre*

DICKY TURNER (*standing, centre, in short jacket*)
COINS THE WORD 'TEETOTAL'.
(THE CHAIRMAN IS JOSEPH LIVESEY)

*Harris Public Library, Pre*

THE FIRST TEETOTAL PROCESSION, PRESTON, 1833, LED BY
DICKY TURNER AND THOMAS SWINDLEHURST (*on horse*)

over the candles or let the glue get cold. Qualifying as a journeyman was also costly. A newly-qualified hatter paid a 'garnish', among coopers there was a 'brothering' ceremony and in foundries 'loosing' cost the former apprentice £3 or £4. One man estimated that compulsory usages during his apprenticeship had cost him £9.

This elaborate network of usages was kept in being by a ferocious system of bullying. A coal porter who failed to pay the ten shillings due when he first used a cart would find the wheels removed. A non-paying tailor would have the point of his scissors broken off and a triangular hole cut in the rim of his hat. Among printers the offender was identified by filling the sleeves of his coat with printers' ink, so that his shirtsleeves were indelibly stained, and 'preparations of gunpowder with burning matches attached to them' might be hung from his coat buttons. A man might find the pockets into which he had been slow to dip his hand glued together, or discover a pawn-ticket in place of his coat, pawned to buy his workmates the missing drink. The worst sufferers were apprentices. In Ireland, Dunlop was told, 'any boy refusing to pay the footing would be knocked about like a pair of old boots'. An apprentice shipwright who failed to pay was flogged with a handsaw. In the furniture trade a boy was 'cabbed'. A heavy cloth was thrown over him from behind, 'his hands are then tied and he is laid on his face along a bench, his shoes are taken off and he is sharply beat on the soles of his feet with a flat board . . . He remains after this the object of unrelenting abuse and spite . . . and is finally sent to Coventry.' Even domestic servants were not exempt. One maid who failed to bring with her the expected bottle of whisky found that her colleagues 'refused to help her in the washing for the family, told unfounded stories to their mistress' and 'managed to make her life so miserable that in a fortnight she quitted her service'. 'The perfection of compulsory drinking usage' was, in Dunlop's opinion, to be found in the tailoring trade. When two tailors were caught drinking only a modest amount together they had to buy a similar drink for every man in the shop, sometimes amounting to sixty half-pints.

John Dunlop considered it 'wonderful that there are any sober men in the mechanic class at all, when such perpetual drinking domineers over them'. Yet experience showed that even a small determined group was usually sufficient to break a usage. In one large Scottish town the refusal of thirty-six families to serve drink at funerals had been enough to end the practice. In a printing works the members of a temperance society had organised a meeting at which a majority had resolved, 'No drink, but a mechanics library'. Public opinion, said Dunlop, was already changing. When he had begun his enquiries he had been threatened with violence; now there was a general willingness to provide information. But who could still stay unmoved at the familiar sight of wives on 'cold wet nights . . . searching up and down desolate streets for their husbands, sometimes accompanied by several crying, half-sleeping little children'?

What finally persuaded the government to amend the licensing laws, however, was the capricious way in which they were being administered. Petitions were always being laid before the House of Commons protesting about licences unfairly withheld, and rural justices who left villages without an ale-house, for fear it might become a resort of poachers, radicals or trade unionists. By an accident of history both parties in 1830 favoured liberalising the law, the Tories because increased sales of beer would benefit the farmer, the Whigs because they favoured free trade on principle. The brewing trade itself was divided, fear of a decline in the value of tied houses being counterbalanced by the hope of new outlets for their products.

On Thursday, 8th April 1830, the Paymaster-General, John Calcraft the younger, a former Whig turned Tory, rose in the House of Commons to introduce the Sale of Beer Bill, designed to give 'the poor and working classes of the community a chance of obtaining a better, cheaper and a more wholesome beverage'. This would be done by 'throwing open the trade' and giving anyone who paid a two-guinea excise duty the right to sell beer, without a justices' licence.

The opposition was largely disarmed by the fact that the

government intended at the same time to abolish the duty on beer, a universally popular proposal, and Calcraft, on the second reading on 4th May, held to the essential point: 'By giving a free trade in beer, it was expected that competition would introduce among the labouring classes a good old English beverage, which could not now be got in any part of the country, nor in many parts of town.' He stressed the need to prevent adulteration and the 'avowed custom' of watering beer down by 25–30%. 'In the country', he explained, 'the brewers owned the public houses and, without that advantage, they would not be able to sell as much bad beer as they now sold.'

Thus cast in the unfamiliar rôle of defender of the working man, the government found itself being praised by the reforming party in the House. Robert Slaney declared that ministers had acted 'with an honest and manly discretion'. Joseph Hume praised them for introducing 'a measure highly beneficial to the community'. Only a few invincible reactionaries like Colonel Sibthorpe forecast disaster. 'The morals of the people must suffer', he warned. The Bill 'would ruin many valuable vested interests'. The Bill 'would convert the whole country into a mere grog shop', predicted another honourable and gallant gentleman. Such unwelcome voices were drowned by the chorus of praise for beer which made it seem that to drink it was a patriotic duty. One back-bencher described it as 'that beverage of which we all boast', while Henry Brougham, a future Lord Chancellor, was equally enthusiastic:

> What they might now expect was that they would have . . . good beer instead of bad spirits; and so long as it might be thought necessary . . . to afford to the people that species of exhilaration . . . so long he thought the lawgiver was best performing his duty by giving to them what under present circumstances might be called a moral species of beverage.

On the third reading, the Bill's opponents made a final effort. 'The better the beer', warned one member, 'the greater would be the temptation.' The Bill, said another, would result 'in destroying that control which country gentlemen now exercised so beneficially . . . over the poachers and other frequenters of public houses . . . The main relief would be to the tailors, shoemakers and artisans of neighbouring towns . . . the men who met in public houses and combined against their masters.'

This blatant appeal to self-interest was uttered in vain, and in the Lords, where the Prime Minister himself moved the Bill's second reading, it had an easy passage. When the Iron Duke gave his opinion that there was no real danger of 'disturbance and riot' while the Bill would cut the price of a quart pot of beer from 5d. to 3d., that was good enough for their lordships and none even troubled to divide the House. On Friday, 23rd July 1830, the Duke of Wellington's Beer Bill, as it was commonly known, received the royal assent.

*Chapter Three*

## SINGING AND SPRAWLING

'The new Beer Bill has begun its operations. Everybody is drunk. Those who are not singing are sprawling. The sovereign people are in a beastly state.'

—The Rev. Sydney Smith, 24th October 1830

On Sunday, 10th October 1830, the Sale of Beer Act came into force. The result was astonishing and immediate. Queues formed outside the excise offices of householders anxious to put their two-guinea fee and get into the gold rush. Some of the new beer-shop proprietors were men of bad character who had previously been refused a public-house licence. Some were unemployed labourers whose parishes advanced the cash out of the poor rates to make them self-supporting. Some were widows whose neighbours held a whip-round to set them up in business. Some were thieves and footpads who wanted a new and convenient meeting place. Some, complained a magistrate, were 'petty tradesmen who would rather get their bread by any other way than by hard labour'. A beer-house mania swept the working classes as a railway mania was to seize the middle classes fifteen years later. Beer-shops threw open their doors to passers-by on the very first day they became lawful. In Liverpool fifty new ones were set up every day for several weeks; by the end of the month the city contained 800. By the end of the year there were 24,000 beer-shops in England and Wales. Twelve months later the number had risen to 31,000; by December 1832 it was 36,000, by 1834 38,000, by 1836 46,000. In the same period the number of licensed public houses also rose, though far more slowly, to a total of 56,000. Thus for a population of about fifteen million in England and Wales there were now 100,000 places at which one could obtain a drink—and almost half of them were under no public control.

The beer-shop explosion was felt in every corner of the country. A Lancashire M.P. complained in 1833 that his constituency contained 2,000, but even a thinly populated county like Norfolk could muster 350. One firm claimed to have opened 200 in Birmingham and its environs. Hanley, Staffordshire, with 16,000, mainly working-class, citizens already well supplied with public houses, soon had 110 beer-shops; Pilkington, Lancashire, for 11,000 people had 48; Cheltenham, a largely middle-class town of 25,000 people, 190. Even the village of Ingatestone in Essex, with only 700 inhabitants, supported ten. Beer-houses blossomed in tiny hamlets where it would not have paid a brewer to set up a public house. Often a cooper or a carpenter, a tailor or a grocer, a butcher or a wheelwright, ran one as a sideline. Blacksmiths set aside a room to sell beer, where their customers could go while their horses were being shod; shoemakers did the same for people waiting to have their shoes mended. Even a labourer or jobbing gardener would set up a beer-house to supplement his income, his wife running it during the day. The very parishes which the gentry had struggled hardest to keep 'dry' were naturally the most popular sites for beer-houses. As one brewer said, the chain of beer-shops he had set up throughout Hampshire was serving labourers who 'hardly know the taste of beer', and he hoped it would become to them 'as it has to the inhabitants of towns, almost a necessary of life'. Agents from the brewers toured the most remote corners of the countryside persuading householders to set up beer-shops in their homes, advancing the two-guinea excise fee and providing the first casks of beer on credit. A statement in the House of Commons that the labourer on his way home 'now has to run the gauntlet through three or four beer-shops, in each of which are fellow labourers carousing, who urge him to stay and drink with them' was clearly no exaggeration. In one row of fourteen houses in a Lancashire town six sold beer. Of fifty houses in an

Essex hamlet five were beer-shops. At Icklesham in Sussex, where the gentry had transferred the licence of a conveniently placed public house to an inaccessible house on the edge of the village, the former premises reopened as a beer-house, as they did at nearby Ringmer, where the licence had been suppressed altogether.

The testimony most commonly quoted to show that the Beer Act was a failure is that of the Rev. Sydney Smith, Canon of St. Paul's, a former supporter of 'free trade in ale and alehouses'. 'The new Beer Bill', he wrote on 24th October 1830, 'has begun its operations. Everybody is drunk. Those who are not singing are sprawling. The sovereign people are in a beastly state.' This, however, was an initial reaction. Once the first excitement had died down public opinion became far more divided, and despite a tremendous outcry in Parliament the government were not, said Lord Althorp in June 1831, 'prepared to abandon the principle of the measure'.

The Act's supporters were unfortunate in that it came into operation in the very month in which a wave of spontaneous riots began to sweep the whole of the south and west of England. Sullen mobs of half-starved men appeared outside the houses of the gentry to demand a living wage. Ricks were burned, cattle maimed, machinery destroyed, a number of people killed, and a series of special punitive courts held reminiscent of Judge Jeffreys's Bloody Assize. Naturally enough the labourers tended to meet to discuss their grievances in the new beer-houses, the only public rooms in their villages, and the more remote the house the better. In the beer-houses, declared more than one magistrate, the labourers imbibed radical opinions along with their beer. It was this, said a Berkshire M.P. in the House of Commons, which was responsible for 'much of the immorality and insubordination' which now prevailed among them, and which, a Buckinghamshire magistrate admitted, led to 'a general disposition to benefit the labourers by an increase of pay', from seven or eight shillings a week to nine or ten.

Although the Sale of Beer Act had 'thrown the trade open'

with a vengeance it failed to break the stranglehold of the great brewers. By 1833, less than three years after the passing of the Act, of 346 beer-houses in Norfolk, more than 300 bought their beer from outside; in the Arundel district of Sussex 46 of 73 beer-houses did the same and a new brewery had had to be opened to meet their needs; at Wantage in Berkshire it paid the beer-house keepers to obtain supplies by heavy waggon from Reading, twenty-four miles away, rather than brew for themselves. It was a joke in the district that two brewers had dolefully told their companions in the hunting field just before the Act was passed that this would be the last season they could afford to ride to hounds. Three years later they were still in the saddle at every meet, but now 'with new coats and better horses'.

Where the brewers did not succeed in capturing a substantial share of the new trade, they set out to compete with it. A London grocer described in 1834 what had happened to 'a low dirty public-house with only one doorway' opposite his home. This was transformed into:

> A splendid edifice, the front ornamented with pilasters supporting a handsome cornice and . . . balustrade and the whole elevation remarkably striking and handsome; the doorways were increased . . . to three, and each of those eight to ten feet wide . . . and the doors and windows glazed with very large single squares of plate glass, and the gas fittings of the most costly description . . . When this edifice was completed, notice was given by placards taken round the parish; a band of music was stationed in front . . . and when the doors were opened the rush was tremendous; it was instantly filled with customers and continued so till midnight.

Inside, the new gin-palaces, as they were quickly named, were equally impressive, as a character in a temperance novel of 1860 discovered:

> Lustrous mirrors in glittering gilt frames dazzled his sight . . . massive pillars, all marble and burnished gold . . . showy timepieces and rich cut-glass chandeliers . . . The taps communicating with the spirit casks were of polished silver or were silver plated . . . Farther on were the beer-taps; and the beautiful shelves behind

> held bottles of various kinds and elegant ornament . . . whose very names were sufficient to tempt the unwary . . . Prime double-stout, mild ale, best cordial gin, cream of the valley, Old Tom, pineapple rum, genuine Scotch whisky, best French brandy . . . rum-shrub.

The publicans who could not afford to give their premises a face-lift often competed by 'opening a dram-shop . . . to make up for the deficiency in the sale of their beer'. The result was that, after a slight drop in the consumption of spirits in the years immediately after 1830, sales were, by 1838, higher than they had been in 1830, and by 1845 very much higher.

The campaign against the beer-houses began almost before the ink was dry on the statute-book. As early as March 1831 complaints were being raised in Parliament of 'an alarming increase of immorality, pauperism and vice among the lower orders arising from the great number of beer-shops' and by March 1833 one M.P. was quoting a duke who thought that 'If the Beer Act was not altered in five years it would demoralise the whole population of the country and make them a set of drunkards and miscreants.' Meanwhile, however, M.P.s from the newly-enfranchised industrial towns were presenting petitions in support of the beer-shops. The Radical John Roebuck introduced one from 4,000 people in Merthyr Tydfil who 'had signed it by affixing not their names but their marks'. This proved it to be 'the petition of the poor man and entitled on this subject to great attention'. Other M.P.s considered 'the new beer-shops . . . a decided advantage to the poor', since 'by the Bill good Beer was made more general and when it was good it did not give persons the stomach ache'.

In April 1833 the Marquess of Chandos moved in the House of Commons for a 'Select Committee . . . to enquire into the state and management of houses in which beer is sold by retail', which began its sittings two weeks later. The members showed a commendable readiness to hear evidence from all quarters, and some witnesses were readily shown to be blinded by prejudice. A former mayor of Arundel, who complained that 'I was obliged to get out of my gig three times for people coming along, waggoners drunk, when I was returning from shooting', revealed under questioning that this incident had actually occurred before the first beer-house had opened its doors and a Hampshire clergyman who dwelt on the poverty caused by the beer-shops was forced to admit that his parish did not contain a single one. A Devonshire M.P. explained away a typical story accusing a beer-house keeper of revolutionary agitation: 'A gentleman who lived in the parish had heard that this person had a newspaper of rather liberal politics read in the house . . . He wanted to substitute one of a very different description; the man would not let him do it, and then, and not until then, he had the party prosecuted.' A clerical magistrate from Itchen Abbas, near Winchester, alleged that 'the delegates from the Political Unions constantly attend those houses and there they enrol their members', finally producing with a triumphant flourish a placard he had confiscated and sent to the Prime Minister:

> The flags of freedom and liberty are flying over the churches and steeples on the Continent; rise, Englishmen, and assert your rights and pull down priestcraft and oppression. The Reform Bill is only a stepping-stone to our future advantages. Down with the tithes! Down with the taxes!

Much of the evidence showed the failure of existing methods of maintaining public order. A Norfolk magistrate disclosed that the chief suspect in a series of rick and barn burnings in one parish had reached an understanding with the overseer of the poor. 'He has told us that if we will give him eight shillings a week he will keep his family with the profits of the beer-shop and will give us no further trouble.' Several clergy, who had tried to reform their parishes by direct action, had been unsuccessful. One in Sussex who had slipped out of church in mid-service on a Sunday morning to catch his parishioners in the act of drinking had merely been invited to 'come and take a drop'. A country vicar in Berkshire who stalked into a beer-shop at 11 p.m. found that despite his admonitions 'the people would not stir or take off their hats'. Another prudently stayed in bed but 'They go and rattle his gates and holloa to him and disturb his family between eleven and twelve... not from dislike for the clergyman, but merely as a lark in the evening.'

Most of the crime alleged against the beer-houses was little more serious than this. An Essex magistrate gave some examples of petty theft.

> I knew a case where a pig was stolen, driven to a beer-shop, valued by the people there, the value written down and drunk out... At the last sessions a man was tried for stealing fowls and rabbits; they were stolen on Saturday night... taken to a beer-shop and dressed... The same thing happened with regard to stealing a lamb.

In Norfolk a man bored with playing cards in a beer-house at 1.30 a.m. had stolen the clergyman's pig and taken it back to be shared out. In Essex a carpenter had stolen from a local farmer the wood to make a bench for the beer-house and was given five shillings 'to the credit of his score' in return.

Little evidence of gambling or prostitution in the beer-houses was produced, although a zealous Excise Officer from Ringwood in Hampshire said he had seen a game of cribbage in progress in one which also employed 'a certain number of girls, perhaps ten', ready to 'resort around the Forest' and 'a fiddler to attract the people'. Almost the only other case quoted was in Lancaster where the beer-house keeper 'had four rooms and... a girl prepared to each', whom you could visit on paying a shilling for a twopenny quart of ale.

The most serious complaints against the beer-houses concerned their unsatisfactory and isolated premises. After 1832, occupying property of £10 annual value qualified a man to vote, but many beer-houses were rated as low as £4 and £5, and even £1 was not unknown. 'Small cottages with generally two rooms', worth 50s. a year, were typical said one witness, but one near Hastings was described as 'a miserable hut' and in Essex, there were 'one or two you can hardly [i.e. almost] get into a cart'.

The location of the beer-houses was equally unsatisfactory, 'in woods, lanes and all sorts of bye-places', in the country, 'up alleys . . . and in obscure corners out of the range of our watchmen and patrols' in the towns. 'We should', said one magistrate, 'never think of licensing an ale-house in the middle of a wood', but beer-houses everywhere lacked 'the same beneficial publicity'.

There was some evidence that the beer-houses were contributing to rural poverty. One wife had complained that her husband's 'round frock . . . hat and . . . high shoes, and . . . all her garments, were in the pop-shop' due to his increased drinking, and an Essex magistrate described how a labourer had taken his four-year-old child to the beer-shop and 'The wife went to look for him and found the man drunk and the child stripped of his clothes', sold on the spot to raise money for beer. There was, however, much to be said in the beer-houses' defence. Labourers who had formerly saved up their money 'for a regular debauch on Sundays' at the distant public house could now enjoy a modest nightly drink at the nearby beer-house. Working-class travellers could often obtain a cheap bed at them instead of being forced 'to go to the twopenny lodging houses or sleep in the streets', since inns often refused accommodation to a man arriving on foot. Many beer-houses provided cheap meals, like a sixpenny snack of tea and bread and butter. At an inn the tea alone might cost three times as much. Beer, too, helped by the abolition of the beer duty, had come down sharply in price. The best beer, costing eightpence a quart before October 1830, now cost sixpence, the most popular, 'fourpenny', marketed at twopence a pint, while the humble 'twopenny' now offered the labourer a pint for a penny.

Many witnesses appeared before the 1833 Committee simply because they liked beer. A commercial traveller in stationery had found the beer-houses far more obliging than the public houses, which were chiefly interested in selling spirits and refused to cook a customer's steak for him. A South London businessman drank at the beer-house with 'a very genteel party'. A Surrey surgeon recommended the beer-shop to his patients. A Lambeth mathematical instrument maker visited one several times a week and had never seen any bad behaviour. He thought it unfair that the beer-shops had to shut at 10 p.m., since many men, like himself, worked till 9 p.m. or later.

The Report of the Committee was laid before the House of Commons on 21st June 1833. While acknowledging that 'considerable evils have arisen from the present management and conduct of beer-shops', it did not propose to abolish them or, a popular remedy, confine them to off-sales. All it suggested was that beer-houses should be of a minimum rateable value, between £7 and £15, that those running them should be required to produce a certificate of good conduct and that hours, especially on Sunday, should be reduced. An amending Act broadly on these lines was passed in the following year and further restrictions on hours and on the type of premises which could become beer-houses were imposed in 1840, but the campaign against them continued. In 1846 the Rev. Thomas Page addressed from Virginia Water Parsonage, Egham, Surrey, *An Earnest Appeal to the Nation at Large on the Mischievous Effects of Beer-houses*, which quoted a critic who had said that, 'if Satan himself had had a seat in the counsels of the nation, the Beer Act was the very kind of measure which the great enemy of mankind would have suggested'. The working classes, alleged Page, from being 'a manly, independent, industrious and thrifty portion of the community, attentive to the interests of their employers', had become 'disaffected, dissolute, impatient of superiority or control, reckless of family duties'. The beer-shops were 'hot-beds of every species of iniquity'. One of his Sunday school pupils had been found by her mother in a beer-shop at midnight. Another 'girl under sixteen years of age, on a Sunday afternoon, was inveigled into a beer-house and treated with beer by a depraved young man, under the influence of which the grossest indecencies were practised'. Another young man, returning from a beer-house one Sunday, 'intercepted in a lonely spot a married female on her way back from public worship and after most grossly abusing her, meeting with another of his dissipated companions, both pursued their helpless victim and repeated their abominable offence'. It was clearly the day almost as much as the deed which offended Page. As he explained, quoting a prison chaplain, a rich source of temperance material, 'The frequenters of these moral pest-houses soon learn to despise the Sabbath; and Sabbath breaking with the farm labourer, very commonly leads to... poaching, fowl stealing and sheep stealing.'

In 1848 an Association for the Suppression of Beershops was founded in Liverpool and offered a £20 first prize for the best anti-beershop essay. The winner, J. Russom, added some new evidence to earlier indictments. 'These moral pests' were, in Russom's opinion, 'seminaries of the idle and the dissolute... Those who visit such places... are induced to become first poachers, then perhaps burglars, next highwaymen and finally assassins.' They also accounted 'in a considerable degree' for 'the increase in juvenile delinquency', and for the decline in religion. As a Bath vicar had said of his parishioners, 'The beershop is their church; they bow down before the beer barrel.'

The beer-house continued under fire for the next twenty years, until the Wine and Beer-House Act of 1869 made the grant of all licences conditional on the justices' approval. This reversed the process by which the beer-houses, already numbering 53,000, were spreading at the rate of 2,000 a year. Existing beer-houses could, however, only be refused a licence in strictly limited circumstances and a few of these 'old beer-house' or 'ante-1869' licences still exist today, the sole survivors of that Act of 1830 which the Duke of Wellington was said to have considered a greater achievement than any of his military victories.

*Chapter Four*

# SIGNING THE PLEDGE

'Next morning my mind was made up and I solemnly vowed that I would never take any kind of intoxicating liquor again.'

— JOSEPH LIVESEY, 1831

THE MODERN temperance movement began in the United States about 1770, when a member of a Quaker meeting at Philadelphia protested that he was 'oppressed with the smell of rum from the breaths of those who sat around him'. The first formal pledge to abstain from drink was taken by those attending a meeting at Moreau in New York State in 1808, though the signatories were still allowed to drink wine at public dinners, or beer and cider at any time, or to break the pledge on payment of a twenty-five-cent fine, increased to fifty cents for getting drunk. The first pledges against all forms of intoxicating drink were probably taken at Boston in 1826 and at Hector, New York State, in 1827, where members who had taken the 'total pledge' were marked by the letter 'T' in the membership roll, sometimes, mistakenly, advanced as the origin of the word 'teetotal'.

In 1829 the captains of various American vessels in the port of Liverpool distributed temperance tracts to local residents, leading to the formation of the Liverpool Temperance Society in March 1830. The first British total abstainers were probably, however, the Cowherdites, an obscure religious sect founded, at Salford, Lancashire, by a former Anglican clergyman, the Rev. W. Cowherd. In 1809 his followers took the name of Bible Christians—not to be confused with the Methodist sect of the same name, founded in 1816—and renounced 'animal food' and intoxicating drink. The pioneer non-religious total abstinence society was founded at Skibbereen in Southern Ireland in 1817 by Jeffery Edwards, a nailmaker and reformed drunkard, which was said to have acquired 500 members but which failed to survive as a separate entity. The real founder of the temperance movement in Ireland was probably Dr. John Edgar, Professor of Divinity at the Royal College, Belfast, who established the Ulster Temperance Society in 1829, launching it on its way by pouring all the whisky in his house, almost a gallon, out of his parlour window into the courtyard outside. By 1830 several similar societies were flourishing in Dublin, the chairman of one, which met in an old coach-house, presiding from his seat on a symbolically empty whisky barrel.

The 'father of temperance societies in Great Britain' was said to be the Greenock magistrate and anti-usage campaigner, John Dunlop. On a Continental visit he 'was greatly surprised to find the working classes of France so much superior in their habits to the same class of people in Scotland' and, having concluded that drink was responsible, founded a moderation society in Greenock in 1828 or 1829—the authorities differ. On 5th October 1829 Dunlop and four other members of the Greenock society, at a meeting in a bookshop, signed the total abstinence pledge, but the society as a whole soon reverted to 'moderation' only. A few days before the Greenock meeting a woman acquaintance of Dunlop had founded a total abstinence society for women in a suburb of Glasgow and six weeks later a separate Glasgow and West of Scotland Temperance Society was launched, with William Collins, a printer and publisher, as vice-president. This later became the Scottish Temperance Society, though at first it was national only in name.

By the end of 1830 temperance had clearly taken root in Scotland. During the first year nearly half a million tracts had been distributed, 130 societies had been formed, with a total membership of 25,000 members, many clergy were actively helping in the cause, and William Collins had launched *The Temperance Society Record*, the first of many temperance periodicals. At Dumfermline there was another portent of a less encouraging kind. The newly-formed Temperance Society having proposed to sell beer in the temperance coffee-house and reading-room it had set up—considered essential if it were to pay its way—the extremist faction had seceded, to form a rival Dumfermline Association for the Promotion of Temperance by the Relinquishment of *all* Intoxicating Liquors.

The pioneer of temperance south of the Border was also a Scottish businessman, Henry Forbes, who in March 1830 founded the Bradford Temperance Society. Its first public meeting, in June, was the real start of the movement in England. Local manufacturers released their employees early to attend, the hall was packed with 1,800 people, and the star speaker, Dr. John Edgar from Belfast, held the audience until almost midnight. Soon afterwards all the doctors in the town issued a joint declaration condemning spirit-drinking and twenty-six local grocers agreed to cease to offer them to their customers. Meanwhile, in April 1830, a society had been started at Warrington, which in the same month issued a tract making the revolutionary assertion that 'Temperance Societies will abolish various diseases . . . increase the strength and longevity of mankind . . . prevent numerous crimes being committed.'

In May 1830 a temperance society was formed in Manchester and reporters and printers from *The Manchester Times*, *The Courier* and *The Chronicle* flocked to sign the pledge. Equally surprising, on the proposal of Henry Forbes from Bradford, which sent agents all over the north, the first occupational association was formed, the Commercial Travellers' Temperance Society. In September the new movement spread to Leeds, then to Bolton, Birmingham, Newcastle and Bristol, soon to become the stronghold of the movement in the west. During 1830 William Collins, who had attended the great meeting at Bradford, visited London to try and launch a society there and his third attempt, in November 1830, led to the creation of the London Temperance Society, which in the following July became the British and Foreign Temperance Society, under the presidency of the Bishop of London, Charles Blomfield, a champion of many good causes, including sanitary reform.

The progress of all the early societies depended largely on chance and on the vigour of individuals. Interest in the ailing, original society in Liverpool, for example, was dramatically revived by the loss of a steamship in the Mersey in August 1831 with heavy loss of life, due to 'the mad folly of the drunken captain'. Here, too, as elsewhere, the campaign against drink was only one aspect of a general movement to improve the condition of the poor. A leader in both fields was John Finch, an enlightened iron merchant who never thought 'of giving less than three shillings to a man who can do a day's labour . . . for . . . no man can support a family in Liverpool . . . properly unless he receives as much'. Finch succeeded between July and December 1830 in persuading 160 working men, mainly dockers, to sign the moderation pledge, and in setting up groups of workers, each with their own president, secretary and foreman, who bargained for them with merchants and shipowners. The groups shared out their earnings in a dock-side office, not at the public house, and Finch also started free libraries and a school for the men, but the venture failed and the schoolroom forms were bartered for drink in the public house.

Undeterred, he now attempted to reclaim from drunkenness a business contact, Thomas Swindlehurst of Preston. Swindlehurst, a roller-maker, could earn £4 or £5 a week when he was sober, but he rarely was and he had run up a debt of £110 for iron supplied by Finch's firm. When Finch visited Preston to try and collect the debt, he found Swindlehurst drinking his business worries away in the public house. Striking while the, unpaid for, iron was hot he persuaded Swindlehurst to sign the moderation pledge, talked his partners into advancing £350 to pay off Swindlehurst's debts and two months later, in June 1831, went personally into partnership with him. Seldom can an investment have looked less promising or have reaped such gratifying dividends. The new business prospered; the debts were soon repaid; and Swindlehurst became a devoted servant of the temperance movement, his account of his experiences making a great impression on working-class audiences.

In his new-found enthusiasm for the cause, when he received

a bundle of anti-drink tracts from John Finch, Thomas Swindlehurst passed some on to an acquaintance, a young tallow-chandler, John Smith, who distributed them in the street. Here one caught the eye of a local cheese-merchant and reformer, Joseph Livesey. The man, the place and the cause had at last come together.

Despite its nickname of Proud Preston, Preston in 1830 was a place of smoke-blackened mills, throbbing with the life of the new steam-driven machines, and terraces of mean houses, thrown up to accommodate the soaring population, which had trebled, from 12,000 to 34,000, since 1800 and was to double again by 1850. As in other boom towns of the Industrial Revolution, amenities were few. A resident recalled how 'There were no national schools, no Sunday schools, no mechanics institutions, no penny publications, no cheap newspapers, no free libraries, no penny postage . . . no railways, no gas.' With the cotton-mills drawing in their 'hands' at six in the morning and not setting them free till at least 8.30 at night, there was, in any case, little leisure for self-improvement. Many working-class families found recreation from toil in the church or, more commonly, in the chapel; more patronised the public house or beer-house—Preston acquired 190 of the latter between 1830 and 1834. Here was spent a high proportion of working-class wages, from the 24 shillings a week of a prosperous mechanic to the 10 shillings of someone practising the dying craft of home-weaving. An average wage for an adult mill-worker was around 18 shillings; for a youth 8 to 12 shillings, and for a younger child (its hours of labour limited to twelve a day by the 1819 Factories Act) 3, taken by its parents. Some kindly employers also paid a child twopence for itself, a market catered for by the publicans with infant-sized glasses of gin, called 'squibs', at a halfpenny a time. To tempt in the adults there were fiddlers, hornpipe competitions, and 'special offers' of rum at fivepence a noggin instead of sixpence.

Preston was, however, basically a beer-drinking town. There was, a witness told the Select Committee on Drunkenness in 1834, 'ten times more drunkenness in Preston from the consumption of beer than either wine or spirits'. The cotton trade, like others, was riddled with drinking customs and, John Dunlop had noted, 'Those operatives who demure to acquiesce in these usages are considered d——d low, mean, mangy souls and liable to every species of insult.'

In politics, Preston maintained a sturdy independence, with an unusually wide suffrage. The militant reformer, William Cobbett, had fought the seat in 1826 and four years later an extreme Radical, 'Orator Hunt', who had presided at the meeting which ended in the 1819 'Manchester massacre', was actually elected. On this occasion Joseph Livesey stood on the platform beside Henry Hunt and narrowly escaped being laid out by a half brick.

'Joe' Livesey, thirty-six in 1830, had been born in Walton, near Preston, in 1794, the son of a handloom weaver. Both his parents died when he was seven and soon the young orphan joined his grandfather and uncle at the loom. From the age of ten until he was twenty-one, Livesey slaved away in a damp, dark cellar, winding the weavers' bobbins and, after his grandmother's death, acting as housekeeper. As he bent over the rattling loom Livesey taught himself to read, scribbling words on the nearby wall to help his memory.

> I was allowed no candle and for hours I have read by the glare of the embers left in the fire-grate, with my head close to the bars... There was no public library and publications of all kinds were expensive; and if I could succeed in borrowing one I would devour it like a hungry man would his first meal.

Livesey learned by hard experience the physical difficulty of life for the poor. Water for washing he fetched from the river; to obtain milk meant a one-and-a-half-mile walk; but everywhere there was alcohol. At the dame school which he had briefly attended as a small child, the pupils were regaled with spiced ale and wine at Christmas and reeled home drunk. 'We had', he recalled, 'a sad, wet lot connected with the church. The grave digger and his father were both drunkards; ringers and singers, both were hard drinkers... The parish clerk was no exception.' It was a joke in the district that when the church clock stopped the reason was 'the clerk was drunk again last night'.

At the age of sixteen, Joseph became a ringer himself and soon discovered there were fines for arriving late or for ringing a false note, spent at Christmas on a supper at *The White Bull*, where mulled ale, rum-shrub, or punch, and raspberry brandy flowed freely. The following year he joined the Baptists, but was shocked when, after he had walked fourteen miles to Accrington to attend the induction of a new minister, both minister and congregation adjourned at the end of the ceremony to drink spirits. At twenty-one he became involved with a more rigid sect known as the Scotch Baptists and decided to seek a wife among them. 'I heard', he wrote, 'of Miss Williams as an amiable, religious girl and, before seeing her, my choice was decided.' Miss Williams fortunately raised no objection and three times Livesey walked the thirty miles to Manchester to see her, weakening once and travelling the last ten miles 'outside' on a coach, at the cost of five shillings, which he still begrudged sixty years later.

Livesey's marriage proved ideally happy. His wife, Jenny, ultimately bore him thirteen children, of whom nine survived. 'I used', he remembered, 'to play with them, run with them, romp with them and, when sitting by the fireside, sometimes I should have one on each knee and one or two climbing up the chair back, perhaps combing my hair or pulling my whiskers.' He later delighted in his twenty-seven grandchildren, acknowledging in old age that 'even now as I pass . . . in . . . the street . . . those who can just toddle about I feel as if I could form one of their party. I would still drive the hoop, play the ball or strike the shuttlecock.'

In 1816 the Livesey family moved to Preston, renting a small cottage at half-a-crown a week, and working at the loom until ten in the evening or later. Soon afterwards Livesey fell ill, and his doctor prescribed a diet of bread and cheese and 'a sup of good malt liquor'. Livesey discovered that cheese in the local shops cost sevenpence or eightpence a pound, but at the cheese fair at Lancaster he managed to buy the last two cheeses from a farmer for 4¾d. a pound. He borrowed a sovereign to finance the deal and a pair of scales from a draper friend and spent the Saturday evening selling the cheese in small portions to his neighbours, making one-and-sixpence profit, more than his weaving would have brought in during the same period. The following Saturday he repeated the experiment, offering cheese at 5½d. while his competitors charged 7d. The business flourished; soon Livesey was able to dispose of his loom and was to be seen every Saturday selling cheese in Preston market, while on other days his pony, Billy, carried him to markets as far afield as Blackburn, Wigan and Bolton, and on buying expeditions into the countryside.

At this stage of his life Joseph Livesey enjoyed his drink with the next man. His deals with farmers were often sealed in gin and after a long day at his market stall he took a glass of ale with his fellow traders. Twice, however, drink nearly cost him his life. Once he had to leap to safety when two drunken carters raced their heavy waggons on either side of his light gig, and on another occasion he was nearly drowned by a drunken ferryman. Eventually he decided to serve only milk or water in his own house and to give no alcohol to his children, while in 1824 he addressed a pamphlet on drunkenness to the poor, entitled *The Besetting Sin*.

But Livesey was not content merely to write tracts. There were few good causes in Preston with which he was not involved, whether it was helping at a soup kitchen for the hungry, providing bedding for the destitute, running a free Sunday school and Mechanics Institution, organising an annual day out for the old people, or providing work for the unemployed. His consuming energy was always seeking some new and useful outlet for his talents. 'I had a restless spirit', he later wrote, 'and was always projecting something new. After seeing an institution fairly and successfully started I began to feel indifferent.' In 1831 that 'something new' was temperance. The tract he had been handed in the street, the evidence all around him on his charitable visits to the back streets, and finally a glass of whisky offered him by a friend all influenced him in the same direction. Livesey was fond of referring to this drink as 'the best I ever drank, because the last . . . It took hold of me,' he wrote, 'I felt very queer as I went home and retired to bed feeling very unwell. Next morning my mind was made up and I solemnly vowed that I would never take any kind of intoxicating liquor again.'

*Chapter Five*

# JERUSALEM, LANCS

'Preston was soon recognised as the Jerusalem of teetotalism, from which the word went forth in every direction.'

— JOSEPH LIVESEY, *c.* 1832

THE TEMPERANCE movement at this time drew its support from businessmen, clergy, and the more prosperous section of the middle class; working men, who were the chief victims of drink, had so far barely been affected. Joseph Livesey's chief work, however, had been among the poor and on New Year's Day, 1832, he founded a temperance group within his Sunday school for adults, many young men signing the moderation pledge. One who wished them to adopt the 'total' pledge was overruled, for as Livesey later explained, 'among the middle classes, this was considered a dangerous doctrine... To forbid wine and beer was declared an innovation upon... temperance orthodoxy.'

Livesey himself by now considered 'the liberty to take wine and beer in moderation... a fatal source of backsliding', and many working-men recruits to the temperance movement agreed with him. One of them, a cobbler called James Teare, of whom more will be heard, later claimed to have been the first man in England to preach total abstinence, at a meeting in the Grimshaw Street chapel, Preston, on 18th June 1832. This speech, if delivered, made little impact and was not reported by *The Preston Chronicle*, which in June gave a glowing account of the work of the Preston Temperance Society:

The society seems to be flourishing greatly in Preston. The weekly meetings are numerously attended by the operatives... The

> speakers are chiefly the operatives themselves, who relate in their own simple language the benefits which they or their acquaintances have derived from relinquishing . . . intoxicating liquors . . . The greatest harmony and good feeling has pervaded these assemblies and . . . at the close of the meeting on Tuesday, 73 individuals became members of the society.

The Preston Temperance Society had come into being in March 1832, after a visit from Henry Forbes of Bradford, and in May a series of meetings began in the Old Cockpit. In the same month Livesey advocated total abstinence in his paper *The Moral Reformer*, returning to the subject two months later, when he developed what was to become a favourite theme:

> A man who drinks a quart of ale will take nearly two ounces of pure spirit . . . nearly equal to half a gill of brandy . . . It may be asked, if you deprive people of spirits, wine, ale, porter, cider, perry, etc., what must they drink? . . . Drink . . . we would say, water, if you would be wise, virtuous, happy and healthy; or, if you will gratify your palate, a little tea, coffee, lemonade or any other undistilled and unfermented liquor.

Livesey's insistence that the alcohol in wine and beer was identical with that in spirits, and equally harmful, was his distinctive contribution to temperance thinking and it led him to the step which marked the real birth of the temperance movement.

> On Thursday, August 23rd 1832, John King was passing my shop in Church Street and I invited him in, and after discussing this question, upon which we both agreed, I asked him if he would sign a pledge of *total* abstinence, to which he consented. I then went to the desk and wrote one out . . . He came up to the desk and I said, 'Thee sign it first.' He did so and I signed after him . . . In the course of a few days notice of a special meeting was given, to be held in the Temperance Hall (the Cockpit), the following Saturday night, September 1st, at which this subject was warmly discussed . . . At the close of the meeting I remember well a group of us gathering together, still further debating the matter, which ended in *seven* persons signing a new pledge.

This document, engraved and widely reproduced,[1] became a sacred relic of the temperance movement, of which it was the founding charter:

> We agree to abstain from all liquors of an intoxicating quality, whether ale, porter, wine or ardent spirits, except as medicine.
>
> — John Gratrix, Edward Dickinson, John Brodbelt, John Smith, Joseph Livesey, David Anderton, John King.

Apart from John King and Joseph Livesey, none of the 'seven men of Preston', as they were soon labelled, made much further contribution to the movement and two actually broke their pledge.

The new policy had at first little effect on events, and total abstainers and 'moderates' who drank beer continued to work side by side. Preston had already been divided into twenty-eight districts, each under a 'captain', responsible for making new members and visiting existing supporters to prevent backsliding. Sunday morning was the favoured time for obtaining recruits. 'Let the missionaries go where the hard drinkers reside', advised Joseph Livesey. 'Dirty doorsteps, broken windows and other indications of the effects of drink will not be long to seek.' He recommended, too, a promising line of argument for 'If drinking ale really gives strength and vigour ... the man who gets his quart on a Saturday night ought to be ... active on a Sunday morning ... instead of ... thirsty and depressed and scarcely able to get from his bed to his big chair, where he usually sits unwashed till after dinner.' The aim was less to make immediate converts than to persuade a man to attend a meeting, and for Livesey at this time winning supporters to the temperance cause was merely part of his general charitable work.

Unlike many of their successors, the early reformers were under no illusions that getting rid of drunkenness would abolish poverty, and as John Finch of Liverpool wrote of some of the desperately poor families he and Livesey visited together, 'It was unnecessary for us to ask them to join the Temperance

[1] See page 51.

Society . . . for they have not one penny to spare for drink.' A few years later, Finch, by now virtually a socialist, was expelled from the local temperance society for this and other alleged heresies, but his advanced political views were typical of the early temperance reformers. Almost all, like Joseph Livesey, were Radicals; many were Chartists. Symbolically, the chairman of one West Country society presided from the seat once occupied by the local Chartist leader. They believed that signing the pledge was the prelude to self-improvement, by which the working class would fit itself for political power.

Although the total abstinence issue was already becoming troublesome in 1833, the pioneers were still content to disagree. 'He must be indeed an ultra-advocate of temperance', said John Finch, 'who would refuse to the toiling and sweating porter . . . a draught of what in his own phraseology is termed "heavy wet".' This was surely preferable to him taking 'a flash of lightning', several tots of spirits. In Preston, meanwhile, the total abstinence party was rapidly gaining ground. Night after night the Old Cockpit, off Stoneygate, was thronged with their supporters. The building, which seated 900, had been built by a former Earl of Derby to enable the population to enjoy the now illegal sport of cock-fighting, and in the next few years it became the forum of Chartists and Corn Law Repealers. In 1832 it was the turn of the temperance men and when not at the Cockpit, 'the Preston friends' were preaching the new doctrine in the surrounding villages. On the morning of Monday, 8th July 1833, the start of Preston race week, a local holiday, a party of seven, led by Livesey and including James Teare and Thomas Swindlehurst, set out by hired horse and cart to convert Lancashire to the cause. From the cart flew a white flag, made by Mrs. Livesey, bearing the words 'Temperance meeting' and a summary of their teaching: 'Malt not, brew not, distil not, buy not, sell not, drink not', and loaded inside were nearly 10,000 tracts. As they approached a town two men would go ahead to book a room and put up posters, and then the whole party would drive through the streets, waving the flag, ringing a handbell, and scattering tracts, while Teare announced the meeting in a voice which brooked no interruptions. At Stockport no one would hire them a hall, so they used the Methodist Chapel and drove round the town beating a borrowed drum; the hall was packed out. At Rochdale even the use of a chapel was refused, but an open-air meeting next day was a great success. Similar meetings were held everywhere they went, from Manchester to the smallest village. 'In the early days', wrote Livesey, 'we felt that we were really engaged in a "Temperance Reformation", we gave heart and soul to it . . . We seemed as if we could turn the world upside down.'

By now the movement had a new name, first heard in the Cockpit in 1833 from the lips of a former drunkard, 'Dicky' Turner. As a child Dicky had worked in the mills but had since slid steadily down the social scale from plasterer to fish hawker, later returning to the textile trade as a carder. In the previous October, now aged forty-two, he had rolled into a schoolroom where a temperance meeting was in progress, half-drunk and intending to cause trouble; instead, as so often happened, he had signed the pledge. Though possessing a 'dark ruddy complexion and an earnest gaze' he was only five feet four in height, but he made up in vehemence what he lacked in physique. On this famous night he was so carried away that he shouted out: 'I'll have nowt to do wi' this moderation, botheration pledge; I'll be reet down and out tee-tee-total for ever and ever.' At this Joseph Livesey leapt to his feet, exclaiming 'That shall be the name', and the name it duly became.[1] The public at large soon began to use 'temperance' as a synonym for 'teetotal', to the annoyance of the 'true temperance' or 'moderation' party, who pointed out that this was like a vegetarian calling himself a temperate meat eater.[2]

Dicky Turner later became in demand as a blunt, no-nonsense speaker, and he was famous for his mixed metaphors

[1] *The Oxford English Dictionary*, 1933 edition, specifically rejects suggestions that the word had existed in Lancashire dialect before 1833.

[2] Throughout this book I have followed the normal usage of employing the word 'temperance' to describe the movement as a whole, or any society that so described itself, even when it was in fact teetotal.

like 'We will go on with our axes on our shoulders and plough up the great deep and then the ship of temperance shall sail gallantly over the land.' In 1846, at the age of fifty-six, he walked to London to attend the first World Temperance Convention, preaching teetotalism all the way. Soon afterwards he died, his tombstone recording his claim to immortality: 'Richard Turner, author of the word teetotal'.

The roller-maker Thomas Swindlehurst was another popular speaker, becoming known as 'the king of the reformed drunkards'. He was often jocularly referred to as 'His majesty', and after an informal 'coronation' at Preston in 1836, addressed a mock proclamation to a temperance rally, 'From our Palace in Great Shaw Street, Preston', referring to 'the extension of our dominions and the extirpation of our moral foe'. Swindlehurst became rapidly disillusioned with the 'moderation' pledge. 'Your moderation allowance of three glasses per day', he told Finch, 'does not prevent me from going to public houses and ... I have schemed to get drunk on several occasions. Sometimes I have taken ... none at all for several days, and then I had eight, ten or twelve glasses due. This made me a good fuddle.'

It was, however, Finch's son who finally caused Swindlehurst to take the total pledge, by presenting him with a valuable new hat, costing twenty shillings, to be forfeit if he exceeded his moderation limit. Swindlehurst later described how, when tempted to take a fourth glass 'at the Plough Inn ... I bethought me of ... my new hat ... and ... ran out of the house, and home as fast as my poor legs would carry me.' He never went back. Two years later Finch himself became a passionate advocate of total abstinence, acquiring his own nickname, 'king of the teetotallers'.

Another popular figure at meetings was William Howarth, a fat man ironically known as 'Slender' or 'Slender Billy', a walking disproof of the belief that beer was essential to health. A different type altogether was 'the temperance poet', Henry Anderton, born in the same village as Livesey, where his mother kept a seed shop. Anderton was a lively young man, very fond of dancing, but his surviving work hardly suggests overwhelming poetic talent:

> Don't quaff the first pot,
> And the devil can not
> Compel thee to swallow a second.

Nor was Anderton very successful as a saddler. 'Teetotalism drove my trade away', he wrote sadly, for his chief customers, coach-proprietors, were also publicans. One of Anderton's great admirers, who edited an edition of his poems, was another famous Preston personality, Edward Grubb, at first known as 'the little drunken tailor' but later labelled 'the philosopher of the movement'. Despite this reputation Grubb did not despise more direct methods of argument. When some publicans produced a free barrel of ale to tempt away his audience at an open-air meeting in Blackburn in 1835 Grubb persuaded his hearers to stave it in. The enraged drinkers thereupon pelted him with rotten eggs, one of which ruined his new white hat. Grubb, however, won the final round. The crowd dragged up to the platform the man responsible and, according to legend, 'a well-merited punishment was then administered before their eyes by Mr. Grubb, after which nobody ventured to disturb the meeting'. Three years later Grubb scored an even greater triumph in a public debate with a 'moderation man' at Liverpool, who admitted himself beaten and signed the pledge on the spot, being followed by 2,000 members of the audience.

Also awarded nicknames were George Okell, 'the rector of the Obelisk', who preached teetotalism from the obelisk in Leigh market-place, flourishing his wood-cutter's axe, with which he proposed to hew down 'the tree of intemperance', and 'the Birmingham blacksmith', John Hockings. Hockings, having recruited seventy nail-makers at Belper in 1836, founded the Leicester Total Abstinence Society, with 400 members, and 'raised the standard of teetotalism' in the Midlands. When challenged at a London meeting to prove himself a blacksmith, he made three horseshoes in the time it took his challenger to make two. Hockings was one of the first to benefit financially from his temperance work. He attributed much of his success to charging for admission to meetings, later cashed in on making temperance medals and eventually emigrated to Canada to seek a wider field for his business talents.

But although teetotalism was spreading fast, it was the Cockpit at Preston which was the heart of the movement. 'We have', wrote Joseph Livesey, 'no select place for speakers, no platform. The speakers rise up in their different places and tell their plain and honest tales.' These normally described how the individual had been snatched back from the pit of drunkenness, but Livesey, who had always been abstemious, chose a different theme, to expose 'the great delusion', that beer and spirits were essentially different. This 'Malt Liquor Lecture' was to become the great oratorical set-piece of the movement, and Livesey illustrated it with a wealth of visual aids. On a blackboard he displayed the results of his enquiries to a local brewer, which showed that ale contained 5% alcohol, 3.8% barley, traces of some other substances, and 91% water. 'Two shillings worth of barley', he told his audience, flourishing a large loaf and a quart of ale, 'gives you two shillings worth of food; but two shillings worth of ale gives you one pennyworth of food . . . Ale is simply the juice of the pump, coloured, flavoured and fired.' The climax of the lecture was the ceremonial burning of the spirit distilled from a quart of beer, the effect of which, Livesey commented, was 'to destroy the coats of the stomach and to injure the livers of those who drink it . . . I much mistake my audience if there are not hundreds here, the bottom of whose pockets it has burned out many a time.'

The Malt Liquor Lecture ultimately became a ritual of the movement; no major temperance occasion was complete without it. In the next few years Livesey went on tour with it, travelling all over the north and Midlands. Sometimes the meeting ended in uproar but there were gratifying successes, as at Burnley, where the burning of the spirit caused one man to leap up, exclaiming: 'I have drunk as much of that as would have lit all the lamps in Manchester.'

Although constantly absent from Preston on his missionary

tours, Livesey successfully stood for the new Preston Borough Council in 1835, soon afterwards carrying a motion to sell the former Corporation's wine. Preston must have had a good cellar; the wine fetched £226 3s. 7d. and, on Livesey's insistence, the Council also disposed of its 'two japanned wine waggons, five dozen wine glasses, ten decanters and a cork-screw'. His fellow members probably heaved a sigh of relief when at the next election he was, in his own words, 'beaten by the mighty electioneering lever, cash and beer'.

In 1834, after publishing several teetotal tracts, Livesey launched *The Preston Temperance Advocate*, an eight-page monthly, costing a penny, which soon became the movement's paper of record and the foundation of the Livesey family's prosperous printing business. Besides advertisements for temperance, i.e. teetotal, hotels and coffee-houses, *The Advocate* carried a lively gossip column, *Varieties*. This gleefully recounted how an anti-temperance society, crowning a 'king of the drinkers', had tipped a bowl of blazing punch over its new monarch's head, and how two ex-teetotal lead miners, refused more drink at a Northumberland inn, had thrust a 'cask containing 25 lbs of gunpowder . . . into the fire, saying "Then we'll all go to hell together."'

In the same year Livesey decided to carry his message to the capital, expecting, he admitted, 'to produce a revolution in the great metropolis'. The British and Foreign Temperance Society, however, rebuffed him, its porter, who found Livesey the bread, barley and scales he needed for his lecture, being warned that if he gave any further help he would lose his job. Livesey finally obtained 'a sort of cellar chapel, about three steps underground' near Finsbury Square in the City, and engaged two sandwich-men to parade outside, but, in a hall big enough for 400, only twenty-five people turned up. In September 1835, Livesey tried again, but the hall, in Red Lion Square, Holborn, was as empty as before, and eventually 'Slender', in desperation, went out into the streets, ringing a bell to advertise the meeting. This had usually worked wonders in the north; in London it produced only a tap on the shoulder from a policeman, who told him to

*Harris Public Library, Preston*

THE PRESTON MISSIONARIES ARRIVE AT BLACKBURN, 1833

*Harris Public Library, Preston*

A MEETING IN PRESTON MARKET PLACE BROKEN UP BY A PRIZE-FIGHTER WITH A BEAR

*Harris Public Library, Preston*

JAMES TEARE ATTACKED IN THE MARKET PLACE AT STREE
SOMERSET, 1836

THE MOB STORMING THOMAS WHITTAKER'S MEETING AT
HARLOW, ESSEX, 1840

*Harris Public Library, Preston*

stop ringing under threat of arrest. But the incident attracted attention, the hall filled up, the authentic voice of 'the true Preston' was heard in the capital by an audience of hundreds, and the British Teetotal Temperance Society was formed. It was, however, to be several years yet before the teetotallers would move out of the obscurity of a dingy hall in Holborn into the spacious splendours of Exeter Hall in the Strand.

THE PRESTON PLEDGE

We agree to Abstain from All Liquors of an Intoxicating Quality, whether Ale Porter Wine or Ardent Spirits, except as Medicine.

John Gratrix. Jno: Smith.
Edwd Dickinson. Joseph Livesey.
Jno: Broadbelt. David Anderton.
Jno: King.

*Chapter Six*

# THROWING OFF THE SHACKLES

'We are all at fours and fives here about teetotalism and moderation. We shall soon, I expect, have got rid of the shackles of the moderation plan.'

— Letter from Huddersfield in *The Preston Temperance Advocate*, January 1836

THE COMING of total abstinence breathed new life into the temperance movement. It provided an effective reason for declining invitations to public houses, weddings and funerals, and prevented the movement being discredited by the heavy beer-drinking of its supporters and by the lapses of reformed drunkards whom only a renunciation of *all* alcohol could save.

The teetotallers were inspired, too, by a conviction that their work was God-given and it was not only Joseph Livesey who saw Preston as a new Jerusalem from which salvation was to be spread abroad. The contemporary literature is full of references to the 'Preston apostles', to 'preaching the word' and 'spreading the gospel'; the sudden eloquence which turned unlettered working men into powerful speakers was compared to 'the gift of tongues' displayed at Pentecost and to St. Paul's conversion on the Damascus road. Significantly, such men described themselves as temperance missionaries. Often they had painfully gained their education in Sabbath schools where the three Rs meant reading, writing and religion, and the Bible was the one book they had thoroughly studied. The language used by the secretary of the Warrington Total Abstinence Society, writing to Joseph Livesey in May 1835, was typical:

> Though we are but a few youths we hope in the strength of our God to stay, like David, the lion and the bear and to rescue the lambs from the lion's mouth. And though we have but our slings and stones yet we feel confident that Goliath, the great and daring monster, Drunkenness, will verily be slain.

Livesey's friend, John Finch of Liverpool, wrote in similar terms in 1836:

> Go, teetotaller, again, therefore and tell the modern Pharisees the things they may see and hear, 'the blind receive their sight, the lame walk, the lepers are cleansed'. Take our yoke of total abstinence upon you and learn of us to go about doing good . . . Come then to us all ye that are weary of a life of intemperance and heavy laden with sorrow, poverty, disease and crime and the love of strong drink, and God will give you rest.

Such language did not sound out of place in the nonconformist chapels which were the site of so many early temperance meetings, nor on the lips of men who were active members of dissenting sects. Without the widespread support of the free churches the infant movement might not have survived. Although temperance, in the 'moderation' sense, commanded great support in the Church of England and among the Roman Catholics, teetotalism was distrusted from the first, especially by the higher clergy, partly no doubt because it was so often preached by extreme evangelicals. Many converts to teetotalism tended to speak of the moment they signed the pledge as one of spiritual rebirth, resembling a second baptism. An extreme case was Captain Bailey, a Manchester 'flatman' or barge-owner, who recounted his experiences to a temperance festival in 1836.

> He stated that when he gave up his drunken career and became a teetotaller he was determined to make a complete job of it, so he took the opportunity one day when he was alone in his cabin to wash off all the filth of drunkenness. He stripped and washed himself from head to foot, he then took a dose of physic, to purge, as he said, the corruption of drunkenness out of him. But this

did not fully satisfy him; he felt anxious to get rid of his drunken blood, so he applied to a surgeon and requested him to bleed him almost to death . . . as he was going to take in a cargo of good tee-total blood.

To many teetotallers the refusal of the existing temperance societies to embrace the new doctrine seemed like the rejection by the Jews of the teachings of Christ. Many teetotallers said openly that they preferred a drunkard to a moderate drinker: the one was a walking witness to the perils of drink; the other, to use a favourite phrase, was 'a drunkard-maker'. Livesey wrote of knowing ten drunkards who 'were all moderation persons once . . . Matthew Moderation, Billy-Little-drop, John Odd-glass, Nathan Never-to-excess . . .' and so on. 'I have said and mean to say', thundered Henry Mudge of Bodmin in a sermon in 1839, 'that the example of moderation drinkers is worse and more dangerous than that of drunkards. The former are decoys to lure us into, the latter are beacons to warn us off from, the whirlpool of intemperance.'

Between 1834 and 1836 the teetotallers, by a combination of ruthlessness, persistence and persuasiveness, seized control of the temperance movement. The experience of a leading Huddersfield moderate, William Haigh, was typical. After rashly agreeing to speak at a rally at Haslingden, with Henry Anderton and John King, he found that it was he, and not the drunkards, who was under attack. He described how Anderton's 'keen satire made me writhe . . . and my face crimsoned with shame as he made the audience laugh at my folly in coming all the way from Yorkshire to teach the Lancashire folks "the great delusion" that ale and wine drinking in moderation was the best cure for drunkenness'. At the end of the meeting he told his tormentor, 'I cannot do with you taking the shine out of me in this way', and signed the total pledge.

Nor was he alone for long. Huddersfield had had a flourishing temperance society since 1832, but after Joseph Livesey had lectured its members in 1835 the old tranquillity was lost. A local correspondent wrote to *The Preston Temperance Advocate* early in 1836:

We are all at fours and fives here about teetotalism and moderation. We shall soon, I expect, have got rid of the shackles of the moderation plan . . . I have been perpetually pestered by the moderation men finding fault with us. We have scarcely had a meeting without some remarks from the moderation people to damp the zeal in favour of teetotalism.

One year later the society went teetotal.

The transformation to teetotalism marked a change in the social character of the temperance movement. It lost its respectable, middle-class image; it gained a tougher, working-class approach, less subtle but far more effective. Wrote Henry Anderton early in 1834:

Where none but privileged and educated people are permitted to speak and where ale is preached as a nutritious beverage, or at least as a necessary evil, the societies . . . are dying or dead . . . Where uneducated, reformed drunkards have full liberty to tell their round unvarnished tale, and where abstinence, unqualified abstinence . . . is held forth . . . those societies are progressing with a glorious rapidity.

In September 1834 a conference of delegates from societies all over Lancashire and Cheshire, held in Manchester, unanimously decided that all societies in future should offer the teetotal pledge as well as the moderation one, since many potential members were refusing to join unless the former were available. Already the first exclusively teetotal society had been formed, at Miles Platting, near Manchester, in July, several other places following soon afterwards. The case of Warrington, where an exclusively teetotal society was formed in October, was particularly significant. The old Temperance Society here, founded in 1830, had regarded beer so highly that when an ex-drunkard asked for a 'total' pledge to sign one had had to be specially drawn up for him, and a friend had tried physically to prevent him signing, calling out 'Thee mustn't, Richard, thee'll die.' In 1834, however, the Warrington Total Abstinence Society effectively replaced the old temperance society, and by the following year it even had a flourishing band which, according to one report, 'from the superiority of the music did very great credit to teetotalism'.

In Preston itself the cause was also flourishing. On Whit Monday, 3rd June 1833, what was later claimed as the first teetotal procession in the world marched through the streets a thousand strong, with bands playing, led by Dicky Turner carrying a flag, Thomas Swindlehurst on a white horse and Joseph Livesey in an open carriage. The marchers were greeted with shouts of applause, but Preston was not always so welcoming and one meeting in the market-place was broken up by a notorious prize-fighter, Touch Duckett, and his performing bear, before whom the audience fled in terror. The Preston Society finally discarded the moderation pledge in March 1835 and in September delegates from societies all over Lancashire, Cheshire and Yorkshire decided to form a national organisation, the British Association for the Promotion of Temperance, commonly known as the British Temperance Association and, after 1854, as the British Temperance League. At first 'two-pledge' societies were allowed to join but this concession was short-lived; in July 1836 a further meeting at Preston decided that all affiliated societies must become exclusively teetotal within three months. In the following year the Association adopted a 'total' pledge renouncing drink 'except in cases of extreme necessity', but this was denounced by such teetotal strongholds as Preston, Warrington and Liverpool as 'vague and ill-advised'. Several threatened to secede unless it were dropped and for years any reference to 'extreme necessity' was good for a laugh on temperance platforms. By then the teetotallers had won their main battle. In some places, like Bolton and Sheffield, an existing society expelled its 'moderation' members; in others, like Liverpool, a separate teetotal society was founded which soon eclipsed its rival. At Blackburn the Temperance Society, founded in 1831, had had a notoriously accommodating pledge, which allowed its members to drink wine and beer 'in great moderation' and even spirits 'when necessary for refreshment in travelling or transacting business away from home'. Now its active members deserted it to embrace the sterner doctrine of the Total Abstinence Society, which by October 1834 claimed 1,200 supporters. At Halifax, recorded one teetotaller, 'In 1832 we formed a temperance society on the moderation pledge; the effects were scarcely visible, no drunkards were reclaimed and not many reduced their daily consumption of wine or porter. In 1835 the total abstinence pledge was introduced. The first society dwindled away and the teetotallers gained strength and now reckon 700 members.' The evidence from Bradford, birthplace of English temperance, was the same: 'Here the first moderation society was formed', wrote a disillusioned member, 'and there was no want of zeal, talent or piety in working that system, yet in five years we did not succeed in reforming one solitary drunkard.' John Cadbury's experience at Birmingham was similar: 'On the moderation plan', he wrote, 'I never knew one drunkard reclaimed; whilst on the teetotal plan we have reclaimed hundreds.' At Southampton the Temperance Society, founded in October 1835, was short-lived. One of its members began to distribute *The Preston Temperance Advocate*, to which he reported progress in July 1836:

> The moderation, or rather botheration, society here is dying of a rapid consumption. At the last monthly meeting not one of the secretaries—for there are three—were there. One of the members said to me, 'I shall propose that this meeting be adjourned to this night six months and that the teetotallers take their place.' We did so. Oh! Sir, how can they go on with such a miserable system to keep men on the verge of such an awful precipice? Teetotalism gives a man wings to fly, a tongue to speak, feet to walk, eyes to see, in a word gives liberty to breathe. Who can describe the blessings of teetotalism?

It was in London that the most bitter battles of what was known as 'the war of the pledges' were fought out. Teetotalism was slow to take root in the capital and the British and Foreign Temperance Society, founded in 1831, was an ultra-respectable body, which regarded 'the Lancashire fanatics' with deep distaste. Preston men in their turn distrusted this well-connected but idle body, characteristic, in their view, of the sophisticated softness of the south, and especially of the capital. As Livesey wrote, 'I would rather have one good, plain disinterested teetotaller, who gives every week what time he has to spare to the cause, than fifty vice-presidents who do little or nothing.'

The stronger the teetotallers became, the more ineffectual grew the British and Foreign Temperance Society. During the winter of 1834–5, while teetotalism was carrying all before it in the North, the Society's officials were vainly struggling to put down this 'new and dangerous doctrine' and by the end of 1835 the most active societies had withdrawn their support and affiliated instead to the teetotal and Manchester-based British Temperance Association. By now the gulf between teetotallers and moderation-men was widening. As the Liverpool Temperance Society warned in April 1836, 'The end of such societies would never be gained while moderators and teetotallers were confounded together and so long as such an ill-starred union existed there would be an unceasing jarring of interests and consequent distrust among the members.' A letter in *The Liverpool Temperance Advocate* later that year pointedly drew attention to the renewed failure of the British and Foreign Temperance Society to produce an annual report, or to prevent its magazine 'falling off in circulation'. The writer went on:

> If something be not shortly done . . . the British and Foreign Temperance Society must inevitably and finally fall . . . Our meetings are addressed almost entirely by teetotallers, who fail not on all occasions to rail most violently and crabbedly at the British and Foreign Temperance Society and attack those who support it, thereby causing great disgust and often disturbance. The principal speakers at the last May meeting at Exeter Hall were teetotallers and there was no one upheld the society which they met to support. The very agents in their lectures and speeches and private discourse about the metropolis are in the constant habit of recommending the teetotal pledge as superior to the British and Foreign Temperance Society and even speak point blank against the Society which pays them to talk.

The Society in fact staggered on for a few more years. In 1840 its annual meeting retreated to the humbler surroundings of the Hanover Square Concert Rooms; the teetotallers met in

Exeter Hall. By 1848, despite its wealthy supporters, the Society's annual income had shrunk to £200, compared to £1,630 in 1836. That year its magazine ceased to appear and Bishop Blomfield resigned as President. Two years later the Society was formally wound up. Its leaders, explained a teetotal historian, 'persistently refused to walk in the light... Their determined antagonism to teetotalism proved their ruin.'

What made the teetotallers regard the 'war of the pledges' as a holy crusade was their growing belief that it was not merely inexpedient to drink alcohol but morally wrong, since drink was, as Livesey put it, 'the devil in solution'. The original pledge for twelve months was extended to cover lifelong renunciation and a campaign launched to replace the 'short pledge', of personal abstinence, by the 'long pledge', which added a promise 'neither to give nor offer' drink to others. But even this was insufficient for the real enthusiasts, as the history of the other principal London-based organisation, the New British and Foreign Temperance Society for the Suppression of Intemperance, soon revealed. This had been established in 1836, as the successor to the British Teetotal Temperance Society, founded in the previous year after Joseph Livesey's second visit to London. Its president was Earl Stanhope and it had many well-known supporters, among them James Silk Buckingham, the water-drinking M.P., and John Dunlop, the 'anti-usage' authority, while it did its best to cater for all tastes by accepting both moderation men and teetotallers as members, offering the latter both the 'short' and the 'long' pledges. The extremists, however, increasingly demanded the 'American pledge', a comprehensive undertaking aimed at drinking-usages and the whole licensed trade. 'We will not', promised the signatories, 'use intoxicating liquors as a beverage, nor traffic in them... We will not provide them as an article of entertainment or for persons in our employment and... in all suitable ways we will discountenance their use throughout the community.'

The Society's annual conference in May 1839 at Exeter Hall was the occasion, according to an eyewitness, of 'perhaps the most extraordinary and tumultuous meeting ever held within the walls of that building'. Amid the uproar, Earl Stanhope threatened to walk out if a resolution in favour of the American pledge were carried and eventually declared it defeated by 256 to 337, but the teetotallers were not beaten yet. Overnight they regrouped their forces, planning a take-over of the Society at its public meeting next morning. Their tactics succeeded. Amid general uproar the proceedings were held up while Edward Grubb, the 'Preston philosopher', called for the American pledge to be put again to the vote. Eventually Earl Stanhope, unable even to make himself heard, walked out and John Dunlop took over the chair and announced the motion carried by a large majority. The minority then marched out, joining Lord Stanhope in a new organisation, the British and Foreign Society for the Suppression of Intemperance, or 'Suppression Society', which, while teetotal, did not insist on any particular form of pledge. Eventually in 1842 both Societies were dissolved and replaced by the National Temperance Society, which in 1856 merged with the London Temperance League to become the National Temperance League.[1]

The controversy over the pledges helps to explain the proliferation of organisations and titles which is so confusing a feature of temperance history. Societies appeared, coalesced, split into two, were dissolved, re-formed—sometimes under names previously used by rival bodies—and changed their names with bewildering frequency. But, despite all these upheavals in the mid-eighteen thirties, the movement went on growing. In 1834 there had been about 100,000 members of temperance societies, almost double the total of a year before, in England and Wales. Twenty-eight thousand of them lived in Lancashire, though Cornwall, with 11,000, had most in relation to population. North Wales, too, was becoming a stronghold of teetotalism, which it has remained until the present day. In 1837 it was said to contain 100,000 teetotallers, a number probably including all ages, for the secretary of the Rhyl

[1] The National Temperance League and the British Temperance League were united in 1949 as the British National Temperance League. Its headquarters is now in Sheffield.

Temperance Society wrote proudly that 'Our children, yea, as young as three years of age, refuse intoxicating liquor when it is offered them saying "No wicked ale!"' Two years later half the population of Anglesey were claimed as converts and 2,500 of the 8,000 people in Caernarvon. One Society estimated that in the whole United Kingdom in 1883 there were half a million teetotallers, a not unreasonable figure if children were included.

There were, too, other encouraging signs of a change in public opinion. In 1834 the judge at Lancaster Assizes bound a man over to join a temperance society, remarking that 'from Preston . . . there has not been a single case these Assizes'. In the same year Lloyd's of London reduced their usual 6% insurance premium on a ship sailing to China to 5% as it had no spirits on board. In 1836 the first temperance boarding house and the first Mechanics Temperance Institution were opened in London and the first temperance hotel appeared, in Aldersgate Street in the City, financed by William Janson, who was also known as 'Barley-water Billy'.

Most encouraging of all, the agitation against alcohol was beginning to make an impact on the medical profession. The escape-clause in the earliest pledges, 'except as medicine', had proved a constant source of back-sliding and the later substitution of 'except when ordered by a doctor' had proved only partially successful. Medical declarations against alcoholic excess, or against spirits, were readily forthcoming, but it was not till 1834 that the first medical teetotaller was recruited. This was Ralph Grindrod, a twenty-three-year-old Manchester general practitioner, who had realised while working as medical officer to several sick clubs that drunkenness was 'the working man's curse'. He celebrated his conversion by delivering an open-air lecture in a square surrounded by workmen's cottages, using two borrowed tables as an impromptu platform, on which he burned some alcohol. The resulting 'blue blazes', he told his audience, resembled the combustion constantly in progress in the stomach of a heavy drinker. Soon afterwards Grindrod challenged to a public debate the landlord of a popular local inn, famous for its home-brewed 'tenpenny'. On three successive

August evenings in 1834 a huge crowd, estimated at 10,000–15,000, packed Stevenson Square in the centre of the city, to watch the contest. The publican described his opponent as 'a graphic personification of a waterdrinker. Look at him! Does he look as if he had ever indulged in port, hock, sherry, turtle, venison or even oyster sauce? No! More likely *soup maigre*.' Grindrod's supporters retorted with a procession exhibiting 'the fruits of teetotalism'—a 60 lb loaf, a 65 lb ham and an 85 lb cheese. At the end the crowd voted overwhelmingly in their favour, but the drinkers had the last laugh, if a rather grim one. In the following January the floor of the nearby Tabernacle gave way during a crowded teetotal meeting. Two people were killed and many injured, and Grindrod, called to treat them, was greeted with cries of 'A judgment is come upon you', and 'This is what you get by temperance.'

At this time anyone on a coach journey who declined the traditional glass of rum or punch 'to keep out the cold' was regarded with curiosity by his fellow passengers, and in 1836 Grindrod published *A dialogue between a surgeon and a moderate drinker* which had taken place in a stagecoach, following this up with *Physician on Total Abstinence*, the movement's first medical textbook. Later he became a pioneer of the water-treatment of illness and one of the founders of Malvern Spa.

Grindrod was also to be remembered for a convert made during the Manchester debates, a gawky young workman called John Cassell. Cassell had been so impressed that he had signed the pledge on the spot and the following year, now aged nineteen, he walked to London, supporting himself by odd jobs, and wherever he stopped ringing a handbell to attract a crowd and preaching teetotalism. On arrival in London after three weeks on the road Cassell contacted some sympathisers at a temperance meeting and within a few months 'The Manchester carpenter' had become one of the most popular speakers in the country. His rendering of poems in his strong Lancashire accent never failed to bring the house down, and his uncouthness became a legend. Cassell's coarse, ill-fitting clothes, his bony limbs, his dark, disordered hair, his rough speech, made even less intelligible by a stammer—all were cherished by audiences, as was his unshakeable good nature. He was given to high-spirited singing and shouting as he trudged along, calling out invitations to passers-by to 'Come and see the jolly teetotallers'. Ten years after his arrival in London, John Cassell began to publish *The Teetotal Times and Monthly Temperance Messenger*, and other improving works. His first big success was a cheap educational series, appealing to the self-help spirit of the times, and before he died, at forty-eight, he had, like William Collins, laid the foundations of an enduring publishing business.

In April 1835 the teetotallers staged their biggest rally to date, at Wilsden, a village five miles from Bradford, which became the site of an annual jamboree. A crowded meeting in the church, addressed by Joseph Livesey, was followed by refreshments in a marquee, 135 feet long, where 'about five o'clock the sober but exhilarating liquor began to circulate'. Nearly 3,000 people were fed, in two sittings, and the elaborate décor was much admired. This became a feature of big temperance functions and often the public paid for admission merely to see the decorations, which on this occasion included a wooded bower, with lifelike stuffed birds perched on the branches. These were soon to become a status symbol of the movement. A case of them on the sideboard was a sure sign, at least in temperance novels, of a thrifty, non-drinking household, just as the absence of a clock indicated moral decline, this being the first item the drunkard pawned.

Such homes were likely to become fewer if the example of 'several spinsters and widows' at Llanfair in Wales were to be followed. They, *The Preston Temperance Advocate* reported in 1837, had 'signed a pledge to refuse the addresses of any male who is not an out and out teetotaller'.

*Chapter Seven*

## FIRING BOMBSHELLS

'Though Plymouth is forty-five miles from Exeter, in the name of God I shall be there on Monday... Tell them at the Cockpit that I am firing my bombshells as warmly as ever.'
— JAMES TEARE, Exeter, to JOSEPH LIVESEY, 1836

BY 1835 many local societies, their struggle with the 'moderation men' won, were beginning to consolidate their organisation. In Preston 'temperance academies' were set up in cottages, where classes were held in temperance doctrine, and in the Cockpit a room was set aside for training speakers—there were soon eighty ready to face a real audience. All these volunteers were now about to be reinforced by paid agents, for whom temperance was not only a way of life but a living.

The first such missionary, James Teare, had been born in the Isle of Man in 1804 and apprenticed to a bootmaker. At the age of nineteen, while waiting at Liverpool to emigrate, he had visited his brother at Preston and decided to stay. Teare, a keen Methodist, was 'a strong-built, healthy, vigorous man', with 'a brusque, dogmatic manner', hence his nickname of 'honest James Teare'. Joseph Livesey's dictum, 'A kiss is worth a thousand kicks', made no appeal to him; he preferred 'a tee-total row', when he could 'give it to the soakers hip and thigh'. He had won his spurs as a speaker during the famous Race Week mission in 1833 and in the winter of 1835–6 he twice returned to his native island, to bully, rather than cajole, the inhabitants into signing the pledge. Four Manx breweries went out of business, and in one parish alone thirty-two public houses closed for lack of support. 'This island', *The Preston Temperance Advocate* recorded, 'has already caught the teetotal fire', a fire stoked up by energetic follow-up visits from Manchester and Preston. One such visitor was shocked to see 'huts with boards and slates hung over the doors, upon which were rudely cut or daubed such notices as "Shoes mended and spirits sold"'.

His experiences in his native island were a dress rehearsal for Teare's real mission and on Monday, 4th April 1836, he set out from Preston determined to introduce teetotalism into every town and county in Great Britain. He carried a certificate from the Preston Society commending his mission, but travelled at his own expense, nowhere asking for money but not refusing it if offered. His average income as a professional speaker, he later calculated, was never more than £65 a year, and at first he lived on his savings.

This first missionary journey later became a legend and every self-respecting society in the west of England dated its foundation from Teare's arrival. When, after twelve months on the road, he appeared at the Cockpit in Preston to report on his work, he received an ovation. Despite spending long periods in London, Bristol and Birmingham, he had travelled 8,000 miles, held 400 meetings, and carried the message into twenty counties from Yorkshire to Devon and from Kent to Denbighshire. Soon afterwards he was off again, concentrating on the Midlands and North Wales but getting as far afield as Somerset. By now the teetotal movement was everywhere putting down roots, and temperance halls, where societies could meet without being dependent for a room on suspicious clergy or hostile publicans, were beginning to spring up in many places. The first such hall, at Garstang in Lancashire, was in a temporary hut; the first permanent, converted building was opened by Teare at Burnley on Christmas Eve 1837, and the first custom-built Temperance Hall began operations at Bradford early in 1838. Another sign of the times was the founding at Salford in 1835 of the first English branch of the temperance friendly society, the Independent Order of Rechabites. Like other societies, the Rechabites provided sick benefits, burial grants, and medical care, as well as some harmless ceremonial, but no meetings were held in public houses and only teetotallers could belong. After a slow start, the 'tents' or branches of the Order sprang up everywhere; within four years there were nearly 200; within seven years three times as many, representing a membership of 25,000, growth continuing throughout the century.

By 15th August 1836, four months after he had set out, Teare was sending back a cheerful report to Joseph Livesey from Bristol:

> Since I wrote to you last I have been at Swansea ... where I held four meetings, one in the Town Hall and the other three in the largest chapels in the town. A society was formed on the teetotal principle and nearly 100 signed the pledge. I held one meeting in the Town Hall at Neath, the church minister in the chair. In the course of my address, he got up and opposed me, saying that our Lord made wine and that it contained alcohol ... But, I do assure you, I beat him down with fair argument and no little mortified he appeared to be. He was supported by a liquor merchant, who told me to sit down; but instead of sitting down, I spoke for nearly two hours. I felt I could have spoken all night ... I have held meetings nearly every night these last twelve weeks and have had opposition at nearly every meeting ... One wicked man told me to go home again; to which I replied, 'Never, so long as there is a drunkard in England!' ... The cause is going well at Bristol, Bath and the other places I have visited ... Tomorrow I shall leave this place and go further into Somersetshire.

Somersetshire at first proved little more welcoming. At Taunton the Wesleyans provided the use of their chapel but the landlords and 'moderation people kicked up a row, broke the pews and pulled the hat pins out of the wall and threw them on the platform'. At Street, near Glastonbury, he was attacked at midday, so violently that two of those responsible were sent to the treadmill for six weeks and two others fined £3 each. Moving on to Devon, Teare held three crowded meetings at Exeter, but the temperance society at Plymouth warned him that its members were not yet ready for teetotalism. Teare, however, was the last person to stay away because he was unwelcome. He wrote to Preston:

> But though it is forty-five miles from Exeter, in the name of God I shall be there on Monday. Pray that God may go with me and tell them at the Cockpit that I am firing my bombshells as warmly as ever.

As Teare's fame spread the opposition hardened. As he walked down the steamer gangplank at Bristol he was greeted with groans and hisses and at Plymouth not a single minister would allow the use of his chapel. Teare therefore proclaimed the teetotal message to an audience wedged into the tiny desks of the Free School, but even the use of this was withdrawn soon afterwards. A Plymouth Teetotal Society was duly founded but it met at first in a dingy, unheated loft, each member bringing with him a bundle of candles for lighting. As he walked the streets, the cry might be raised, 'There goes a teetotaller!' and people would hurry to doors and windows to enjoy this rare sight.

Teare's greatest triumphs were scored further west, in Cornwall. Dr. Henry Mudge, a Methodist lay preacher, invited him to visit the county town, Bodmin, and when he arrived, in January 1838, 200 pledges were collected in two nights. When Teare reached St. Ives, a month later, the little fishing port embraced the new faith with an eagerness verging on hysteria. Within three months there were 1,200 pledged teetotallers in a population of under 5,000; within eight months the number had doubled. By August 1838, when a Cornwall Teetotal Association was formed, there were no fewer than 18,000 teetotallers in the county, or one in seven of the whole population, and in many a Cornish cottage James Teare's picture hung beside that of John Wesley.

Bodmin became one of the showplaces of the movement. It was the scene of the county's first 'teetotal harvest supper', when a hundred farm labourers in their Sunday best paraded through the streets carrying their reaping hooks, before sitting down to a meal washed down by water and tea. Afterwards, instead of joining in the traditional country songs, they stood up in turn to testify to the benefits of temperance. Teare on a later visit was met by a band playing 'See the conquering hero comes', and his activities were commemorated in some abusive verses:

The Bodmin cobblers, for their trade
Began to quake and fear
When they were told that Mr. T——
Would labouring be here.

He came, he spoke, or rather dared
His vulgar trash to bawl,
And as a proof of abstinence,
Swore he's renounced his *awl*.

And, faith!, with justice, we cannot
His self-denial blame;
For, for a hundred pounds a year,
Hundreds would do the same.

Although Teare remained the great temperance hero of the west, as the years passed he became increasingly alienated from his old Preston associates. His 'passion for little economies . . . apt to run into meanness', hardened into an obsession that he was almost destitute, and his legitimate pride in his work for the movement swelled into a belief that he had founded it single-handed. This was the cause of the first of many rifts within the teetotal movement. Few contributions to the Teare Testimonial Fund, launched from Bristol in 1860, came from Lancashire and in 1864 three 'Preston teetotallers from the year 1832' published a crushing *Refutation* of Teare's claims, accusing him of being 'left to sound his own trumpet' and declaring that 'some might be uncharitable enough to insinuate that the money had been raised under false pretences'. Four years later, when 'honest James Teare' died, it was discovered that he had been comfortably off, although he made posthumous amends by bequeathing 100 guineas for two prize essays in his memory.

Teare's real memorial was the remarkable vigour of the temperance societies which sprang up in the west. As in

Lancashire, their main appeal was to the working class and a man's trade was his most valuable qualification, for a tin-miner was most effective in convincing other miners and a shepherd other shepherds. 'If the specimen was not ready to hand', wrote one Bristol pioneer, Thomas Hudson, 'it was held to be conclusive that while teetotalism might suit the other man the opponent's own case was exceptional.' Visitors like James Teare, he recalled, created a great impression, when they denounced the 'pooblicans' and

> slapped their pockets with loud boasts of golden guineas saved from the drink shops, who talked of roast beef and plum pudding as if they really meant it. If the 'roast beef' and 'pocket full of money' and 'pig in the sty' business told effectively from strangers, how much more it succeeded when the foregoings of the speaker were known, when the beef and bacon would be actually smelt and seen and tasted and the pig heard grunting in the sty.

The 'teetotal pig' soon acquired in rural Devon, Somerset and North Wales the symbolic significance of the case of stuffed birds in industrial Lancashire. Families saved their pennies towards the proud day when they would own their own pig and a domestic money box became known as a 'piggy bank'.

A famous exponent of this line of argument was a clayworker, Nathaniel Bailey. His speech to a Boxing Day rally was typical:

> Gents and ladies: If anyone had said this day twelve months that Nat Bailey would have stood up to address such a lot of teetotallers like himself, Nat would have told 'em they was liars. I've been a married man two and twenty years; and I never spent such a happy Christmas in my life before; and I never had such a famous piece of beef in my cupboard. 'Twas none of your backshambles stuff, what dogs wouldn't touch, but some of the very best beef in all England... I never had such puddings before, neither, and then all my little 'uns say—'Thank God father's a teetotaller.'

Nat described how he had taken to drink as an apprentice and one Easter 'got mad with drinking':

Well, my friends, I got my razor and went to look for my wife. The old woman . . . thought I was up to no good, and so off she ran. I . . . ran after her; but I couldn't catch her . . . and it was a good thing I couldn't, for if I had caught her, I should have been hung for her, instead of being here to tell you teetotallers about it . . . Look at my wife and children before you. Instead of being ragged and deserted, they looks tidy and comfortable; and then, for a working man, I've got a middling good coat on. If you'd seen me this day twelve months, 'twas such an old 'un that you wouldn't have picked 'im up in the streets . . . So you see what I've got by being a teetotaller.

This was always a popular type of argument. At Modbury, near Plymouth, a speaker produced in turn 'a nice coat for father', 'a new gown for mother', and 'new boots for the children', finally referring to the crowning benefit of temperance, 'a good plum pudding', the cue for two men to stagger in with a giant pudding, which was sliced up and served to the audience. Some gestures by new converts were even more dramatic. One former beer-house keeper uncorked all his barrels and flooded his cellar with beer. A businessman at Street, Somerset, used the contents of his wine cellar to moisten the cement for his new house. At Cirencester, Gloucestershire, one teetotaller somewhat ironically bought up *The Hole in the Wall* public house and pulled it down, erecting a temperance hall on the site, with a floor made of chopped-up beer vats. But even this was not the worst outrage charged against the teetotallers. 'The greatest excitement', a local correspondent told Thomas Hudson of Bristol, 'was caused by the cutting down by their owners of apple-trees used for making cider. This was looked upon with awe and horror as a wicked sacrilege, rendered worse by the subsequent impiety of giving apples to pigs.'

Not surprisingly, the teetotallers in the West Country, as in the North, became violently unpopular. The open 'jaunting car' in which the Bristol group travelled to meetings often attracted a shower of rotten eggs and the hall and school-room in which they met were 'not infrequently besieged by a gang of rowdies made ready for the job by strong potations'. Fortunately the society possessed one working-man member, Thomas Bodset, 'a red-faced, hot-headed, devoted teetotaller' who was 'pre-eminently a man of action. At this exciting period there was seldom a meeting held, the proceedings of which were not additionally enlivened by a fist encounter between Thomas Bodset . . . and some beery bully.'

At a meeting in October 1836 one regular trouble-maker, 'a low-minded, dissipated master-sweep named William Bulphin', pushed his way through a police cordon to attack the platform, only to be driven off by several blows from a heavy, brass-headed cane, wielded by a Quaker. Bulphin took his attackers to court, where the pacifist, teetotal Quakers were denounced as 'bellicose', counsel remarking that 'If such were the effects of temperance he would advise the defendants in future to take a little . . . wine.' They were fined £10, plus costs, but the publicity was cheap at the price, for the battling Quakers, tea-pot valiant on water, became a local joke. At Camborne, too, in 1838, the waterdrinkers hit back after some drunken rowdies had broken up one of their meetings and 'mustered . . . within view of the different inns and beer-shops in the evening, hissing and hooting anyone who dared to enter'.

Often the publicans were said to be behind the attacks on teetotallers. In rural districts, where the publican was often also a retail corn merchant, many public houses displayed notices: 'No yeast or grain sold to teetotallers'. A publican who inadvertently raised his hat to a temperance speaker riding past, 'threw down his hat into the road and, trampling it underfoot, swore that he would never wear it again and forthwith walked away bareheaded'. In one Cornish village a farmer who lent his cart for a platform found it next day at the bottom of a mine-shaft. The chapel caretaker in another village told Thomas Hudson, the visiting speaker, 'If you are going to preach I shall light four candles in the pulpit, but if you give a teetotal lecture only two—and every alternate candle over other parts of the chapel.' At Penrhyn, the doors of the Wesleyan chapel were locked against James Teare and the teetotallers 'turned out to grass on the bowling green'.

In the 1840s, at the height of the railway boom, a popular West Country speaker was Samuel Garnett, 'the teetotal navvy' who 'appeared on the platform in his usual velveteen jacket, breeches and hobnailed boots, his sunburnt ... neck being adorned by a huge white collar'. Hostile audiences relished his grammatical mistakes and mispronunciations, though some connoisseurs preferred a schoolmaster who denounced 'intostication' and 'fomented liquor' and a reformed drunk who boasted that 'I have made hundreds of convicts to the cause'. Another target for interruptions was Joseph Eaton, of Bristol, an extremely thin iron merchant, who, as he bent over the candle to read his notes, would be greeted with cries of 'Now then, old Iron Hoop, if thee doesn't mind thee'll burn thy nose!'[1] A popular Somerset double act were an elderly couple of Primitive Methodists from Nunney near Frome, since the husband 'kept up a running commentary' on his wife's oratory, exclaiming, 'That's true, Betty! Well done, Betty!' Even better known was John Shapcott, who ran the Exeter to Tiverton coach service and taught each of his large family to play a musical instrument. The brass band of 'Shapcott and Sons' was often in demand at temperance meetings.

The Bristol pioneers, being town-dwellers, were not infrequently accused at village meetings of knowing nothing about country life. At first, until teetotal farm labourers were available as speakers, they were constantly assailed by the questions, 'If it be wrong to drink beer and cider, what did the Almighty send barley and apples for?' and 'How could a fellow do a day's mowing or reaping without a gallon of cider or beer?' The vexatious question of what would happen to the barley if no more beer were brewed was answered by a Bristol merchant who evolved a recipe for barley pudding, portions of which were handed round at the tea-parties for fish wives and other working women which he organised. At the end the guests were asked to affirm that they had enjoyed the pudding more than beer.

[1] 'Old Iron Hoop' had the last laugh. When he died in 1858 he left more than £16,000 to temperance organisations, probably the movement's largest bequest.

Rowdy meetings, often with noisy mobs outside trying to break in, helped to advertise the movement in the west in its early days and additional publicity came from processions of witness, like that first held in Bristol in 1837. By now some 3,000 people in a population of 120,000 had signed the pledge and 1,000 of them marched through the streets 'to the strains of martial music and banners uplifted to the breeze'. Despite some jeers, the bystanders were, said Thomas Hudson, struck by 'the favourable contrast... thus presented between the smartly-dressed, jolly, well-conducted men, women and children... and the blear-eyed, foul-mouthed representatives of the pipe and the pot'. The worst the teetotallers suffered on this occasion were cries of 'Coffee-guts!' and the display of a drawing featuring one of their best-known members, an empty coffee-pot and a coffin—as a warning against coffee-drinking.[1] At Bath, although the town's prosperity was founded on water, they had more to endure, being a favourite target for 'Sam Sly', the local newspaper's resident wit, who later signed the pledge himself. After a mock report of the teetotal tea-party held at the Guildhall at Christmas 1836, 'giving to all who took part in it the drollest names and putting into their mouths the most ludicrous speeches', Sam Sly produced a classic *Sketch* of the temperance procession held in June 1837.

> The teetotallers have been chuckling and rejoicing among themselves at what they term 'A judgment' in Bath, by a brewery having accidentally caught fire... Little did they dream... of the mischief that was *brewing* overhead; and long will they remember the day when they got... washed away in their favourite beverage... Just as these swill-tubs were in full sail... one of the most tremendous storms in... memory... came showering down upon them like waterpots with the rose off.
>
> Every vehicle, from a fly to a wheelbarrow, was in requisition for the conveyance of the most opulent and *inveterate soakers*... The procession was headed by the bearer of a tin tea-kettle on a crimson cushion... then

[1] At Minehead a teetotaller was said to have died as a result of drinking several quarts of coffee a day, a post-mortem allegedly revealing 9 lb 14 oz of it in his body.

A COFFEE-POT on a Tea Tray.
A PUMP, on two men's shoulders, handle bound with blue ribbon.
A boy, with his head in a bucket.
Two young ladies, with a set of tea service . . .
Four men, carrying a hogshead, inverted . . .
A cart-horse . . . and water cart.

The teetotallers had also other opponents to contend with. One man told Thomas Hudson cheerfully that together they would shut up the public houses, 'What with you not drinking anything at all and I not paying for what I drink.' Even more embarrassing was an Irish impostor, 'Father Moore', who wandered through the West Country using Hudson's name, leaving behind him a trail of drunkenness and petty thefts, and the behaviour of Hudson's borrowed horse, which stopped without prompting at every public house on the road. Fanatics within their own ranks proved troublesome, too, like the Independent Order of Horabites at Fowey, who would drink nothing but neat water, as 'every attempt to improve it . . . only tends to injure it', and the extreme sabbatarians who considered it disrespectful to the Almighty to shave on the Lord's Day.

Perhaps the greatest trial the early speakers suffered was having to stay at temperance hotels, which were often opened by those who had failed at normal inn-keeping and by reformed drunkards, who, with no aptitude for the job, were set up in business by local sympathisers. The management of the very first temperance hotel, opened in London in 1836, was, a teetotal historian admitted, 'not altogether satisfactory', and even the Preston hotel was only saved from bankruptcy when Mrs. Livesey moved in to run it for a year. Thomas Hudson, in the West Country, complained dyspeptically that 'among the qualifications the . . . advocate was expected to possess was the ability organically to assimilate whatever was set before him'. At one hotel he caused offence by leaving the uneatable ham and peas. At another, near Penzance, he found the hotel consisted of a room over a general store and his dinner tray contained only a badly cooked mutton chop, ill-baked bread and a mountain of candle-grease. Stories of similar experiences filled the temperance press and provided a popular subject of conversation at temperance rallies. One much-travelled American complained of 'swindling in the sacred name of temperance ... "Temperance House" has been only another name for dirt, discomfort and overcharging with civility'. He recalled 'a table where the cloth looked like a map of the United States, stained with mustard, coffee and grease' and meat which 'reminded you of the man who refused to partake of a similar steak on the ground that it was an infringement of Goodyear's patent for indiarubber'. A temperance historian acknowledged that by 1865, when there were nearly 200 in England, 'temperance hotels had, in many cases, brought a reproach upon the movement, because of their mean appearance and unsuitable management'. A new era was said to have begun with the opening in Manchester that year of *The Trevelyan*, costing £17,000, the building of 'one of the finest hotels in the kingdom' in Dundee in 1867, by a successful hotelier, Thomas Lamb, and the formation in 1872 of Temperance Hotels Ltd., to open a chain of better-class establishments. As late as 1899, however, it was being suggested to the North Wales Temperance Association that 'a prize should be given for the best name to indicate a hotel or an inn established on temperance principles but not to include the word "temperance"'. The name could 'be registered and placed in the hands of a powerful temperance authority', there could be three grades of hotel, each with a maximum tariff and minimum standards, and an inspector would be employed to withdraw registration if he discovered the familiar 'want of cleanliness and ... unsatisfactory provisions for the comfort of the public'. The scheme, however, came to nothing. With a few exceptions, temperance hotels continued to come in their traditional three grades, bad, very bad and appalling.

*Chapter Eight*

# GOING ON GLORIOUSLY

'In London we are going on gloriously... large as London is I hope before long there will not be a soul in it who has not heard of teetotalism.'

—THOMAS WHITTAKER to JOSEPH LIVESEY, 10th July 1837

WHILE JAMES TEARE was rousing the south and west against alcohol, another professional teetotaller, of very different personality, was stirring up the east and north. Thomas Whittaker had been born near Grindleton on the Yorkshire border in 1813, one of nine children of a small farmer, and after a disastrous lawsuit and various moves, the Whittakers finally settled in Preston. Here, now aged six, young Thomas was roused at 5 a.m. to walk a mile to the mill. He got home again at 8 p.m., earning two-and-sixpence a week, less twopence every time he was late. Here, at thirteen, he heard of machine-breaking mobs roaming the textile districts and saw his father issued with a blunderbuss to defend the mill. Here at fourteen he got so drunk one Saturday that he could not remember getting home, with a 'face... so cut and bruised I was not fit to be seen'.

Whittaker was a pet of the women at the mill, who pressed drink upon him, and a popular competitor in hornpipe competitions in public houses, but when, at eighteen, he proposed to get married, his fiancée's father forbade the match. Whittaker made a bet, in drink, that he would be married within a month. One weekend he persuaded his sister to borrow £3 from the grocer, got up at 4 a.m., dressed in his brother William's Sunday suit, and walked twelve miles to Stockport. Here he knocked up the vicar to get a special licence, smuggled his bride out of her home, and by breakfast-time was married. Next day Mr. and Mrs. Whittaker were both at work at the mill, but before long his drinking cost him his job and soon Whittaker was seeking work in other towns.

In Preston he had attended Joseph Livesey's night school but admiration for his old teacher did not prevent him going 'to join the disturbers and enjoy the fun' when Livesey attempted to deliver his Malt Liquor Lecture in the Theatre Royal, Lancaster, in 1834. 'Lancaster ale', Whittaker acknowledged, 'was of a much more potent character than that to which I had been accustomed and it made sad havoc of me.' It made sad havoc of the meeting, too:

> The place was very crowded. The chairman . . . was Squire Dawson . . . The meeting had scarcely commenced when a man's legs came through the ceiling over the pit and down tumbled the plaster . . . Presently an old paint-pot was suspended through the hole made and paint dropped from it on to the people below . . . The squire . . . exhorted the people for the credit of the town to listen to Mr. Livesey. A dusty, stuffed imitation fish was hurled at the squire's head; he was hit across the nose, his sight dimmed by dust, and his spectacles disordered . . . at this point someone got to the main gas tap and left us in darkness; then we had imitation thunder and lightning.

The following year, during Livesey's mission to Blackburn, Whittaker was attracted to another meeting by the names of heavy drinkers he had known on the posters. He was deeply impressed, for despite the absence of hymns, prayers and Bible reading, 'the preaching ran like fire among dry stubble'. When his brother William challenged him to sign the pledge he agreed. 'I . . . made a clean sweep of the whole business . . . I have simply closed the account and done with the shop.'

Instead of drinking in the evenings, Whittaker now taught himself to write, but at work his teetotalism made him unpopular, his workmates believing 'it was a system got up by the masters to ascertain how little working men could live upon'. His fellow workers 'secretly spoiled my work and damaged my machinery' and were so indignant when he refused to collect his wages from the public house that he was finally asked to leave.

Whittaker's thoughts now turned to 'the model town' of Preston 'and its band of brave teetotallers', and with the help of Joseph Livesey he became a full-time agent of the British Temperance Association. On Monday, 9th May 1836, four weeks after James Teare had left on a similar venture, Thomas Whittaker set out on his first missionary journey, on the *Flying Packet* canal boat.

> I then left Preston for Lancaster, a raw Lancashire lad, twenty-three years of age, well supplied with Livesey's *Malt Liquor Lecture*, *The Temperance Advocate* and a good assortment of temperance tracts . . . There was a licence to sell drink on board and . . . I untied my tracts and began to distribute them and there was soon a hot discussion. The captain did not like it at all, for it interfered with the sale of drink.

Soon afterwards, Whittaker encountered further opposition at the small town of Burton in Westmorland.

> Saturday afternoon was the time fixed for attack and the Market Cross for the centre of action. The square in which it stands was pretty well covered with public houses and hotels. The principal one, nearest to the Cross, had a good sized window looking right upon the meeting from one of its best sitting-rooms. In that room, with the sash of the window lifted up, sat the parson of the parish, the leading lawyer of the place, and one or two others . . . While I was speaking . . . the lawyer and the clergyman sent a man . . . with a large mug of ale to ask me to drink . . . He came close to me and offered me the mug . . . Of course I declined the offer, upon which the contents were thrown in my face.

This Saturday saw the first appearance of Whittaker's famous rattle, for the town crier at Lancaster had been 'made drunk by the publicans while on his round' and his colleague at Burton 'would not disgrace himself by crying a teetotal meeting'. It was made for him by a friendly joiner and soon proved its worth, not merely because 'town criers in that part of the country, at that time of day, as a rule were either just getting drunk, quite drunk, or just getting sober', but for its curiosity value, for 'everybody seemed inclined to learn what the end of the rattling job would be'. At Bishopswearmouth, Sunderland, when Whittaker was rattling, 'a crowd met me headed by the town crier in his official robes', and, though drunk, 'with what dignity he could assume, forbad my usurpation of *his* office'. That night, however, he attended Whittaker's meeting and later signed the pledge.

When Whittaker arrived, by invitation, at Penrith on the coach from Kendal, he was met by a 'gentleman... in yellow top boots and smalls, a large flapped, beautifully embroidered waistcoat, a blue coat with bright buttons and large silk velvet collar', who was clearly shocked at his guest's 'check shirt... brown coat... fustian trousers and ankle jacks... wardrobe ... tied up in a large blue cotton handkerchief' and 'contemptible' speech. The discovery that Whittaker was a teetotaller 'almost knocked the breath out of him... They had no teetotallers there and did not want any. Theirs was a Temperance Society... and if I spoke at the meeting I was not to say a word about it.' Whittaker was finally abandoned 'in the street at 5 o'clock that day, eighty miles from home, not railway days, nor ten shillings in my pocket', and eventually found a tradesman who, though 'fearing the loss of his business', agreed to 'run the risk of lodging me'. Whittaker then collected an audience of hundreds for an open-air meeting, but when he tried to borrow a chair to stand on its owner refused, saying that 'if you talk teetotal on my chair I shall never see it again'. She only relented when he 'became responsible for damages'. He finally spoke to such effect that a drunkard who was 'a terror to the neighbourhood' refused to wait till the end of the meeting to sign the pledge, declaring 'Nay, I will sign *now* or you shan't speak.' A society was founded with forty members and Whittaker walked back to Kendal 'in fullness of joy. At times my delight was so great that I shouted and literally ran and jumped. The cattle started in the fields and the men working in the ditches looked up in wonder at the sounds.'

At Keswick, despite learning that the last attempt to preach temperance had resulted in the Town Hall being wrecked and a warning 'that they would *kill* me if I talked teetotal', Whittaker's meeting, in the Wesleyan chapel, 'was filled with an excited multitude' and one minister afterwards generously gave up half his bed to the speaker.

In the small town of Brampton, Cumberland, all the chapels and public halls were shut against him and he was forced to hire a room for half-a-crown in *The Shoulder of Mutton* public house. The meeting was interrupted by relays of drunks from the bar downstairs, but two days later the publican abandoned her trade.

After walking eight miles in the rain to the village of Aspatria, near Maryport, Cumberland, Whittaker found an audience of seven. One of them was the butler from the local 'big house', Brayton Hall, who took home some temperance tracts and gave them to his master, Sir Wilfrid Lawson. Sir Wilfrid was so impressed he burned his brandy, tipped his gin into the fish pond, and made his whole household 'dry', his son and heir, also named Wilfrid, later becoming the most famous teetotaller in the country.[1]

After the Aspatria meeting, Whittaker occupied the only bed in a Methodist widow's cottage while she sat up all night mending and washing his travel-worn clothes. Six years later, when he came back to the district, it was as a guest of Sir Wilfrid, and his clothes were taken away for overnight valeting by a footman. Embarrassingly, Whittaker, waking to find them missing, thought them stolen and soon 'the whole establishment was set in commotion'.

Whittaker also encountered some excessively austere hosts. At Shotley Bridge, near Newcastle, he was entertained by a farmer who only served tea 'made from herbs gathered in the field' and who was 'horror-struck' at one of the 'frilled and ruffled shirt-fronts' given to Whittaker by a female admirer.

[1] The conversion of Sir Wilfrid, senior, has also been attributed to a Methodist preacher from Manchester, William Pollard, in 1834. Possibly he recruited Sir Wilfrid to the temperance cause and Whittaker made him a teetotaller.

Laying hold of it with his dirty fingers and tearing it off, breaking the strings and exposing my plain check shirt beneath, he exclaimed, 'What on earth hast thou got there? Thou wilt lose thy soul! The Canaanitish women down yonder at Sunderland... have ruined thee!'

Once Whittaker arrived at a meeting at Shotley Bridge 'faint, cold and hungry', his 'one horse Irish car' having taken four hours to make the fifteen-mile journey through snowdrifts, but when asked for 'a nice suitable hymn and... a lively tune ... Harry... proceeded to give out

"And am I born to die?
To lay this body down?"'

A very thin Wakefield teetotaller was also a poor advertisement for the joys of teetotalism.

Biscombe was as hungry-looking a dog as could be met in a day's march. He was also badly pitted by small-pox... While low in flesh he was in colour bad... During the procession the parish sexton came running with a large, rusty key, represented to be the key of the 'bone house' and offering it to Biscombe begged that he would go and 'lock himself up again. What was he doing out, frightening the women and children? Go back,' said the sexton, 'thou wilt get me into trouble. I had only just gone to get a bit o' dinner.'

Another character Whittaker encountered, the proprietor of a temperance hotel, if invited to speak, 'was very much exercised to know... if there would be a platform erected to speak from', so that he could show off his 'yellow top boots, the relics of better days'. Once, to display them better, he leapt on a table. 'The boots were beautiful; the people applauded... He forgot the frail foundation on which he was standing... the table collapsed, and the boots, books and speaker lay in one confused but harmless mass on the floor of the singing pew.'

Through all his adventures Whittaker remained incorrigibly optimistic. 'I generally get from ten to forty names each night', he reported to Preston on 21st June 1836. 'Though I am in a poor country I have set the fire of teetotalism burning.' Between mid-July and mid-August 1836 he established fourteen new societies and revived many others, and his fame spread all over the north-east, until 'the two counties of Durham and Northumberland were . . . covered with this strange story and in some of the colliery villages we seemed to carry the entire population'.

At Newark, however, a centre of the malt trade, his reception was very different. 'The room on my arrival was packed with maltsters' and brewers' men . . . Several climbed on the backs of the seats . . . and broke them . . . The legs and arms of these flew at my head and . . . the men then danced with delight and jumped "Jim Crow". In the scuffle . . . someone managed to pin an old newspaper to my coat-tail and apply a light to it.'

Many clergy were also hostile. At Sunderland, Whittaker saw the preacher, in front of a congregation of 1,600, tear up a leaflet announcing a temperance meeting and stamp on it in the pulpit. At Kettering, Northamptonshire, two nonconformist ministers preached sermons on the Sunday before his arrival on the texts 'Be not righteous overmuch' and 'Beware of false prophets'. One later took the chair at Whittaker's meeting, announcing that 'he hoped the day would come when every working man would have at least two pints of ale a day. Upon that several of the men began to flourish bottles and ask questions . . . At length someone set fire to some loose shavings lying on the floor . . . A cry of "Fire!" excited the people and the roughs made a rush at me and jammed me against the wall.' This meeting broke up in disorder and Whittaker was only rescued by a maltster, who took one arm, and a wine merchant, who took the other, and led him 'through the streets of Kettering followed by that howling mob', eager to throw him in a nearby pond. Both his rescuers then signed the pledge and the next time Whittaker spoke in Kettering it was from one of the pulpits from which he had formerly been denounced.

By now, Whittaker had evolved an effective technique for dealing with hecklers. At Newcastle, in reply to a troublemaker who shouted, 'A quart of ale is better for a hardworking man than a quart of water', Whittaker demonstrated so convincingly that the sixpence spent on ale would be better used to buy meat

GEORGE CRUIKSHANK'S IMPRESSION OF A LONDON BEERSHOP, FROM *The Drunkard's Children*

A LONDON GIN PALACE, FROM THE SAME SOURCE

*Blackie and Son Ltd.*

JOHN FINCH

*Blackie and Son Ltd.*

JAMES SILK BUCKINGHAM

*Blackie and Son Ltd.*

JAMES TEARE

*Mr. Meredith Whittake*

THOMAS WHITTAKER, IN MAYOR'S ROBES

and potatoes that 'the crowd burst out like a thunder-clap, "Beafsteaks for ever, Whittaker!"' At Market Harborough, where 'there was great interruption . . . coming at one time to a free fight', Whittaker discovered that one of the ringleaders was a bricklayer from Preston. His constant references to the town finally caused his fellow Prestonian to leap on a form and challenge anyone to lay a finger on the speaker. At Carlisle he was interrupted by a drunken shoemaker, who constantly repeated 'If I like to drink, I'll drink; and if I like to be teetotal, I'll be teetotal.' Whittaker's remarks about Carlisle needing men like this 'who have a will and a purpose', turned him into an ally. At Shildon, near Bishop Auckland in County Durham, Whittaker 'rattled' to such purpose around a crowd watching a company of strolling players at the local fair that the actors abandoned their performance and went, with their audience, to listen to him instead.

During these seven years, from 1836, Whittaker later calculated that he had addressed more meetings than 'any man living or dead in the same time'. His income averaged around twenty-five shillings a week, leaving little for coach fares or postage. He spent only twenty weeks at home during the whole period, and messages to his wife were squeezed in at the end of his official reports to Joseph Livesey. After rousing the north he set off in the spring of 1837 for London, travelling 'on top' from Manchester, a journey which took twenty-two hours and cost £3 10s. Even here, however, he was not off duty for 'in Leicester about midnight . . . supper was spread for the passengers and I alone took water'. His fellow passengers 'set up a great horse laugh and the waiter could not or would not understand what I meant' and 'kept saying "Porter?"'

Whittaker knew no one in London, but two days after his arrival attended a large temperance meeting in Kennington, presided over by James Silk Buckingham. He was given the chance to speak for twenty minutes and 'went off like a rocket! My youth, my dialect, my experience, was an astonishment to the Londoners . . . The next day I was selected to second the first resolution at the great meeting in Exeter Hall.' Despite shouts of 'Name!', meaning 'Who is he?', Whittaker seized his chance: 'I held them for forty-five minutes as between my finger and thumb', he recalled. 'My soul was fired and my tongue loosened as they have seldom been fired either before or since.' By the end of the week, during which 'there were other meetings . . . at all of which I spoke in company with men of note and eloquence', he had 'a name and a status' that 'made it impossible to ignore me as a teacher of temperance'.

By July 1837, only two months after his arrival, he was able to send back to Joseph Livesey a gratifying progress report:

> In London we are going on gloriously . . . During the last week I have held nine meetings and distributed 2,000 tracts; and large as London is I hope before long there will not be a soul in it who has not heard of teetotalism . . . On Saturday morning, I distributed 400 tracts on the Margate steamer; and in the afternoon, accompanied by several friends, went to Greenwich. On our way in the steam-boat we preached up abstinence and the consequence was no intoxicating liquors could bc sold, although they cried out 'brown stout, ale and porter'. We held the first teetotal meeting ever held in Greenwich Park, and a good one it was. Returning home, I distributed tracts and gave admonitions at the dramshops.

Shortly after Whittaker had arrived in London his wife died, but he successfully proposed to a young Sunday school teacher, Louisa Palmer, a few months later on their way home from a watch-night service on New Year's Eve, 1837, 'giving her two weeks to consider the question, for I had no time to spend in courting'. Immediately afterwards he set out on a tour of Essex. In sophisticated Central London, used to bizarre doctrines, the teetotallers had met little active opposition, but meetings in suburbs like Tottenham, Barnet and Uxbridge were often 'in the hands of loafers, hangers on and rowdies' and in the barley-growing districts of East Anglia hostility reached a peak. The local societies, where they existed, tried to visit every town and village at least once a month, but it was uphill work. 'The common mode of annoyance and interruption', noted Whittaker, 'was to let off sparrows and these poor things would fly about the meeting in all directions, not unfrequently bobbing against the candles and putting them out. Occasionally we were favoured with a crow and sometimes fireworks.'

At Framlingham, Suffolk, the minister, a plump beer-drinker, objected to candles being provided for Whittaker's meeting in the chapel, although his chief officials were tee-totallers. The rival parties climbed over the pews, until 'The race between light and darkness became quite exciting.' It 'was won by the man of light' when the 'preacher . . . had to puff for breath'.

Often no chapel was available. In one village Whittaker spoke in a sawpit; in another in a bakehouse; at Luton, Bedfordshire, in a hay-loft. Lofts were not, however, ideal meeting-places since rowdies might gather at the foot of the ladder and nervous speakers had been known to leave instead via the window. Hospitality was also a problem, for Whittaker's hosts were often too poor 'to stand the entire cost of entertaining an agent during his visit . . . We would take tea at one house and supper and bed at another and next morning go out to breakfast at a baker's and help eat up the stale bread.'

Harlow in Essex in the winter of 1840 provided 'the most serious riot and disturbance' of Whittaker's whole career. The offer of the local schools for a meeting had been withdrawn after threats 'from the maltsters and farmers . . . that their future subscriptions would be withheld'.

> We had to fall back upon an old building standing in the middle of a field . . . In the upper part of this was a long room, the lower part was let off in tenements. The room was taken possession of by a drunken mob . . . The first signal was the flying of a sparrow, and then another, and another; at one time there must have been nearly twenty sparrows flying about. Then a can of beer was introduced, followed by fireworks—squibs and crackers! . . . They then broke the forms, and began to dance and jump on the floor like wild Indians. Outside, in the distance, was heard the sound of a horn . . . blown by a 'gentleman' who . . . brought with him an additional mob; on their arrival the windows were broken, and the people inside became more frantic than ever. The floor of the room was somewhat rotten, and not considered safe, so the people

> in the dwellings below began to remove their furniture...At length the parish constable arrived, and offered to conduct me through the crowd...The fields on each side of the road were filled with turnips...and the crowd gathered them and threw them at my head: I was tripped up twice, but recovered myself. At length I got a good start, and ran like a hare, and they followed me like a pack of hounds! However, I got to cover...and reached the house of my host... We sat down to supper...but in the midst of it there was an awful yelling up in front of the house. Some sixty men armed with sticks and other weapons, having been further primed with beer, were instructed to 'demand my body'... They formed a complete circle round the dwelling in conjunction with the stream flowing round the back part of the premises. They rang the bell, and broke the windows; they then burst open the door, and two of them came into the house, and demanded my body... Poor Mrs. Barnard [his hostess] fainted ... I ran upstairs and the men made an attempt to follow... In my excitement I sought to escape by the chimney, but I could not manage to climb it and I was for the first and last time in my life in great bodily fear. I lost all power for the moment of life and limb and I lay flat on the bedroom floor unable to move or stand.

The constable finally came to the rescue and the ringleaders were put on trial. The whole affair brought the teetotallers a good deal of sympathy, and one maltster even organised a further meeting for Whittaker in the name of fair-play, although this time, too, 'a crowd of people gathered near the inn and pelted me on the coach as we drove out of the place'.

Whittaker later wrote that 'During the years from 1837 to 1845 London and the neighbourhood was thoroughly worked', and he also made his way through the West Country, penetrating as far as Plymouth. Cornwall he left to Teare. His life at this time was a curious combination of luxury and poverty; on one journey he was delivered to the stagecoach near Bristol by a 'splendid pair of horses and in a handsome close glass carriage', and met outside Taunton by a man with a donkey cart, so that his fellow passengers now 'looked down their noses ...while I could have sunk in my shoes'. He felt ashamed of his embarrassment, however, when he found that his new escort, a poor shoemaker, had lost a day's work and made a round trip on foot of seventeen miles to provide him with transport. By such sacrifices the temperance movement grew.

It was at Street, Somerset, that Whittaker made his star convert, John Clough, an itinerant Scots heckler, who hired himself out to publicans as a wrecker of temperance meetings. The local teetotallers had found him 'dry' work and lodgings, but he was always having a relapse, when he would, he claimed, become a moderate drinker, and was soon taking sixteen quarts a day and being carried home in a wheelbarrow. Whittaker, however, persuaded him to sign the pledge in earnest, Clough reformed, was reunited with the wife he had not seen for twenty-two years, and under the pen-name 'Colin' published a highly successful autobiography, *Remarkable Adventures*.

In 1849 Whittaker set up as a temperance hotel keeper in Scarborough, though the business was largely run in his absence by the faithful Louisa. Eventually, however, he settled down in the town, founding several successful local newspapers, and becoming a prominent local figure, active in campaigns for better public services, for enfranchising working men and for Home Rule. In 1861 he rashly wrote to *The Scarborough Times* to blame the loss of the Whitby lifeboat, with twelve of its crew of thirteen, on the fact that 'the men had, from mistaken kindness, been supplied . . . with spirits', thus losing 'that self-control and sobriety essential to safety in such a storm', the worst in living memory. The Scarborough men's heroism had left forty widows and orphans unprovided for and Whittaker's comment that there was 'more destruction in the bottle than in the fury of the waves' provoked a furious public reaction. He was denounced in the local press for 'a wrong that the people of Whitby will never forget'. An angry crowd demonstrated outside his house and an effigy labelled 'Witty-cur' was hanged from a ship's yardarm in the harbour, flogged in procession round the town by the fishermen, and burned on the sands in front of a cheering crowd.

Six years later, however, Whittaker was elected a councillor and in 1880, on becoming mayor, he was chaired through the streets and photographed in mayoral robes and chain with his famous rattle in his hand, being 'determined that the rattle which had been the companion of my obscurity and shame should be the companion of my distinction'. At sixty-seven he married for the third time and at seventy-five, when speaking in Hyde Park, he challenged any drinker of the same age 'who has lived in a public house' to race him to Marble Arch for the prize of a new hat, a Workington publican having to be dissuaded from entering his ninety-three-year-old whisky-loving father in the contest. Whittaker did not die until 1899, at the age of eighty-six, outliving most of his nine children. His surviving sons were both knighted, one becoming a Radical M.P. and leading prohibitionist. The newspapers Whittaker founded still flourish, while in Scarborough churchyard his gravestone still fires a final posthumous salvo—'Strong drink . . . is Britain's curse'—and bears the obituary he would have valued most: 'Thomas Whittaker, Temperance Advocate'.

*Chapter Nine*

# THE DRUNKEN COMMITTEE

'I hear it said by honourable members, "What can be done by a Committee?" . . . Sir, almost every measure of improvement which has proceeded from this House has been preceded by enquiry.'

— JAMES SILK BUCKINGHAM, M.P., in the House of Commons, 27th May 1834

WHILE THE temperance agitation was making progress all over the British Isles, on Parliament, during the eighteen thirties, it made remarkably little impact perhaps because the drunkenness of the poor made a convenient scapegoat for indifference to social evils.

The first Parliamentary teetotaller, Joseph Brotherton, was like his successors, a Radical. A cotton manufacturer, he was also a pastor of the teetotal sect, the Bible Christians, and in 1821 he published, as one of several *Letters on Religious Subjects*, what was later claimed as the first British teetotal tract. 'The drinking of intoxicating liquors', it declared, 'is the root of almost every evil in society . . . What a tremendous collection of misery and mischief is to be ascribed to this single cause! Poverty! Disease! Villainy! Murder! Good God, can this be read without concern?' Evidently it could, for Brotherton's eloquence fell on deaf ears and when elected to Parliament for Salford, in 1832, he became known, not for his teetotalism, but for invariably moving the adjournment of the House at midnight, a proposal 'met with a chorus of cheers, groans, hootings, cock-crowings, bellowings and other discordant cries'.

A similar reception tended to greet the contributions of his more colourful parliamentary colleague, James Silk Buckingham. 'James Silk' had been born at the Cornish fishing village of Flushing, near Falmouth, in 1786, of a long line of seafaring men. As had happened to Joseph Livesey, the drunken scenes he witnessed as a child made an indelible impression on his mind. 'At this period,' noted Buckingham later, 'no one... thought intoxication unbecoming but... indicative of high breeding.' Spirits, particularly brandy, were the common drink in Cornwall for smuggling was almost universal. As a choirboy, Buckingham witnessed a dinner for 100 guests where, after 'almost every man at the table had drunk three or four tumblers of hot spirits and water... it was... proposed to send for the parish choir and sing anthems'. He also saw many drunken funerals. It was the custom to lay the coffin on a bench 'of chairs reversed... Here a hymn or psalm was sung and glasses of brandy handed round... to everyone present... This frequently stimulated the leader to give out a second hymn or psalm and another round of brandy was served as before.' The coffin was then carried a short distance to another house, by four or six bearers, where this procedure was repeated, and so on at other resting places until 'by the time the parties reached the parish church, some two miles distant, they were nearly all muddled and stupid'.

At nine Buckingham was as big as many boys twice his age and badgered his mother to let him go to sea. On his first trip he was made drunk as a joke and he soon became disgusted with the heavy drinking both on board ship and on shore, noticing that English sailors laced their wine with brandy, while foreign sailors diluted theirs with water. After various adventures, including a spell in a French prison and desertion from the Navy, after seeing a press-ganged sailor flogged to death, Buckingham set up in business selling charts and navigational instruments. His great relaxation was women's company; he acknowledged feeling 'such susceptibility to the influence of female fascination... as to bind me continually in fetters, till these were loosed by some new charm', and at nineteen he married, only to find himself ruined by a reckless trustee. James worked his passage to London and eventually obtained a post as chief officer on a ship sailing to the West Indies. On the voyage home the captain and second officer became incapably drunk, so that Buckingham had to take three watches in succession, an experience he turned to good account, by writing a popular song, *Starboard Watch Ahoy*. Later the line 'with joy he drinks the cheering grog' caused him some embarrassment. 'At this period,' he explained, 'no one apprehended the least evil from a moderate use of spirits . . . in times of storm and rain.' Soon afterwards, on becoming captain of his own ship, Buckingham applied a rigid rule of no spirits on board, describing them as 'the source of nearly all the accidents, quarrels and breaches of discipline that occurred at sea'.

In 1811 Buckingham began a long series of exciting journeys in the Middle and Far East, surviving attacks by tigers, pirates and brigands and some hair-raising escapes disguised as an Arab from places where no European had ever set foot before. Finally he settled in Calcutta, where he founded a highly successful paper, *The Calcutta Journal*, before being expelled in 1823 for attacking the East India Company's administration.

Back in England, and reunited with his family after a ten-year separation, Buckingham supported himself by journalism, publishing travel books and founding *The Athenaeum* and other magazines. Through lecturing up and down the country on the iniquitous tyranny of the East India Company he rapidly became a national figure. His Asian travels had caught the public imagination and a Buckingham boom began. Local East India Associations were formed to help his campaign, the House of Commons appointed a Committee to investigate his charges, though it came to nothing, and in 1832 he was elected to Parliament as member for Sheffield. His platform included free national education, stricter laws against child labour, and 'taxation on rank', under which anyone could become a duke by paying £30,000 a year. Once in Parliament he was soon espousing innumerable reforms, from the abolition of capital punishment to the provision of 'asylums and hospitals maintained at the expense of the country' and the support of the aged, the sick and the unemployed out of public funds. This programme was dismissed by his fellow members as 'visionary' and Buckingham was nicknamed Lord Hum, because he was never silent. When he also began to challenge the sacred traditions of Parliament itself, questioning the value of the House of Lords and suggesting that all speeches should be limited to twenty minutes, he became, like his fellow teetotaller Joseph Brotherton, a parliamentary joke. As he rose to speak an anticipatory titter ran round the Chamber.

Buckingham's experiences in childhood, at sea, and among people forbidden to drink by their religion, had made him a teetotaller. In 1832 he signed the pledge and in May 1834 he began to present a series of petitions calling for a Select Committee on Drunkenness. The gin-shops, he declared, were a 'far greater evil' than the beer-houses, to which so much Parliamentary time had been given. 'I hear it said by honourable members, "What can be done by a committee?" . . . Sir, almost every measure of improvement which has proceeded from this House has been preceded by enquiry.'

Much of the opposition to Buckingham came from his fellow Radicals. Some, like Joseph Hume, distrusted the temperance campaign as distracting attention from their panacea for all social evils, education. Others, like William Cobbett, saw it as an attempt to impose yet more restrictions on the working man. But due to Buckingham's persistence and a skilful mustering of the temperance forces, the Committee was finally set up in June and under Buckingham's chairmanship. Much of the ground covered by it had already been gone over by the Select Committee on Beerhouses of the previous year, but the Committee did collect some new material on the gin-shops including first-hand accounts of men who had pawned their shirts for gin, women who had stripped off their petticoats in the bar and children who had been kept from Sunday school because of shoes at the 'pop shop'. One relieving officer estimated that 30% of parish relief, often known as 'gin money', was spent on gin the same day. Ample evidence was produced, too, in support of Buckingham's campaign against drinking on board ship. 'I have', said one naval captain, 'known the gunner and his crew, in filling powder, go drunk into the magazine. I hold spirituous liquors more dangerous than gunpowder.'

The 450-page volume of Evidence heard by the Committee provided ammunition for temperance reformers for the rest of the century. One passage in which George Wilson, a grocer, described the Sunday morning scene in Tothill Street, Westminster, was quoted constantly.

> I arose about seven o'clock and looked from my bedroom at the gin-palace opposite to me. I saw it surrounded with customers. Amongst them I saw two coal-porters ... with women who appeared to be their wives; and a little child, about six or seven years old. They got to the bar and came out again in a short time, one of the women so intoxicated as to be unable to walk; she went against the door-post, and then fell flat on the pavement, with her legs partly in the shop and her person exposed; the three who were with her attempted to raise her, but they were so intoxicated as to be unable to perform that task ... After a considerable time they succeeded ... and placed her against the door-post ... the little child ... endeavoured to arouse her by smacking her on the legs and ... on the face, but she appeared quite insensible.

Probably the most useful of the Committee's revelations concerned the extent to which men were virtually forced to drink. A Bradford witness described how the current shortage of sovereigns and small denomination paper money compelled an employer to pay his men as a gang, with a £5 or £10 note, which could only be changed at the public house. A London police witness said that in the Covent Garden area tailors who finished work on Saturday between five and seven p.m., were kept waiting until ten or eleven for their wages. Hence by midnight the police were laying drunks in rows on the station floor 'like so many logs of wood'. The greatest sufferers from compulsory drinking, however, were the coal-whippers, who unloaded the coal ships from the north on which the capital depended for heat and power. The whippers were employed by some eighty 'undertakers' or contractors, mainly publicans, who controlled the whole trade from Limehouse to the mouth of the Thames, and their exactions, nominally to bribe the coal-ship captains to give their gangs work, swallowed up from a third to a half of a coal-whipper's wages; one man, the Committee heard, had, after such deductions, received only six shillings of the twenty-four he had earned. Another explained how he was often kept waiting three or four hours in the public house before starting work. 'Those that . . . drink the most . . . are the people that obtain employment first', he summed up.

Several witnesses put forward practical suggestions for combating drunkenness. A naval lieutenant described a 'dry' employment office for coal-whippers he had opened at Wapping. Edwin Chadwick, of the Poor Law Board, urged the need for coffee-houses, parks, and 'zoological repositories', to be open free on Sundays. Francis Place recommended reading-rooms in every district and the creation of parish libraries. A Liverpool corn merchant wanted more public buildings to enable the poor to attend 'scientific and mechanical lectures and experiments', while a wine and spirit merchant advised that 'If you gave half a dozen bands of music in different districts on a Sunday evening you would improve the people's morals.'

The report of the Select Committee on Drunkenness was laid before the House of Commons on the 5th August 1834. 'It appears to your Committee', it began, 'that the vice of intoxication has been for some years past on the decline in the higher and middle ranks of society, but has increased . . . among the labouring classes.' In eight brisk pages it spelt out the consequences from 'the irritation of all the worst passions of the heart' to 'the retardation of all improvement, inventive or industrial, civil or political, moral or religious', and listed some immediate remedies. The Committee proposed four types of licence, all to be granted by the justices: the beer 'on' licence, the beer 'off' licence, the spirits 'off' licence, and the inn, catering for travellers and selling all types of drink. The gin-shop, or the ordinary public house serving spirits, would disappear, while on Sundays the spirit 'off' licence would shut completely and the beer-shop for all but one hour. The Committee also favoured fewer licences; earlier closing; the abolition of the spirit ration in the armed forces and on board ship; the prohibition of the payment of wages, or the meeting of friendly societies, in public houses; and a legal obligation on an employer to pay each man his exact wages. Buckingham and his colleagues recommended, too, a reduction of the tea, coffee and sugar duties; the provision of public parks and gardens; state publicity for the dangers of drink; and the creation of 'a national system of education'. To these proposals for 'immediate' reforms, Buckingham added an 'ultimate remedy': a total prohibition on the manufacture or importation of spirits, once public opinion was ready for the change.

The suggestion that the Englishman should be forbidden to drink gin and the Scot to drink whisky ensured that the Report, the first comprehensive attempt in British history to lay down a rational licensing policy, should founder in a gale of laughter. Poor Buckingham had had a rough passage when he first tried to get his Committee set up. He had an even rougher one now, in trying to persuade the House to order the Committee's Report to be printed. One member reduced the House to hysterics by commenting on the evidence given by three sub-sheriffs, that 'he believed that such a thing as a sober sub-sheriff was never heard of'. A member who said he 'could quote many racy passages' from the Report was interrupted by jocular cries of 'Read! Read!' Eventually, as *Hansard* recorded, 'The Clerk read the Report, which was accompanied by much cheering and laughter.'

Not all of those who attacked Buckingham were buffoons. Some were disillusioned supporters who had resigned from the Committee in protest against his allegedly biased selection of witnesses. Others were outraged at the proposal to make spirit-drinking illegal. Lord John Russell said he would never be a party to such a law, and Daniel O'Connell, the Irish 'liberator', called it a 'silly, absurd suggestion', whose sponsors 'wanted a guard . . . If they allowed this Report to be printed they would encourage every drivelling legislator.' A few members stood up for Buckingham. Joseph Brotherton attacked O'Connell for making an unworthy use of his talents; another speaker complained that 'The Report ought not thus to be treated with contempt' and the House finally relented sufficiently to allow the Report to be printed.

The chief result was to enable the whole country to share the joke. *The Times* said that the Committee had seen double. *John Bull* proposed that it should report every month to keep the nation merry. Even the Radical Francis Place commented that the Committee's proposed legislation would be in the repressive spirit of the Six Acts, and would make 'this gay earth as gloomy as the cells of the inquisition'. *The Spectator* nicknamed the Select Committee on Drunkenness 'The Drunken Committee', a label which stuck, and provoked Buckingham to write to the editor to point out that it was 'easier to laugh than think'. His staunch heart, which had sustained him through so many perils, did not falter now. In the Parliamentary recess he toured the country lecturing on behalf of the British and Foreign Temperance Society, and everywhere crowds turned out to hear him. In Liverpool he made such an impact that the council decided to close the local liquor shops on Sunday mornings, and in Sheffield, for the first time in living memory, no spirits were served, and no one got drunk, at the annual Cutlers Feast. In the following year he unsuccessfully introduced a Bill empowering meetings of local ratepayers to authorise the construction of public walks, baths, libraries and museums 'to draw off by innocent pleasurable recreation and instruction all who can be weaned from habits of drinking'. Two years later, in 1837, the final failure of his long campaign for compensation from the East India Company forced him to resign from the House of Commons, but he remained active, and derided, in public life—it was jocularly suggested that if Buckingham were ever knighted his crest ought to be 'a cuckoo proper'. He was supported by a small annuity, raised by public subscription, by the proceeds of some highly successful temperance lecture tours in the United States, and, after 1851, by a well-deserved Civil List pension. He played an important part in the amalgamation of many smaller societies into the National Temperance League in 1843, and in 1846 drafted a grandiose international appeal from the World Temperance Convention. 'O rulers and potentates of the earth,' it began, with a tact rare for Buckingham, 'We entreat you . . . that you unite with us in doing whatever in your wisdom may seem best calculated to arrest the progress of intemperance in your respective dominions.' He became an elder statesman of the temperance movement, ever ready to act as a draw at a temperance rally or to enliven some staid function with a few tactless remarks and by the time of his death in 1855, many of his contemporaries were ready to give Buckingham his due. *The British Banner* wrote of him in 1849: 'Mr. Buckingham would seem from his youth to have been in a great measure divested of the prejudices which are natural to man', and another writer paid him an even more handsome tribute: Buckingham, he said, was not merely 'before his day, he was above it'.

*Chapter Ten*

# MISCHIEF AT ST. IVES

'The guilt and mischief of teetotallers in some parts of Cornwall, and especially in the St. Ives circuit, are far too great even to be imagined, except by those who have witnessed their proceedings.'

— THE REV. JONATHAN TURNER, *Teetotalism Illustrated by Facts*, 1842

THE WAVE of enthusiasm for teetotalism which swept across the country from Preston in the decade following 1832 made nowhere a greater impact than in the far west. In other places the temperance movement had become associated with radical or reforming politics; here it was speedily identified with revivalist religion. It was in Cornwall that, in 1743, John Wesley had scored his greatest successes and now the new, eagerly proselytising faith of teetotalism was to recall the triumph of Methodism. Teetotalism first appeared among the clay and tin miners and fishermen of St. Ives with the arrival of *The Preston Temperance Advocate* in September 1837, and after a visit from James Teare in the following February a teetotal society was formed. Within three months it had more than a thousand members and was holding crowded meetings in alternate weeks in the two Methodist chapels, belonging respectively to the Wesleyans and the more rigid Primitive Methodists. Within two years nearly 3,000 in a population of about 5,000 had signed the pledge. The society's second annual report was a catalogue of successes:

Almost the entire mining population of this parish are teetotallers and of the 88 vessels belonging to this port 74 . . . sail without the use of the poisonous draught . . . 44 of the masters are pledged members; upwards of three-fourths of the fishermen . . . So great has been the renovation that during the last pilchard fishery . . . we saw scarcely a drunk man . . . Four public houses have closed.

There were, claimed the jubilant teetotallers, 'many instances . . . proving the connection of teetotalism with . . . the extensive revival of religion' which had occurred during the year and soon many Methodists were demanding that their clergy should give a lead against drink. *The Wesleyan Methodist Magazine* had pointed out in 1836 that 'More of our ministers and members have been degraded by the sin of intemperance than by any other . . . This single sin is destroying more souls than all the ministers in Britain are instrumental in saving.' In St. Ives a porter transporting a five-gallon barrel of beer was trailed through the streets by a suspicious Wesleyan, who 'raised the hue and cry' when he saw it delivered to a minister's home and an agitation began for the expulsion from church membership of everyone connected with the drink trade.

By 1841, although no nonconformist church had officially condemned drink, the moderate drinkers were everywhere on the defensive. That year a Primitive Methodist conference actually celebrated communion in non-alcoholic wine and the national Wesleyan conference, while forbidding this practice, agreed to let the Superintendent of each circuit decide whether to allow teetotalism to be preached in its chapels. The conflict which followed at St. Ives was typical of the strife now rending the dissenting churches as a determined body of teetotallers tried to capture them for the cause. The St. Ives representative at the national conference discovered on his return home that in his absence the secretary of the teetotal society, called Docton, had threatened that if the Wesleyans continued to use fermented communion wine there would be a mass secession to the Primitive Methodists, and his successor, the Rev. Jonathan Turner from Shrewsbury, had hardly taken up his new post before there was an open breach. On the morning of Sunday, 19th September 1841, Turner paused at the end of his sermon, and told his crowded congregation: 'I perceive on the wall of the chapel a placard announcing that what you call a teetotal meeting will be held in this chapel on Tuesday next; but I have to say that the teetotallers will not have the chapel, as it was built for the comfort and instruction of *our* people and not for the teetotallers.' At this the service broke up in uproar, though Turner, according to a teetotal account, 'When he beheld so many leaving his chapel . . . cried out: "Stop, stop! Hear me out!" ' News of the mass walk-out at the Methodist chapel ran rapidly round the town and that evening Turner preached mainly to empty benches, the teetotallers pointedly attending evening service elsewhere.

Next day the teetotallers' spokesman, Docton, called on Turner in a distinctly truculent mood, referring to all non-teetotallers as 'lovers of strong drink', criticising various members of the congregation for having made their fortunes out of beer or having 'wedded . . . spirit merchants' daughters' and finally alleging that Turner's colleague, Mr. Allen, kept a barrel of beer in his house. A further meeting failed to improve matters, particularly after the beer-drinking Allen had denounced Docton as 'an ignorant fellow', at which the teetotallers were 'filled with disgustful wonder'. On the following Friday they decided to found an entirely new chapel, the Teetotal Wesleyan Methodists of St. Ives. About 250 members thereupon seceded from their existing church, followed by 150 others in nearby St. Just.

The new sect had by the following year built its own chapels both at St. Just and at St. Ives, where it was now 600 strong.[1] It had acquired, too, a new and stricter set of rules, which not merely forbade drinking but also 'the putting on of gay apparel . . . unprofitable conversation', and, an onerous commitment in Cornwall, 'the buying or selling uncustomed goods'. By 1869 the St. Ives circuit reached twenty miles away and would still only accept pledged teetotallers as members.

In 1841, before moving to Exeter, Turner expelled all members of his congregation who also attended the teetotallers' services and a bitter pamphlet war followed. The opening salvo,

[1] The St. Ives Teetotal Methodist chapel is now a Territorial Army drill hall.

*A Vindication of the Teetotal Methodists of St. Ives, Cornwall, with an incidental exposure of the domination of the Wesleyan Priesthood*, declared that he 'fancied himself some mighty dictator, to whose will the judgement of all mankind must bow'. As for poor Mr. Allen, he had behaved like 'an unholy ruffian who had never heard the gospel'. Turner replied two months later, in October 1842, with a forty-two-page tract, *Teetotalism illustrated by facts, including a brief view of teetotal sayings and doings in St. Ives*.

> I lament the irreparable mischief which it has done to individuals, and to Christian churches, the strifes, alienations, contentions, schisms, divisions, the declensions, backslidings and apostacies, which are its melancholy fruits . . . The guilt and mischief of teetotallers in some parts of Cornwall, and especially in the St. Ives circuit, are far too great even to be imagined, except by those who have witnessed their proceedings.

Turner was highly critical of temperance society membership, which could 'consist of Jews, Turks, Heathens, Infidels, Socialists, Chartists, Arians, Socinians or Antinomians, of liars, swearers, slanderers, Sabbath breakers, adulterers, robbers and manslayers'. At St. Ives the teetotal faction's 'crudities and prejudices . . . uncharitableness, detraction and slander' had been enough to drive people to 'puseyism, popery or infidelity'. He objected, too, to the attacks made on the Methodist clergy, often from their own pulpits, and to 'the shameful profanation of the house of God', when reformed drunkards gave their testimony so that there 'were related the most filthy and disgusting scenes of depravity, in which the relators professed to have been actors'. It was, however, in dealing with 'the unfounded calumnies and the abusive rhodomontade of this wretched pamphlet' and 'the cowardly and paltry imbeciles' responsible for it, that Turner surpassed himself:

> I have now no doubt that they have been thus Providentially permitted and Satanically incited to this act of insanity, for the important purpose of unmasking the real, nature, tendency and effects of their mischievous delusions; and that the case of St. Ives will be

held up as a beacon, which by its frightful glare will, I hope, give an effectual warning to others against the admission of such a pestilence to desolate their peaceful and united churches.

Although his very vehemence weakened his case, Turner did disclose some useful examples of teetotal excesses. One speaker had argued that since 'four pints of beer would make a man drunk, two pints would make him half-drunk . . . and a half-pint would make him half a quarter drunk, consequently they were all drunkards'. Another had said that heavy and moderate drinkers were both drunkards, since a man who stole a little was as much a thief as a man who stole a lot. To quote such statements was to discredit them, but Turner was not the man to leave well alone. 'When will the common sense of Cornishmen', he thundered, 'drive such half mad, incendiary quacks . . . back again to occupation more harmless and better suited to their brainless skulls?'

Turner was far from having the last word, however. A few months later one of his new congregation, 'a teetotal Wesleyan Methodist of the Old School', published *A Letter to the Rev. Jonathan Turner*, which accused him of harming the church by his 'headlong over-heated zeal for your darling little drop system' and demanded to know whether ministers carried out their pastoral duty better 'when they have taken a glass or two of spirit-stirring, soul-invigorating old port wine'. From Penzance, the author of *A Lancet for a Knife or Jonathan Turner Bled to Death*, reminded his readers that his subject had 'been by chance or superior hypocrisy, elevated either from the anvil of a smithy or the superior desk of a pettifogging lawyer'. He proposed a suitably worded memorial tablet on the wall of the new Teetotal Chapel:

> This chapel was founded by the tyranny and injustice of one Jonathan Turner, Wesleyan Priest, who superintended the St. Ives circuit only one year. 'The death of the wolf is the life of the lamb.'

The Jonathan Turner controversy brought the teetotallers valuable publicity, but also led to a hardening of opposition against them. Resistance to the waterdrinkers had so far been sporadic, though many men refused to work with teetotallers and some employers would not engage non-drinkers on the grounds that they could not stand up to heavy labour. Near Oswestry, Shropshire, in 1838 eighty miners who had signed the pledge had actually been dismissed to protect, said the colliery owners, the agricultural interests of the country. Such actions were exceptional, but during the 1840s more widespread and sustained resistance began. Up till this time the temperance propagandists had almost had the field to themselves, but now anti-teetotal tracts began to appear. *A medical, moral and Christian dissection of teetotalism*, published in 1846, ran to eleven editions. The illustrations were by the popular artist Phiz. One showed a teetotaller, complete with religious pictures on the wall, drinking spirits from a medicine bottle. Another, *Effects of Tea*, contrasted a jovial, wine-drinking Elizabethan family with a miserable-looking Victorian couple clutching tea-cups. *John Bull Recovering from his Watery Humour* hinted that the teetotal craze might be nearing its end, and showed his servants hurrying to rescue their sadly shrunken and dejected master with meat and ale. In the supporting text an anonymous doctor, Democritus, charged the teetotallers with meanness, hypocrisy and dishonesty. Their refusal to provide a drink 'when a bill is paid them' was due not to principle but 'a mean spirit of avarice'. The whole system was 'one of the many tricks . . . inflicted on poor Master Bull, to dazzle his eyes while his pockets are being picked'. And what happened to all the money collected at temperance meetings? 'Water and water gruel can't require all that everlastin outlay of your money.'

A more serious blow to the teetotallers was the apostasy of one of their best-known converts, Thomas Smeeton, who, after a dissipated youth, had won a prize for a teetotal *Essay to Young Men*, and worked all over the British Isles as a paid agent for the New British and Foreign Temperance Society. In 1849 he suddenly recanted, launching a violent attack on his former colleagues in a long pamphlet, *Confessions of a Convert from Teetotalism to Temperance*.

> I have known such advocates . . . at a London theatre one evening and on another in the pulpit. I have known another who was very sharp on 'the Church' about teetotalism, who went off on a sudden with a girl he had seduced, leaving his wife and children destitute . . . The Rechabite Societies are nearly all broken up through the wranglings and intemperate squabbles of the brethren. The meetings of many temperance committees, as I painfully know, are little more than arenas for the display of hatred and all uncharitableness.

Smeeton also drew attention to the inconsistencies of teetotal speakers:

> One says 'You will save money by teetotalism', another says, 'You must expect to be a loser in business, but you must bear it for the truth's sake' . . . On the one hand the teetotaller says 'Oh! The doctors and ministers are ignorant and prejudiced, they must not be appealed to', and in nearly the same breath shouts, 'Have you read *our* Medical Certificate and our Ministers' Testimony?' . . . At the same meeting . . . a red-faced teetotaller will say 'You see by my looks that teetotalism is a famous thing' and . . . will be followed by some gaunt, sepulchral-looking friend, who glories in his paleness and thinness . . . One speaker boasts of the enormous appetite he has acquired through teetotalism and talks of 'teetotal pills' . . . signifying meat puddings, dumplings, etc.; whilst another rises and says he is not always craving for food as he used to be.

The teetotallers, said Smeeton, were always ready to 'kick the floor and clap their hands' when anyone said he felt better for being teetotal, but for every person who found it beneficial two gave it up as harmful. Above all, it was unscriptural. St. Paul's advice to Timothy to take a little wine, though dismissed with 'a hearty laugh of derision' by the teetotallers, stood 'as an impregnable fortress, defying all the assaults of ridicule and time'. The teetotallers had their revenge in the following year when Smeeton was jailed for embezzlement, and soon after his release he died of cholera, while serving with the Civil Corps in the Crimea.

An even more sudden change of front occurred with a

magazine called *The Teetotaller*, started in 1840, which came out as usual in September 1841, but was followed later the same day by *The Anti-Teetotaller*, produced in the same office by the same staff, though it lasted only a few months. More serious was a long attack made by Charles Dickens in 1851 in his weekly magazine *Household Words*. Under the title, *Whole Hogs*, Dickens wrote a description, far less effective than that of Sam Sly in Bath, of an imaginary temperance procession, from the Bands of Hope, 'the Infantine Brigade of Regenerators of Mankind', to 'the gentleman with the massive watch-chain who smiles so sweetly on the surrounding Fair'. The teetotallers, who attacked society for tolerating moderate drinking, were, said Dickens, like a lunatic who believed all men insane but himself. 'Society won't come in and sign the pledge . . . Therefore Society is fond of drunkenness, sees no harm in it, favours it very much, *is* a drunkard—a base, worthless, sensual, profligate brute . . . Against this sweeping misrepresentation, I take the liberty of entering my feeble protest.'

More damaging to the temperance movement than any verbal attack, however, were the strikes and lock-outs which swept the country from 1840 onwards. None was more disastrous than the Great Pitmen's Strike, which for five months in 1844 threw more than 30,000 Durham miners out of work. A temperance historian described how the miners' comfortable homes, with 'in a prominent position . . . the well-framed Rechabite emblem or certificate and the family pledge-card . . . were broken up . . . and all idea of thrift for ever abandoned. The once neat, industrious housewife became a broken-spirited, listless and careless woman, sighing for rest in the grave or . . . seeking consolation in the spirit-bottle. Men who, before the strike, were earnestly trying to reform their lives . . . lost heart and faith . . . driven by desperation, or allured by the temptations of the ever-open dram shop.'

'From 1837 to 1845', recorded the same writer, 'the greater part of the colliery districts of Northumberland and Durham were alive with active, earnest, temperance workers.' Now the local temperance societies foundered, Rechabite 'tents' broke up, their funds exhausted, and temperance workers lost heart or were scattered far and wide, many emigrating after being black-listed by the employers. It was a disaster from which the movement in the north did not recover for many years. This and similar strikes left behind, however, an important legacy. The old distrust of working men for the teetotallers began to disappear, for many of the men's leaders in these battles were also active temperance workers. Henceforward the most active trade unionists, the most progressive politicians, were often teetotallers, in whose minds hostility to the mine-owners and other ruthless employers was often linked to a growing hatred of the licensed trade.

*Chapter Eleven*

# THE GREATEST MAN IN IRELAND

'The Very Rev. Mr. Mathew . . . the really greatest man that Ireland ever produced.'
—Daniel O'Connell, Killarney, 17th January 1845

DRUNKENNESS, THE first temperance reformers had clearly shown, was often linked to poverty, insecurity and violence, and no part of the British Isles in the late 1830s was more poor, insecure and violent than Ireland. The national drink was whiskey. In 1831 a population of under eight million had put away nearly nine million gallons. Five years later, though the population had risen by only 200,000, official consumption had increased by nearly 50%, while much home-made 'poteen' was produced in illicit stills and dispensed in illegal 'shebeens'. Rivalling whiskey in popularity was porter and sales of Guinness alone increased by a quarter in the same five years to two-and-a-half million gallons. They had clearly not been harmed by an allegation made in 1813 that 'poisonous doctrines . . . totally subversive of the Catholic faith were propagated through the medium of . . . anti-Popery porter', with 501,000 cartloads of Protestant hymn books and catechisms mashed up in the brew. 'Happily', it was said, 'Pim's ale was an antidote to the heresy porter.'

The condition of Ireland presented a challenge to the temperance movement in England and Scotland and, in addition to many visitors from Preston and elsewhere, John Finch had toured the country in 1834 and John Dunlop in 1837. Neither they, nor resident reformers like Dr. John Edgar of Belfast, made much lasting impact, partly, perhaps, because they were

Protestants. A successful campaign in Ireland needed to be Catholic-led, ideally by a priest. Now, as so often, the hour was to call forth the man.

Theobald Mathew, known to his family as Toby, was born in 1790 at Thomastown Castle, near Cashel in Galway, where his father was agent to his cousin, Lord Llandaff. As a boy he was always charitable to beggars, disliked field sports and was never known to use a harsh or improper word. His eight brothers unkindly called him 'the pet' or 'Miss Molly'. At sixteen Toby entered Maynooth College to train for the priesthood, and at Easter 1814 was ordained and joined the Capuchin Order, whose watchword was 'humility'. After a successful brief ministry at Kilkenny, Father Mathew moved to Cork, a city of 80,000, nearly half of them illiterate.

The Capuchin convent, or 'little friary', lay in the heart of a poor district. It consisted of two small rooms and a cupboard, with a chapel only forty-three feet long, and even on St. Patrick's Day a collection raised no more than one-and-sixpence-halfpenny. In charge of the convent was a man of rough manners but conspicuous goodness, known as 'the apostle of tolerance', Father Donovan. Father Mathew found only a bare bedstead in his room, as Donovan had given away the sheets and blankets to a poor family, and was dumped on strangers for a meal, as the convent larder had also been emptied. He was delighted at these proofs of his superior's charity and the two priests were soon inseparable. Donovan was a first-class cook and Father Mathew loved company, and often the two holy men entertained, drinking punch and port with their guests.

Father Mathew's reputation as a kindly confessor spread fast and he was often in the confessional from 5 a.m. till breakfast time, and again in the evening until 10 or 11 o'clock. The tiny chapel soon reeked of fish-oil from the clothes of his lamplighter penitents, and the odours peculiar to butchers, sausage makers and candle-makers. His sermons, too, became famous. 'His voice', acknowledged his first biographer, who knew him well, 'was shrill, weak and puny . . . At High Mass or Vespers his voice was a croak and his performance was mournful and dismal beyond description.' But 'they crushed into that little temple to listen to the word of God preached by a man of God'.

For gradually it dawned upon the people of Cork that they had an uncanonised saint among them. Many reformers loved causes; Father Mathew loved people. He treated the dirtiest street urchin or the most degraded slum-dweller with the same courtesy that he gave to the rich and powerful: 'They will', he said, 'be as high in heaven as the highest in the land.' When he visited the sick he would often press a banknote into the patient's hand, whispering 'You will seriously pain me if you refuse', and during the 1832 cholera epidemic he begged to be allowed 'as a favour' to take the unpopular midnight to 6 a.m. shift in the hospital. It was truly said of him by a contemporary, 'His life is a sermon.'

One of Father Mathew's fellow governors of the House of Industry, or workhouse, was William Martin, a Quaker businessman, who had become a passionate teetotaller after hearing reports of a meeting in Dublin in October 1836. He tried to persuade his own Temperance Society to do the same but the crowd regarded the suggestion as an insult to the tradition of Irish hospitality, shouted the speakers down and smashed up the furniture. At a later meeting only thirty people turned up and these were mostly brewery employees who had come to resign their membership. However, the handful of survivors agreed to the change and teetotalism in Cork was launched on its career.

Though now nearly seventy, 'Billy' Martin's 'speech was at times rather a war-whoop than an appeal to the reasoning faculties', wrote a sympathetic observer. His favourite technique was a series of rhetorical questions: 'What does the race-horse drink? Water! What does the elephant drink? Water! What does the lion drink? Water!' and his shop window was decorated 'with flaring placards and startling pictures, which forcibly advocated his darling cause'. These included 'a prodigious plum-pudding bristling with huge almonds, or a mammoth round of beef', and 'an internal scene, in which a gentleman was represented in the act of administering a second and evidently a superfluous blow to his wife, with a poker of gigantic dimensions'. When they met at the workhouse, Martin would make pointed comments like 'Strong drink is the cause of this', and at last Father Mathew, who hated to say 'No' to anyone, gave in. At 7 p.m. on Tuesday, 10th April 1838, in the loft over a Cork school, Father Mathew signed the pledge, exclaiming loudly, 'Here goes, in the name of God.'

Although the teetotallers were widely criticised for 'pestering and bothering the poor man', they plastered the city with placards boasting of their latest convert. The effect was immediate. Temperance mania swept Cork. The bars emptied, the slum streets became peaceful and the school loft became so thronged with eager converts that the floor threatened to collapse and meetings were transferred to the Horse Bazaar, a roofed-in, open-sided shed that could accommodate 4,000. Soon twelve clerks were busy copying down the names of the pledge-signers. In three months, it was claimed, 25,000 had signed; in five 131,000; by the end of the year nearly 200,000. Recent research suggests that the true total was nearer 7,000, but the exaggerations were believed at the time and added to the excitement. The small house in Cove Street, to which Father Mathew had moved from the friary, was besieged until long after dark by people eager to take the pledge at his hands. Others arrived from Kerry and Waterford, from Limerick and Tipperary, even from far-away Galway, 'lame and footsore after their long journey ... with their little bundles in their hands'.

Father Mathew did not look like a great popular hero. His appearance was agreeable rather than striking, a colleague in 1826 remarking on his 'finely formed middle-sized person of exquisite symmetry ... the countenance intelligent, animated and benevolent ... eyes of dark lustre, beaming with internal peace'. He was usually dressed in a 'long, black frock coat, with a cloth vest of the same colour and black small-clothes with polished Hessian boots'. His reputation, however, soon spread all over Ireland. December 1839, when he paid what was intended to be a private visit to his brother-in-law in Limerick, sixty miles away, provided a warning of what was to come. 'On the day before he was expected to arrive the principal roads were black with . . . people . . . the steamers plying on the Shannon brought up each trip human cargoes varying in number from 500 to 1,000. The holds of the vessels were literally crammed; and wherever standing room was to be found on the decks it was at once occupied.' Some people came from 100 miles away and although 'the public rooms were thrown open for their shelter', that night 5,000 of the visitors lacked a bed, two shillings was paid for standing room in a cellar, and the price of bread and potatoes doubled.

Father Mathew arrived late on the Saturday evening, along a road lined with people for three miles, and when next day he attended mass 'the crowd at the chapel . . . was immense', the police, who tried to keep order, being 'struck over and over again, amidst cries of "Kill the rascals"'. The police had a rough time on the Monday morning, too, for 'missiles and blows were dealt bounteously on them' from the 'dense mass of the people, all pressing forward to take the temperance pledge' outside the house where Father Mathew was staying. 'At length, from the great pressure, the iron railings in front of the house yielded and a number of people were precipitated into the area; when one woman was so severely injured, that she afterwards died; another had her thigh broken.' There were several other casualties, too, for the weight of the crowd eventually broke down the main door and the people in front were pushed inside and up the main staircase, which collapsed. Eventually a party of dragoons escorted Father Mathew to the Courthouse, where he was to give the pledge. A local priest observed that 'Some of the horses, with the riders, of the Scots Greys . . . were . . . lifted from the ground and carried away for a short distance by the rushing multitude; and so densely were the people crowded that several . . . ran along . . . on the heads and shoulders of the vast assemblage.' At the Courthouse 'the pressure of the mob . . . was so great that the entire railing which surrounded the building gave way and several persons fell into the river and many more were taken to the hospital severely injured by the falling of the rails and trampled on by the crowd'. For the rest of the day, a Limerick resident recorded, 'the spacious streets of our city seemed completely covered with human beings . . . many of them in a beastly state of intoxication, after drinking their "farewell to whisky"'. Next day Father Mathew was up at 6 a.m., administering the pledge to detachments of fifty and a hundred at a time who knelt in the street outside. When his voice failed teams of priests recited the words for him, and to save time the new teetotallers were told to give their names and addresses to their parish priest for transmission to Cork. It was said, probably with some exaggeration, that during this visit 150,000 people took the pledge, while Father Mathew's host was left with a bill for £100 for repairs.

Similar scenes occurred in the next few months all over Ireland. At Waterford 4,000 people had been expected, but 60,000 arrived, many of them in contingents which had marched all night through the rain led by their clergy. Three months later a Methodist travelling through Waterford was astonished to witness a sober St. Patrick's Day. 'This may', he wrote, 'properly be called St. Mathew's day. I have . . . not met as much as one individual . . . affected by liquor . . . I looked in all the public houses but in most of them there was not a person to be seen but the landlady leaning over the counter with sorrow pictured on her countenance.' At Parsonstown, armed troops knelt outside the chapel where Father Mathew was giving the pledge, 'with bayonets fixed and pointed . . . to oppose the rushing multitudes; whilst . . . cavalry . . . with flags waving in the wind moved up and down in slow and measured pace'. At Dublin, which Father Mathew visited in March 1840, he was surrounded by crippled and diseased people who believed they had only to touch the holy man to be cured, although he constantly denied possessing the gift of healing. At Carlow, where the cathedral was crammed during a three-day visit, Father Mathew had literally to run across a park to catch the coach back to Cork, giving pledges as he ran. When it stopped for breakfast next morning at Athy, the cry went up 'Father

Mathew is at the hotel', and soon 'the vehicle was wedged round so completely' by eager pledge-signers that it was delayed for five hours. Some sceptics wrote indignant letters to the papers proposing that this troublesome priest who held up the Royal Mail should be banned from using public transport. The coach proprietors retorted by offering him free travel for life. No doubt Father Mathew's generosity partly explained the reluctance to let him go, for 'It literally rained silver upon these occasions', and when he tried travelling at night, his coach was sometimes intercepted by eager but impecunious pledge-signers at four in the morning.

By June 1840 Father Mathew was said to have two million followers, a quarter of the population, with seventy invitations to other parts of Ireland still outstanding. Among his recruits were many priests, eight professors and 250 students at Maynooth, and innumerable journalists. 'It would be difficult to say whether he prized more, as a convert, a newspaper editor or a peer of the realm', wrote his biographer, and Father Mathew himself attributed his success 'next to God, to the support I have met with from that most mighty moral power on this earth, the public press'. At meetings he liked to draw the attention of the audience to some embarrassed reporter on the press bench commenting: 'There is the hue of health on his countenance, not the flush of strong drink.' Once he insisted on paying the hotel bill of one such 'fine specimen of a faithful teetotaller' only to find it included several brandies and whiskies. Any reporter who clambered up on to the platform to take the pledge was sure to be cheered by the audience, and one such recruit proved of permanent importance. John Francis Maguire, a former law student, who founded *The Cork Examiner* in 1841, appointed himself his hero's Boswell and his classic biography of Father Mathew became an influential work of temperance literature, greatly impressing Mr. Gladstone.

Despite dark threats that he would be murdered by the Protestants, Father Mathew gladly accepted invitations to visit the northern counties, and the result was a triumph. For the first time in living memory in many places Catholic and

Protestant clergy stood side by side on the same platform. Extreme Orangemen, however, remained suspicious. *The Protestant Magazine* in June 1841 warned that the movement was 'a sort of Trojan horse, within whose ribs there lurks an overwhelming phalanx which, some of these nights, will sally forth on the sleeping sentinels of Ireland', and the British Government was pressed, though unsuccessfully, to regulate temperance societies or bands by law.

Daniel O'Connell, leader of the movement to repeal the Act of Union with England, himself signed the pledge in 1840, though soon abandoning it on medical grounds. In 1842 he joined Father Mathew in the Easter Monday temperance procession in Cork, and a crowd of 150,000 went wild with joy as 'the liberator' knelt in the road to receive the priest's blessing. 'Oh, how I love teetotalism!' declared O'Connell in the following year. 'Napoleon boasted of his bodyguards, but I can boast of a more than Imperial guard—a Christian guard of virtuous teetotallers.' This year, 1843, the Repeal agitation reached its peak when a crowd of at least half a million marched to Tara from all over Ireland. Three-quarters of them were teetotallers and all remained astonishingly peaceful. O'Connell was not exaggerating when he spoke of 'the moral miracle of the teetotal movement' and declared that 'The year 1843 was the triumph of Father Mathew not of me.'

The transformation of Ireland during the 'Father Mathew years' was by any test remarkable. The consumption of spirits, 12,300,000 gallons in 1838, dropped to 7,400,000 gallons in 1840 and to 5,300,000 in 1842. By the end of 1841 it was claimed that there were at least five million on the teetotal roll, in a population of eight million. Breweries and distilleries went out of business and publicans deserted their trade. In many areas drunkenness virtually disappeared and everywhere serious crime dropped sharply; when the judge arrived for Cork Assizes in autumn 1841 he found only one prisoner awaiting trial. The Chief Secretary, Lord Morpeth, said in 1840: 'The duty of the military and police in Ireland is now almost entirely confined to keeping the ground clear for the operation of Father

FATHER MATHEW'S
MEDAL

FATHER MATHEW

PARTURE OF FATHER MATHEW FROM CORK FOR
AMERICA, 1849

THOMASTOWN, THE STATELY HOME WHERE FATHER MATHEW WAS BORN

THE FRIARY, COVE STREET, CORK, WHERE FATHER MATHEW LIVED AND WORKED

Mathew.' Two Irish Protestants living in London who toured their native land that year found 'sobriety to be universal throughout Ireland . . . From first to last we employed perhaps fifty car-drivers; we never found one to accept a drink. The boatmen of Killarney, proverbial for drunkenness . . . declined the whiskey we had taken with us and after hours of hard labour dipped a can into the lake and refreshed themselves from its waters.' Two years later a Bristol man recorded that 'in the most inferior parts of Limerick he found scarcely a cabin without a clean and comfortable bed', while the secretary of a mining company in County Waterford, where 800 of 1,200 employees had taken the pledge, reported: 'From being a most dissolute, idle and intractable set of workmen . . . clothed in rags and living in many respects worse . . . even than the beasts of the field, they are now the most industrious, orderly and well clad people in the empire.'

As news of events in Ireland crossed the Irish Sea, Father Mathew received many invitations to visit Scotland and England. His first public visit, to Glasgow in 1842, yielded 10,000 pledges in one day and though he had been away only ten days, he was welcomed back to Cork with 'one wild outburst of feeling—one prolonged shout of joy—as the coach . . . passed through a living lane of human beings . . . During the whole evening the city was in a state of wild commotion.' On 1st July 1843 he landed at Liverpool, where soon afterwards Thomas Carlyle saw him 'distributing the temperance pledge to the lost sheep of the place, thousands strong of both sexes, a very ragged and lost-looking squadron indeed. Father Mathew is a broad, solid looking man with grey hair . . . The very face of him attracts you . . . I almost cried to listen to him.' At Liverpool more than 40,000 signed the pledge, in Manchester 60,000. In Bradford, Huddersfield, Halifax and York the crowds forgot their anti-Catholic, anti-teetotal prejudices and knelt before the Irish Papist. At Wakefield, to avoid disappointing would-be hosts, Father Mathew declined all invitations to stay, but a Quaker enticed him in by labelling his house 'Temperance Hotel'.

A month after landing, Father Mathew reached London, and for the next six weeks worked his way across the capital. Jane Welsh Carlyle was at one meeting on a patch of waste ground off the Commercial Road, Mile End, and was as impressed as her husband had been. 'Thousands of people', she wrote to him, 'all hushed into awful silence . . . and in the face of Father Mathew . . . the mercy of heaven seemed to be laid bare.'

At Parsons Green, in mid-August, Father Mathew first encountered the noisy opposition long familiar to other temperance speakers, a determined attempt being made to break up a meeting of 3,000 people, including many gentry in their carriages. A fortnight later, in Bermondsey, a group of about seventy men and 200 boys surrounded the platform and booed Father Mathew so effectively that a crowd of 20,000 was unable to hear him. The men, hired by local publicans, carried cans of beer, wore hats inscribed 'Member of the Hop and Malt Society' and, recorded *The Morning Chronicle*, 'some of them bore staves and were decorated from head to foot with hop leaves'. When the intruders, using their fists, attempted to storm the platform, 'a general conflict took place', and after being driven back they 'mounted a large pile of bricks', used 'the most gross language' and threw beer 'in the faces of their assailants'. Father Mathew was smuggled away to safety in a cab, but the meeting was wrecked, and the London Irish thereupon formed a bodyguard, including women 'with shillelaghs inside their umbrellas'. At future meetings there was no more trouble.

Meanwhile, Father Mathew had scored a tremendous hit in London society. He met the Prime Minister, Sir Robert Peel, the Duke of Wellington and many other noblemen, secured as a convert the future Duke of Norfolk, who later recanted on medical grounds, and gave Lord Brougham a medal to pass on to a notoriously drunken peer, who made the immortal reply: 'I tell you what . . . I will keep sober for this night.' 'Father Mathew', commented *The Times*, '. . . is an example in his own person that cheerfulness and good humour can be reconciled with total abstinence from all intoxicating drinks.'

During his ten-week visit to England it was claimed that Father Mathew had made 600,000 new teetotallers, from small children to a woman aged 102, though the real total was probably nearer 200,000. On his return to Ireland he was greeted at Kingstown by a crowd of 20,000, and a band playing *See the Conquering Hero Comes*, and the Mathew Tower was erected on a hillside outside Cork to commemorate his recent triumphs. The parlour of his little house in Cove Street, Cork, was now more crowded than ever, the visitors often including teetotallers wishing to be released from their pledge. Some, less courageous, pushed their temperance medal under the door or through the letter-box, whereupon Father Mathew would rush out in pursuit of the backslider. Another hazard of a visit to Cove Street was an encounter with Father Mathew's servant, John, 'a dried-up, wizened-faced, dapper old bachelor . . . sour of visage and sour of speech'. It was an open secret that John drank, but Father Mathew always accepted his explanation that the water smelt of whisky because John had used spirits to polish the jug, and when John had to retire incapable to bed Father Mathew would explain to visitors that he had been taken ill. John was 'eminently aristocratic and hated to be bored by the poor . . . It was', wrote Maguire, 'a pleasant sight to see Father Mathew invading John's pantry in search of a piece of cold beef or mutton' for hungry visitors, while 'John would groan as if he were the victim of some atrocious burglar'. Father Mathew also refused to hear any ill of his beloved cat, Madam Pinky, or of his dog, Sober, a bad-tempered beast finally destroyed after biting a woman's leg. His pet sparrow, Peter, suffered a more bizarre fate, being sat on and squashed to death by a fat friar.

Father Mathew's 1,000 correspondents were as demanding as his visitors, and daily 100 letters poured through his letter-box. Many were from teetotallers asking to be allowed 'some two or three pints, glasses or tumblers', or hot buttered punch for their winter ailments. Other correspondents begged for money to buy out of the Army sons who had joined up while drunk, and one publican wanted Father Mathew to persuade the farmer's sons to whom he had given credit to settle their debts, for they had turned teetotal and said their principles would not allow them to pay. The most persistent begging letters were on behalf of temperance bands, and they amply bore out Thomas Whittaker's view that 'Temperance bands are a folly and a mistake ... Buying instruments and dressing up people at a society's expense ... sooner or later brings trouble.' In theory the bands provided a harmless occupation for young men and were useful at temperance rallies, but equipping a band was only the beginning, for trumpets and flutes were for ever being lost or damaged or stolen. 'The question now is ... ', ran a typical letter, soliciting £10 for new instruments, 'shall we continue a temperance band or shall we not? Shall we, must we, after all be driven to give up our pledges?' Father Mathew had, in fact, no ear for music but Maguire, who had, acknowledged that he had 'listened with a kind of amused horror to the first performances of a temperance band':

> Your whole nervous being is assailed with a crash of sounds... Shriek and squeak... roar and clash, with a blending of all and an occasional predominance of some—this is the band executing 'Love Not'... The tumult is awful... The walls, you imagine must shortly yield to the stupendous reverberations created by the big drum, which is under the able hands of the muscular blacksmith. The performers proudly persevere, their master beating time and swaying his head from side to side, with a gravity worthy of the bandmaster of the Coldstreams... If the big drum yielded to the merciless vigour of its lusty operation... a subscription from the President for the purchase of a new one was expected.

The bands were only one of the many demands on Father Mathew's income. He could never refuse a donation to a temperance reading-room or a temperance library, and, though his own staff was modest, by the summer of 1844 he owed his printers alone £3,000. Even more serious was the failure to charge a realistic price for the medals which every teetotaller wore—the first converts were known as 'medal men'. One man in Dublin received 42,000 medals, for which he never paid; two boxes containing 1,400 more were simply mislaid; while John Hockings, 'the Birmingham blacksmith', did very well for himself on a tour of Ireland, preaching temperance and selling his version of the medal. Father Mathew himself constantly gave away free not only the standard copper medal, worth a shilling, but also silver medals costing him fourteen shillings, although said to be worth only six, and even on at least one occasion a gold medal, value £15. £1,500 worth of medals were distributed free in England alone, many to rich noblemen.

The crash came one day while he was administering the pledge. 'I'm sorry, father', said a kneeling convert and thrust a writ into his hand. Father Mathew passed on as though nothing had happened, fearing the man might be lynched if the crowd learned what had happened, and the bill, for metal for medals, was later paid. Thereafter, however, Father Mathew was never out of debt. A wealthy relation who had promised him a large legacy 'forgot' to mention him in her will. He spent £7,000 he did not possess on building a grandiose new church, and in 1843 a national appeal for him produced many tributes but only £1,100 in cash. A further £8,300, raised in 1844, was soon swallowed up.

Queen Victoria was not, however, encouraging when Lord John Russell proposed in 1846 to award Father Mathew a Civil List pension of £100 a year: 'He has done much by preaching temperance, but by the aid of superstition, which can hardly be patronised by the Crown.' In the following year, however, she approved one of £300, used to buy life insurance to cover his debts.

By now Father Mathew's own problems were submerged in his country's tragedy, for in 1846 the potato crop failed. 'The famine odour', wrote Maguire, 'was in his parlour in Cove Street', and though Father Mathew was soon prominent in relief work the famine and the resulting flight—in the decade from 1841 1,600,000 people left Ireland—struck the temperance movement a blow from which it never recovered. In the same period, despite the drop in population, the consumption of spirits rose from five to seven million gallons. Reading-rooms closed down, bands split up, societies ceased to meet, and where relief works were started, their offices were often in what Father Mathew called 'those pestiferous erections', public houses.

In 1848 Father Mathew had a serious stroke but in 1849 he accepted an invitation to America, spending the long voyage in caring for the Irish emigrants on board. The tour, during which he was entertained by President Polk, who in his honour drank only water, was clouded only by his unwilling involvement in the slavery controversy, each side being indignant that he would not publicly condemn the other. He was distressed, too, that he lacked the 350 dollars to buy the freedom of the negro woman, Molly, and her son Peter, who looked after him during his visit, during which he travelled 37,000 miles, visited twenty-four states and administered half-a-million pledges.

The crowds who welcomed him back to Ireland in December 1851 were shocked at his drawn face and obvious tiredness, and by 1855 his condition had so worsened that he moved away from Cork, to spare his friends and relatives the sight of his last illness. In December 1856 he died and was buried in the cemetery he had founded. That day all work ceased in Cork and the funeral procession stretched for two miles. Eight years later a statue to him was unveiled in Cork, but within a few years, on three of the four corners of the same square, stood public houses. It was said that at least Father Mathew had his back to them.

*Chapter Twelve*

# THE BAND OF HOPE

'Oh we're a youthful Band of Hope,
All pledged strong drink to flee.
Then let our watchword sound afar:
"No drink, no drink for me!"'
— *The New Temperance Hymnal*, 1909

To consolidate its initial success, the temperance movement soon realised that it needed the support of the young. The first Juvenile Temperance Association was founded in Paisley in 1830 and was followed by the first Total Abstinence Society for Boys and Girls at Preston in 1834. In the same year one of the original 'seven men', John Brodbelt, started a halfpenny magazine, *The Youthful Teetotaller*, and when this failed a weekly column was devoted to juvenile activities in *The Preston Temperance Advocate*. This recorded meetings where the speakers were aged twelve or thirteen, and triumphs like that of 'Master W. Garman, who . . . proved himself a hero by refusing a £5 note offered on condition of drinking a glass of wine'. By the early 1840s there were flourishing juvenile societies in several places, notably Edinburgh. Here a wealthy lawyer, John Hope, spent £20,000 on temperance propaganda among children, employing paid agents, subsidising vast fêtes attended by as many as 12,000, and in 1847 founding the British League of Juvenile Abstainers.

The real founder of the juvenile temperance movement outside Scotland was a thirty-eight-year-old Baptist minister, the Rev. Jabez Tunnicliff of Leeds, a former craftsman. Tunnicliff had been deeply impressed by a dying drunkard whose downfall had begun in childhood when a teacher offered him beer after Sunday school. 'It was', he recalled, 'the first glass that did it . . . I want you to warn young men against the first glass.' Jabez Tunnicliff duly delivered this message, to girls as well as boys, and in August 1847 he invited a woman already famous as a preacher of temperance to children to visit Leeds.

Anne Jane Carlile was the widow of a Presbyterian minister. She had been, with Elizabeth Fry, a pioneer prison visitor in Dublin, and an active supporter of Father Mathew. The taunts of female prisoners that, unlike them, she could always afford wine if she gave up spirits, had led her to sign the total abstinence pledge and though now seventy-two she was 'tall and commanding in appearance with lovely grey or white hair done up in stiff curls . . . She had lovely small white hands and always wore handsome black dresses and exquisite white caps, trimmed with white satin.' The crowd of girls from Sunday schools all over Leeds which Tunnicliff had assembled moved her to remark, according to her own account: 'Is it not a cheering sight to see all these dear children? It is in the young people that I have placed my chief hope for the furtherance of the cause so dear to my heart and I think we ought to call this juvenile meeting "the Band of Hope".' According to other versions it was Tunnicliff who first uttered the famous phrase, but whatever the facts the result was as decisive as the coining of the word 'teetotal': the Band of Hope became within a few years a household name.

Mrs. Carlile had little to do with its development, though she lived till eighty-eight, but Tunnicliff had found his life's work. That same evening he wrote the famous song which, to the tune of *Here we come a-gipsying*, was to be heard for generations:

> Come all dear children sing a song, join us with heart and hand.
> Come make our little party strong, a happy temperance band.
> We cannot sing of many things, for we are young we know,
> But we have signed the temperance pledge a short time ago.

The Band of Hope shall be our name, the temperance star
our guide,
We will not know the drunkard's shame, the drunkard's
drink avoid,
Cold water cannot do us harm, strong drink may bring us
woe,
So we have signed the temperance pledge, a short time ago.

We'll ask our fathers, too, to come and join our happy band,
True temperance makes a happy home and makes a happy
land;
Our mothers we will try to gain and brothers and sisters,
too.
For we have signed the temperance pledge a short time ago.

This was the first of many such songs and Band of Hope choirs were soon a popular attraction at temperance functions, particularly the annual demonstration at the Crystal Palace, where the massed-choirs eventually mustered 4,000 voices.

The Band of Hope was formally founded on 16th September 1847 by Jabez Tunnicliff and a committee of ladies. Membership was to be open to all children under sixteen and based on the simple pledge, 'I do agree that I will not use intoxicating liquors as a beverage', though some societies also mentioned tobacco, snuff and opium to be on the safe side. In November 300 children paid threepence to attend the Band's inaugural tea, and twelve-year-old John Mitchell earned his place in temperance history by being the first to sign the pledge.

Leeds was now divided into sixteen districts, each with its woman visitor who canvassed working-class homes and lectured in day schools, and within a few months 4,000 children had been enrolled. Simultaneously, a London draughtsman, John Esterbrooke, was setting up a Band of Hope in Westminster and his pamphlet *Bands of Hope and How to Form Them* provided a blueprint for would-be organisers elsewhere. Many of the first Bands of Hope were started within existing Sunday schools and the movement spread rapidly. In 1851 a fête in Edinburgh, largely financed by John Hope, attracted 30,000 children and in the following year 6,000 crowded into Exeter Hall for a meeting under the chairmanship of James Silk Buckingham. This occasion finally put the organisation on the map, for thousands of children who were shut out stopped the traffic in the Strand, while those within adopted a formal address to the ten-year-old Prince of Wales.

Like its adult predecessor, the teetotal movement among children had its critics. George Cruikshank complained in a pamphlet in 1853 that three children had been expelled from a London Church School for joining a juvenile abstainers' expedition. The curate had previously warned them that in signing the pledge they had committed 'a great sin', because the baptismal vow alone was sufficient for salvation, and had insulted the 'good creatures' sent by God for man's use. Despite opposition, however, the cause made remarkable progress. By 1874 there were at least 5,500 Bands of Hope in the United Kingdom, with 800,000 members; by 1889 the totals had risen to 16,000 societies and two million members, one in every four of the eligible age groups, and by 1897 to more than 3,200,000. Although many children lapsed from their pledge on reaching maturity, these figures help to explain the striking build-up in anti-drink sentiment during the last quarter of the nineteenth century.

The man under whom this expansion occurred was a typical waterdrinker. Stephen Shirley had been apprenticed to a tailor at the age of ten, but at fifteen his diligent attendance at Sunday school caught the eye of the director of a large printing firm, who had offered him a job as a clerk. By 1855, now aged thirty-five, he was a manager in the business and in that year founded the Band of Hope Union in London, a loose federation of all the Bands in the capital. Its first headquarters were a tiny room five feet square in his house and later in the temperance hotel he ran as a sideline—it was unpopular even among teetotallers, since he would eject anyone caught smoking on the premises. The Union eventually acquired a building near the Old Bailey with a large shop front which was filled with admonitory displays for the benefit of people waiting to go into court. It was soon employing paid agents and supplied literature and lecturers to local societies, and in 1863 became the United Kingdom Band of Hope Union. Local societies, however, retained their autonomy and many organisations remained wholly independent, particularly the Juvenile Temples of the Good Templar Order, of which more will be heard later.

One reason for the Band of Hope's popularity was the variety of interesting activities it offered at a time when there was little organised entertainment for children. John Hope's League of Juvenile Abstainers had pointed the way with sight-seeing trips round Edinburgh, country excursions and, in 1854, the use of a park for ball games. In the following year, in London, Stephen Shirley began delivering lantern lectures to young audiences and soon thousands were being given every year, the slides often being based on George Cruikshank's *The Bottle*. A specimen programme for Bands of Hope, drawn up around 1881, suggested a variety of amusements for juniors, from a 'scriptural bee' to lessons in making temperance drinks. For dark winter nights a magic lantern entertainment based on *Jessica's First Prayer* and a talk on 'Fire-water', i.e., spirits, were recommended. The programme for seniors included a 'temperance bee', impromptu speaking practice, and lectures about temperance personalities. The author believed, rightly it seems, that children could be required to attend regularly for several months before being accepted, and would readily pay a penny a month subscription, or twopence for seniors, to supplement the proceeds of bazaars and entertainments.

*The Band of Hope Review and Sunday Scholar's Friend*, an illustrated halfpenny monthly, launched in 1851, soon had a circulation of a quarter of a million and many imitators. John Hope's British League of Juvenile Abstainers had its own magazine, and he also advertised, in 1850, for temperance songs, receiving nearly 400 entries. The best, *We'll win the day*, contained the classic line, 'The little is the sin begun'.[1]

[1] The first Bands of Hope in Scotland were founded in the 1850s and the Scottish Band of Hope Union in 1879. The first Band of Hope in Ireland dates from 1869.

For direct teaching, the Band of Hope relied largely on such publications as the penny *Band of Hope Catechism* which consisted of fifty-two questions and answers to be learned by heart. These led the student on from 'What is the meaning of the word "intoxicating"?' ('"Intoxicating" means poisonous'), to 'Does God make the alcohol in wine?' ('In one sense He does, just as He causes meat to become putrid and pears rotten; but we need not . . . eat the putrid meat or drink the fermented grape juice.') Asked 'Is alcohol of any use at all?', the author replies 'It is useful . . . to painters for varnish and paint', *A New Temperance Catechism for Juniors*, several years later, generously adding 'in museums to preserve specimens and as fuel in spirit lamps or to drive motors'. Many authors were made of sterner stuff. 'Alcohol prevents the growth of the body . . . dulls the brain' and produces 'the trembling hands of many craftsmen', asserted J. Glyn Davies of Conway in his *Temperance Catechism*. The drinker's 'jolly red face is the face of disease', resulting from damaged blood vessels, warned Dr. Benjamin Ward Richardson in *Drink and Strong Drink*. Those who drank would end up 'ad-dicted . . . e-nerva-ted and e-maci-at-ed' and 'im-per-cepti-bly . . . de-gen-e-ra-ted'. Water, or 'Adam's Ale', on the other hand, pointed out A. Joliffe in *The Child's Textbook of Easy Temperance Lessons*, was a 'nour-ish-ing . . . wonder-ful . . . bev-er-age'.

Many writers composed mnemonic verses, as in the Rev. William Spiers's *Giant Alcohol*:

Y east
E ffects fermentation
A lcohol to produce
S upplying strong temptation
T o every silly goose.

F ood in strong drink is never found
O r only in minute degrees
O bnoxious fat it forms around
D isordered hearts to cause disease.

This message was rammed home by gruesome pictures comparing a teetotaller's brain or stomach with a moderate drinker's, a feature of many temperance publications, and one which was particularly convincing in full colour.

The most widely used of all Band of Hope textbooks was *The Worship of Bacchus, A Great Delusion*, by the Band's treasurer, Ebenezer Clarke, first published for adults in 1876, but reissued in a twopenny abridged version for children. Clarke had gained his information by visiting breweries, and his book contained sufficient facts and diagrams about the manufacture of alcohol to enable any intelligent child to set up his own still or brew his own beer.[1] To teach the history of drinking the Band of Hope relied on a solid 300-page volume, *Morning Dewdrops or the Juvenile Abstainer*, first published in halfpenny parts in 1843 and still in print seventy years later. Its author, Mrs. Clara Balfour, led her readers through British history with many a striking anecdote, from the conquest of the drunken Ancient Britons by the 'very temperate' Romans, to the victory in the school playground of a heroic Victorian youth who refused to drink beer.

Anti-drink alphabets also had a great vogue. *The Musical Temperance Alphabet* consisted of a series of simple sentences, each with its own tune. When the teacher held up the letter 'E' the class chirped 'Everybody should always be sober', 'O' produced 'Old and young are better without beer', 'Q', 'Q is always followed by U and drink by drunkenness', and so on to 'Wine is a cause of vice and crime'. Another *Temperance Alphabet for Bands of Hope* relied on rhyming couplets and ingeniously solved the familiar problem of 'X':

> M stands for MODERATE. But surely e'en sips
> Of dangerous poison should ne'er touch the lips.
>
> O stands for ONE. And one glass leads to more
> A fact countless thousands of drunkards deplore.

[1] During prohibition in the United States similar publications were much in demand.

X is the letter which has the strange task
Of showing the strength in each barrel and cask.

For the very young there were temperance picture books, with commentaries contrasting the sober man's weekend with the drunkard's:

Sing a song of Saturday
Wages taken home
Ev'ry penny well laid out,
None allowed to roam! . . .

Sing a song of Sunday,
A home that's black and bare
Wife and children starving,
A crust of bread their share! . . .

Sing a song of Monday
Brought before the 'beak'.
Fine of twenty shillings,
Alternative 'a week'!

Workhouse for the children,
Workhouse for the wife!
Isn't that a hideous blot
On our English life?

Another book in the same series showed an evil-looking publican raking in 'Workmen's Sunday dinners' and 'Market Pennies' until challenged by stalwart temperance lecturers, 'the men, that killed the rats, that spoiled the corn, that grew in the land where Jack dwelt'.

Despite the rapid spread of literacy during the mid-nineteenth century, the need of working-class children for interesting reading matter had largely been neglected and in the 1860s the Band of Hope began to advertise for new children's books which were not 'thinly disguised tracts'. Eighty entries were received for the first competition, the £100 prize being won by the Rev. T. P. Wilson's *Frank Oldfield or Lost and Found*, published in 1869. The tale begins in a tough Lancashire mining village where 'our Sammul', a fourteen-year-old, who works down the pit, and his sister Betty, aged thirteen, are in disgrace at home. 'I'd sooner see you both in your graves, nor have you sticking up your pledge cards about the house', says their drunken father, vowing: 'Ye shall both break your teetotal afore this time tomorrow as I'm a living man.' Sam responds by running away from home and the story now moves to the home of Frank Oldfield, the twenty-one-year-old son of the local squire, who like young Sammul has run into parental opposition on trying to become teetotal, his mother merely telling the butler, 'James, hand the beer again to Master Frank.' James hands the beer to such purpose that soon Frank, now addicted to drink, is being shipped off to Australia, meeting Sam *en route*. After many adventures they return to England. Frank, by now a drunken, dishonest wreck, dies in a Liverpool garret, surrounded by his remorseful family, while noble Sam, who says, 'I'd die afore I'd touch a drop of the drink', is re-united with his still teetotal sister, and his reformed and prosperous father, who prudently live in a 'dry' village with an active Band of Hope.

*Frank Oldfield* was a great success and sold 23,000 copies in three years; in one institution fifty prisoners signed the pledge after hearing it read. The £50 prize-winner in the same competition, Miss M. A. Paull's *Tim's Troubles or Tried and True*, also sold well and in 1879 Miss Paull carried off the first prize in a further competition with *Sought and Saved*.[1] This has a more middle-class setting. The hero, 'Bones', the son of a West Country solicitor, is badly burned at a Guy Fawkes' day bonfire, which he attends with his friend 'Chips'. The surgeon prescribes brandy 'but at the word Bones opened his eyes and with a moan of pain shook his head . . . Chips understood. "He will never touch it, sir," he said.' Bones's widower father, Mr.

[1] Tim's Troubles did not cease with publication for the British Museum copy was destroyed during the war and I have been unable to consult it.

Hampden, and his older brother Arthur, also a lawyer, have other ideas. Mr. Hampden is discovered pressing port upon his idolised infant daughter, Crystal, and Arthur is soon 'lying full length upon the hearth rug, snoring vigorously'. Little Crystal is meanwhile kneeling upstairs praying, 'O dear . . . God, please make my Arthur a better man', apparently without result, for Arthur goes rapidly downhill and tries to cut his throat. He is taken abroad to remove him from temptation, but disappears, eventually turning up on 'a cold, wild night in January, with a torrent of driving sleet and rain' and so changed that he is only recognised by the scar on his neck. Restored to health he signs the pledge, promising if necessary to emigrate to the prohibition state of Maine, while Crystal makes a final appearance at a Band of Hope fête at the Crystal Palace, characteristically remarking: 'When I am singing for temperance, I feel I am singing for Jesus.'

Such books, up to 400 pages long and well produced, were ideal as presents and prizes, but there was a demand, too, for shorter, cheaper volumes a child might buy for himself. Typical of these is Mary E. Murray's *A Bit of Blue Ribbon*, whose hero, eight-year-old Tom Tony, an orphan, is responsible for saving his friend Will Turner, the ploughman, from drink, and for his marrying Tom Tony's Aunt Nan. Will soon 'blesses the day he began to wear "the bit of blue ribbon"', and Tom Tony reveals that 'teacher was asking us all to sign the pledge and we're going to have a Band of Hope and it won't be dull in the winter any more'.

The temperance movement did in fact make a determined attempt to gain access to schools and even after the creation of publicly financed Board schools by the Education Act of 1870, a surprisingly large number of headmasters continued to allow teetotal lecturers into their classrooms. By the 1880s over 200 school Boards, including the progressive London Board, were allowing such teaching and examinations on it, with certificates for successful candidates, and in 1887 a Band of Hope appeal to expand the work raised £12,000. Five paid lecturers were engaged, from 200 candidates, and in the five years the money lasted lectures were heard by 1,400,000 pupils and 50,000 teachers, while 570,000 children, from 13,000 schools, submitted temperance essays. A national examination on one textbook, with £500 worth of prizes, produced 25,000 entries. The campaign in the schools was reinforced by an attack on the home. One Saturday in October 1891, 32,500 Band of Hope visitors each called on thirty or forty houses, contacting altogether a million families and collecting 100,000 new pledges.

These national attempts to indoctrinate the whole working-class child population with teetotal beliefs, were supplemented by individual initiative. In 1906 a Hull M.P., with the co-operation of the local Education Committee, offered prizes of three-and-sixpence and half-a-crown for the best essays on the dangers of alcohol by the pupils in each department of each school in the city. Nearly 13,000 children took part and 200 prizes were awarded. Extracts from the prize-winning essays reveal the extent of the teetotallers' success. 'Before so much alcohol was taken', wrote one boy, 'the British were sturdy, strong, square-shouldered men.' Now they were 'thin, puny, round-shouldered'. 'A man who is under its influence staggers noticeably', pointed out Irene Staples. 'He . . . laughs hideously . . . lets out things about himself that would be better left unsaid.' 'When England lost the rowing championship', explained Edmund Halley, 'the English champion . . . refused to abstain from intoxicating liquor.'

The increasing popularity of science as a school subject from 1870 onwards gave the teetotallers a new opportunity. A national syllabus of *Lessons on Temperance* was adopted by a Liberal President of the Board of Education in 1909, but the most effective propaganda masqueraded as teaching on biology. One such textbook, in 1914, devoted only four out of 163 pages to a direct attack on drink, but included experiments showing that alcohol was harmful to frog-spawn and prevented yeast growing in a test-tube. Another experiment, recalling Joseph Livesey's *Malt Liquor Lecture*, involved heating ale, tonic wine and gin and timing the period during which the resulting vapour burned: five minutes for ale, twenty for tonic wine and twenty-five for gin. A *Manual of Scientific Temperance* published four years later, and officially approved for use in Irish schools, added tadpoles to frog-spawn as victims of premature drinking, and contrasted the luxuriant growth of a vase of flowers fed on water alone with the woebegone appearance of those to which a 1 in 200 solution of alcohol had been added. The point was underlined by a table showing the death rate of barmen to be four times that of gardeners.

Although in 1879 a Young Abstainers' Union was started for the children of the middle and upper classes, the public schools continued to serve beer as an everyday article of diet, with wine on special occasions. In 1890 a conference was held in the Sheldonian Theatre at Oxford to discuss how gilded youth, too, could be taught total abstinence. 'We must', the Archdeacon of Exeter told his audience, 'get at the young of the cultured class and train their habits . . . not . . . the "good boys" only but . . . the cricketers, the boating men, the football players.' It was the athlete—'I speak as an old public school and university cricketer myself'—who had the greatest influence, since 'prowess on the playing fields makes him a god among his fellows'.

At a conference in London in the following year, the school physician of Rugby, Dr. Clement Dukes, warned a distinguished audience, presided over by a bishop and a duke, of the disastrous results of beer-drinking in boarding schools. 'Our great public schools', he thundered, 'are among the noblest institutions of the country . . . And yet words are inadequate to condemn the cruel and pernicious practice which prevails at most of them . . . In those schools where supper with beer is provided at 9 p.m. it is almost a physical . . . impossibility for many boys of a certain age, with their troublesome instincts, to continue pure . . . Beer . . . starts a vice which is as infectious as measles.' Fortunately the remedy was simple. Boys when caught should be told 'your whole character will be damaged for life', and expelled, and there should be a final, meatless meal at 6 p.m. Above all, advised Dr. Dukes, 'Beer and bedtime should be dealt with without further delay. Cubicles also must be abandoned. How is it that the governing bodies of ... our great public schools provide every facility for the commission of secret vice? ... What are we Englishmen doing to remove the blot from our school escutcheon? ... The piteous cry of schoolboys rises up to parents, masters and governing bodies—"Save us from being tempted—lest we fall".'

*Chapter Thirteen*

## THE ACCURSED TRADE

'The traffic in intoxicating liquors . . . is . . . destructive to the order and welfare of society and ought, therefore, to be prohibited.'

— *Declaration of Principles* of the United Kingdom Alliance, 1853

THE 1850s began promisingly for the teetotallers, for alcohol was banned in the refreshment rooms of the Great Exhibition of 1851. *Punch* showed two bewildered yokels who had ordered a pint of beer being told: 'Don't keep it. You can have a strawberry ice', and James Silk Buckingham wrote for the occasion *An Earnest Plea for the Reign of Temperance and Peace*. A great temperance demonstration was planned for the first week in August with Thomas Cook as 'travelling secretary' to assemble supporters from all over the country.

Cook, now aged forty-three, had begun life as a wood-turner, been converted to temperance by 'the Birmingham blacksmith', and published several temperance magazines before, in 1841, finding his true vocation in organising a shilling a head trip for 600 Leicester teetotallers to a demonstration at Loughborough. His work in 1851 was so successful that three years later he became a full-time travel agent and long before his death, at the age of eighty-four, his company was famous all over the world.

The provincial teetotallers whom he brought together in 1851 enjoyed an eventful week, with a mass procession to the Exhibition and a grand fête at the Zoo, attended by 25,000 people. The profits were used to found the London Temperance

League, with Buckingham as its president and George Cruikshank and John Cassell as its vice-presidents. At thirty-four the former 'Manchester carpenter' was now a successful publisher and had so successfully shaken off his legendary uncouthness that mutterings were heard that he got into his carriage at temperance rallies with altogether too lordly an air. The new League organised a series of monthly meetings at Exeter Hall, a building already identified with the temperance movement and described in a verse published in 1850:

> Its front unassuming, straight, formal and square,
> Within it is spacious and lofty and fair,
> The large-hearted, cold-visaged men who meet there
> Well typify Exeter Hall.
> Narrow-browed, gloomy, and frowning on all,
> A most orthodox building is Exeter Hall.

The League also decided to finance an extension of the tour of Great Britain then being undertaken by F. W. Kellogg, a famous temperance lecturer from the United States, where in 1846 the state of Maine, covering an area two-thirds the size of England, had forbidden the general sale of drink. Further laws, in 1851, made it illegal to manufacture drink in the state and gave the police drastic powers of search and arrest. This marked the real start of the struggle for national prohibition in America and it had a marked effect on opinion in Great Britain. Henceforward the British temperance movement was divided into 'moral suasionists', who sought to defeat drink by persuading everyone to sign the pledge, and 'prohibitionists', who favoured legal coercion. Many British teetotallers visited the United States to see the Maine Law at work, and when Neal Dow, its chief sponsor, arrived in Britain on a lecture tour in 1857 he was given a hero's welcome, although among impartial observers the effectiveness of prohibition was already in doubt. In Neal Dow's own town of Portland there were at least 300 illegal drinking dens and so widespread was evasion that already the expression 'bootlegger', for a man who carried illegal drinks for sale in his high boots, had passed into the language.

In 1852 a Quaker businessman, Nathaniel Card, organised a number of private meetings in Manchester, attended among others by Joseph Brotherton, M.P., and the Rev. James Dawson Burns, a Baptist, and the future historian of the temperance movement. These were followed on 1st June 1853 by the foundation of the United Kingdom Alliance for the Suppression of the Traffic in all Intoxicating Liquors, a name suggested by Dawson Burns. 'The traffic in intoxicating liquor is inimical to the true interests of individuals, and destructive to the order and welfare of society and ought, therefore, to be prohibited', explained the Alliance's *Declaration of Principles.* A pamphlet by Dawson Burns, *What the Alliance is and what it is not,* stressed how the 'Maine men' differed from existing teetotallers: 'The Alliance does not wish for a law to prevent any man drinking, but to prevent all men engaging in the sale of strong drink ... It is not the private use but the public traffic which is prohibited.' A man could still 'brew his own beer or import his own wine for anything the Alliance may say to the contrary.'

The foundation of the Alliance was greeted with enthusiasm by many old-guard teetotallers. Joseph Livesey joined its Council, John Cassell, Thomas Whittaker and James Silk Buckingham expressed their support and Father Mathew sent a message welcoming the new movement 'with rapture' as it 'strikes at the root of the evil'. 'To work merely as a moral suasion society without advocating at the same time the Maine Law', said a speaker at one public meeting, 'was but a waste of talent, wealth and time. They had been priming the powder merely. They should adopt the wiser policy of shotting their guns with Maine Law bullets.' Within a year the Alliance was able to support a weekly magazine. 'Our Sebastopol is not yet conquered', acknowledged an early issue during the Crimean War. 'Nevertheless our progress has been astonishing ... During a year of political paralysis we, and we alone, have carried on an agitation that has not lain down and died in its cradle.'

The war had in fact helped the temperance movement, for the public was horrified by the revelations of drunkenness in

G. W. E. Russell's despatches to *The Times*. 'Is the British Army in the Crimea to become, or rather to continue, a model of drunkenness to all nations?' he asked in October 1855. Soon temperance publications were being distributed by the Army's principal chaplain, and on Christmas Day one colonel delivered a temperance lecture to his regiment on the heights above Sebastopol. Further kudos accrued to the teetotallers during the Indian Mutiny in the following year after the attack on Delhi had been endangered by drink and several of the war's heroes were discovered to be non-drinkers.

By 1857 the Alliance was clearly prospering, with nearly 50,000 members, an income of £6,000, and paid agents in eighteen districts. In 1858 it received its first large legacy, £1,300; in 1865 an appeal for a £50,000 five-year fighting fund raised £29,000 on the first day and in 1871 a second appeal, for £100,000, brought in £40,000 within twenty-four hours. The Alliance made effective use of the money collected. More than once it took a full-page advertisement in *The Times* and it was far more active than other organisations in submitting questionnaires to parliamentary candidates, lobbying back-bench M.P.s, and leading deputations to ministers. *The Alliance Weekly News* constantly sought the most readable format and was good value at a penny. No case illustrating the evil effects of drinking escaped its vigilant eye and in 1864 two issues were devoted to 420 such cases extracted from eighty newspapers in one week. These included seventeen deaths and the paper appeared with black borders in mourning for the victims.

The Alliance, though influential, was far from typical of temperance organisations, for it welcomed non-teetotallers as members and was hostile to most proposed reforms in the licensing law fearing these might make the trade more respectable. 'The less the Alliance has to do with legislation providing any facilities for the sale or drinking of intoxicating liquors the better', it declared in 1865. It was equally uncompromising in its relations with other temperance bodies. An offer by the 'moral suasionist' Scottish Temperance League to carry on the prohibition agitation in Scotland was refused, and part of the

League seceded to form a new association to preach the full Alliance line. A suggestion in 1859 that the headquarters of the British Temperance League should move from Bolton to Manchester was turned down because 'there being... little differences at times between some of the teetotallers and some of the Alliance men, the close proximity of the two might have led to more serious consequences'. The League eventually, in 1880, went to Sheffield instead.

The Alliance's indifference to all reforms except its own panacea of prohibition troubled Joseph Livesey, who, from being a nominal supporter, steadily became a persistent critic. He was scathing in 1854 about the 'numerous class who would close the beer-shop, but not their own cellars', and in 1862 he pointed out that 'If it be right to brew your own beer, I cannot see how it can be wrong for your neighbour of the Royal Hotel to brew it for you and take pay for it.' 'With the Alliance it is all "the traffic", "the traffic", "the cursed traffic"', he complained in 1873. 'Buyers are equally to blame with sellers and forty times as numerous... Let themselves and their jugs keep at home... and there is an end of the drink system at once.'

The Alliance continued to insist, however, that 'the real cause' of intemperance was 'the legalised system of temptation' represented by the public house. Hitherto the better publicans and the more moderate teetotallers had often found common ground in wishing to discourage drunkenness. The United Kingdom Alliance wanted nothing except all-out, unrelenting, war on the trade with no terms except unconditional surrender and from the first expressly rejected any suggestion of compensation for a lost licence. Its members spent their spare time collecting evidence against individual public houses, noting down how many children went in and how many drunks came out, and sometimes penetrating hopefully inside in search of further debauchery. One Liverpool licensee sued a teetotaller who entered his house in disguise one Saturday evening for causing a breach of the peace and at Portsmouth another teetotaller was killed by men a publican had hired to attack him.

The victim was hailed as a martyr and £1,000 raised for his family. Clearly there were faults on both sides; one teetotaller who had accepted a glass of beer 'on the house', poured it on the ground but said he would be glad to keep the glass and at Shrewsbury a teetotal railwayman, who had formerly been a good customer at a public house, had a jug of beer poured over him by the landlord, who remarked, 'You shall have it outside or in!'

But it was on paper that the war between licensees and water-drinkers was chiefly conducted. Two books were particularly influential. *An Argument, Legal and Historical for the Prohibition of the Liquor Traffic*, by Dr. Frederick Lees, of whom more will be heard, won a £100 prize offered by the United Kingdom Alliance in 1855, and though 300 pages long, 50,000 copies of it were sold. Cardinal Manning described it as 'a vast Nasmyth hammer, the dint of which has gone into the national ... conscience', and Florence Nightingale read extracts to Queen Victoria at Balmoral. Equally formidable was *Bacchus Dethroned* by Frederick Powell, winner in 1871 of a competition financed by James Teare's legacy, a 250-page textbook justifying total abstinence on every possible ground. There were, asserted Powell, 500,000 drunkards in the United Kingdom and the money now spent on drink would, if the whole population signed the pledge, transform the economy. 'Mills now silent would again send forth the pleasant sounds of working looms ... The 40,000 acres of rich land at present devoted to the growth of hops would be made to wave with golden corn ... Goods and passenger traffic would greatly increase on all our railways.' Drink alone, argued Powell, was responsible for all the nation's ills and 'The day will come when ... those engaged in this traffic shall be deemed pests of society ... shunned by all respectable people ... and ... classed ... with vendors of indecent prints, manufacturers of false life-buoys and rotten cables.'

Such solid works were supported by a host of pamphlets attacking every aspect of the licensed trade. Jabez Inwards in *Pictures on the Traffic* in 1881 even denounced inn signs as a snare, 'devised to trap the young and unwary'. *The Angel*, he suggested, should be renamed *The Destroying Angel* and *The Rising Sun*, *The sun of mental and moral glory set behind the dark clouds of intemperance*. Within the bar, *Old Tom* should be annotated: 'Drink has turned Mr. Thomas into an Old Tom ... We know a man', added Inwards, 'who when he used to drink was known by the name of Old Jack and Drunken Jack but since he has become a staunch teetotaller he ... often receives letters addressed John —— Esq.'

The trade replied with cautionary stories which were little more sophisticated. 'A good young man' which appeared in *The Licensed Victuallers Gazette* for March 1884, described how a father warned his sons to behave respectably during the visit of virtuous cousin Josiah, destined for the church. Josiah proves on arrival to be 'tall and weedy, dressed all in black ... He had lank black hair ... lantern jaws, a greenish-yellow complexion and his eyes were concealed behind a pair of blue goggles.' His young hosts eventually sneak off to the races. To their surprise they meet Josiah there and he reveals that 'I only gammoned the governor to let me come down here for the sake of these races', and that 'I didn't read all the sermons you were so kind as to find me, but I kissed pretty Susan instead'. The story ends with the three drinking champagne together. The same publication carried a series of articles on famous fights which provoked another teetotal pamphlet, *Studies of the Bar, or Beer Bungs and Bruisers*. The trade's typical hero, alleged the author, was apparently 'a vulgar, brutal ruffian, who makes use of his strength ... to swagger about at public house bars and black the eyes and knock out the teeth of any weaker man who has spirit enough not to submit to his bullying ... Can we wonder that men kick their wives to death; that husbands leave their children to starve; that Afghan, Zulu and Sudan massacres are exulted in?'

So bitter was feeling against the trade that the Bishop of Durham protested that 'Licensed victuallers are spoken of sometimes as though they were outside the pale of our common Christianity ... Surely the honest, upright, orderly publican is a man not to be slighted, not to be shunned, but respected?' Nor were such men as rare as the Alliance believed. James Parker revealed in *Mission Work among Licensed Victuallers*, published in 1892, that he had only been refused permission to approach customers in six public houses out of 2,000 he had visited. Some publicans put a temperance society collecting box on the bar because the societies were campaigning for shorter hours and Sunday closing, which most landlords secretly favoured.

The agitation against the public house had indeed the unexpected result of focusing attention on the appalling working conditions in the trade. A temperance handbook stated in 1883 that the average public house in the country was open for 108 hours a week and in London for 123½ hours, and despite several attempts to reduce their hours by law, an enquiry in 1904 revealed that many barmaids still worked ninety to ninety-five hours a week, including Sunday. The average wage in London was only ten shillings a week, less breakages, although some employers also allowed girls eightpenny-worth of drink a day free. Barmaids, the investigators concluded, were not naturally of lower morals than other women, but 'the general character of the occupation renders it unusually difficult for a girl to keep herself unspotted from the world'.

The reply of the trade to the campaign of vilification launched against it was on the whole restrained and reasonable. One Licensed Victuallers Protection Association, formed in 1877, had no more militant aims than to 'seek to promote sobriety and moderation', and pamphlets by licensees sometimes seemed designed to do the teetotallers' job for them. One, by a Welsh publican, asserted that 'half the beer brewed throughout the country is hardly fit for pigs to drink', and that the practice of 'using short measures is carried on to a very disgraceful extent'. The remedy was a national petition by working men to demand that 'the liquor trade be subjected to the same supervision as is now imposed on the milk trade'. M.P.s could be reassured that 'your humble servants have not come to petition for... sparkling champagne, fine old crusted port, light dinner sherries and famous old brown sherry for dessert, with choicest clarets, tokay and other celebrated fancy wines—luxuries we are quite willing to leave to the safe keeping of the members of your honourable House'.

Other writers stressed the inconsistencies in the teetotallers' position. 'When the trade in alcohol is described as a "traffic" the covert inference is that it is morally on a level with slavery and procuration', pointed out a Surrey licensee. The teetotallers made 'the respectable licence-holder an object of the most wanton insult', but would 'flock round the drunkard and ... call him a victim'. In fact the teetotallers wanted to preserve drunkenness, 'like the rat-catcher, who lives by the rat and likes to catch them, but not to exterminate them'.

Prayers against the trade were not uncommon but even here the teetotallers did not have a monopoly. 'Oh, relieve us from the bundle of absurdities, annoying restrictions and anomalies', urged a Publican's Prayer. Its author summed up his views in a poem:

> Oh what a happy land is this, such wisdom, Oh alas!
> If you can't cry your neighbour down, you're but a silly ass!
>
> Non-smokers cry poor smokers down and say it is no treat,
> And vegetarians do with glee, cry down good English meat.
>
> ... Teetotallers cry beer drinkers down, but what seems very queer,
> They cease to pay their share of tax when they stop drinking beer.

No great controversy would have been complete without a correspondence in *The Times*, and in six weeks in 1891 it carried no fewer than a hundred letters on the subject. Many of these revealed growing public alarm at the spread of the prohibition movement. As one resident of Hanover Square put it: 'This fanatical crusade against the drinking of fermented liquors ... has passed beyond the legitimate limits of a fad and is beginning to assume the proportions of a public nuisance.' Other contributions struck a more idiosyncratic note. A member of the Junior Carlton Club disclosed that one working man he knew could get drunk on strong tea, while W. Probyn Devins of the Scottish Club, Dover Street, revealed an unexpected disadvantage of prohibition, since 'If I feel gouty I drink a pint bottle of pink champagne.'

*Chapter Fourteen*

## THE HIGH PRIEST OF THE WATER PUMP

'"Saint Bartholomew" himself . . . I believe to be as rank a hypocrite and as wicked a man, as breathes in the Queen's dominions.'
—DR. FREDERICK LEES, about John B. Gough, Christmas 1857

THE SUCCESS of the tour by the American F. W. Kellogg in 1851 caused his sponsors, the London Temperance League, to issue soon afterwards a far more ambitious invitation. John B. Gough, the greatest temperance speaker of the century, had been born in Sandgate, Kent, in 1817. His father, a retired soldier, was day servant to a drunken and disreputable clergyman, who once offered his tiny congregation a shilling each to adjourn to the public house, which would, he said, do them more good than carrying on with the service. Gough left school at ten and two years later his family paid neighbours who were emigrating to the United States to take him with them. After two unhappy years on their farm, Gough moved to New York, arriving, aged fourteen, with two-and-sixpence in his pocket. Although he eventually learned a trade, as a bookbinder, he also worked as a book-packer and on a fishing boat, and was often reduced to sawing logs or sweeping snow, and to pawning his coat for a meal. After visiting a theatre at the age of sixteen he became hopelessly stage-struck, making his debut in New York with a comic song, *The Water Party*, and appearing at Boston in a farce, *The Temperance House*, in which, as manager of a temperance hotel, he was required to set fire to some bedroom curtains with a candle and be drenched with water by the fire brigade. Gough also tried his hand at ventriloquism, comic songs and tragic monologues, but his speciality was one-man character dialogues in which he acted out such scenes as a squabble 'between a Yankee, Dutchman, Frenchman and Irishman on the subject of eatables'.

Meanwhile Gough was becoming notorious as a drinker, his wife, who might have reclaimed him, dying in childbirth with her baby. Once he was fined, for causing a disturbance at a Methodist meeting, where he had passed the spittoon around in place of the collecting plate, and twice he suffered from delirium tremens. Then, when Gough was twenty-five, a stranger persuaded him to attend a meeting of the Washingtonians, a newly-founded organisation devoted to reclaiming drunkards. On an October night in 1842 Gough signed the pledge, adding his testimony to that of the other newly-recruited teetotallers, but instead of uttering a few halting sentences he delivered a fluent speech which delighted the audience. Gough had discovered the one part he could fill to perfection, that of the reformed alcoholic. Soon he was speaking every week, at first with his overcoat buttoned up to his chin to conceal the shabby clothes beneath. Invitations to speak soon began to pour in from all over the Newburyport area where Gough was living, and one evening a collection, which raised two dollars, was taken up for the new speaker. His career as a professional teetotaller had begun.

During his first year in his new occupation Gough delivered 383 lectures, travelled 6,840 miles and earned 1,059 dollars, far more than in any previous job, in amounts ranging from seventy-five cents to six dollars, although he had, he said, given eighty-three speeches free. By 1845 he was receiving ten dollars a lecture, by 1860, sixty, by 1865, 170, and his annual income, from platform appearances, successive editions of his *Autobiography* and collections of his speeches, was at least 10,000 dollars. All witnesses, including many who disliked Gough, agree on his remarkable capacity to seize control of an audience and his second wife, a schoolteacher, described how at the end of a speech he was 'dripping with perspiration; his clothes were wringing wet . . . He was in a state of collapse.'

When first invited to revisit his native land, Gough was, understandably, reluctant to abandon his lucrative American lecture circuit but he finally succumbed to the persuasions of F. W. Kellogg, and made a bargain with the London Temperance League to lecture them for six weeks in return for his expenses and a free two-week holiday. Rumours of his alleged avarice and secret drinking had, however, gone before him, while the League was widely regarded as an upstart organisation. Many teetotallers secretly hoped the visit would be a failure, and part of the crowd who packed Exeter Hall on the evening of Tuesday, 2nd August 1853, when Gough's tour officially began, had come, a temperance historian acknowledged, 'merely to criticise'.

Although the organisers had arranged for a 500-voice choir to sing 'See the conquering hero comes' as Gough entered, they listened in growing dismay to his quiet and restrained opening remarks, at the end of which there was an audible sigh of disappointment from the platform.

Then, gradually, the atmosphere in the hall began to change. An eyewitness recorded his impressions:

> There stands before the audience a man of the most unpretending air, apparently about thirty-two or thirty-three years of age, five feet eight inches in height, with a dark and sallow complexion; very plainly dressed; his whole mien bespeaking a person who had still to learn that he was somebody . . . The voice of Mr. Gough, too, unites to carry on the deception. At the outset . . . it gives no sign of the inherent flexibility and astonishing resources both of power and pathos. It is in keeping with the entire outer man, who at ease, seems to draw himself down to the smallest possible dimensions; but when fired he becomes erect, expanding in magnitude and stature, so as to present another and entirely new man . . . The conclusion to which we have come is that the merits of Mr. Gough have by no means been overrated . . . Oratorically speaking, he is never at fault.

At the end of this speech, Gough's reputation in England was made. The League, immensely relieved, offered him a new engagement to deliver 200 lectures at ten guineas each, plus all

ANNE JANE CARLILE

*Blackie and Son Ltd.*

REV. JABEZ TUNNICLIFF

*British National Temperance League*

A BAND OF HOPE PROCESSION, SHEFFIELD, C. 1900

A BAND OF HOPE MEETING AT EXETER HALL, 1852

THE ENTRANCE TO
EXETER HALL
FROM THE STRAND

*Radio Times Hulton Picture*

expenses; the six-week visit was prolonged to two years and all over the country temperance societies competed to hire for him the largest halls they could find.

At Dunse, Scotland, where the use of the two largest churches for a meeting was refused, the Total Abstinence Society built a vast, gas-lighted wooden pavilion, accommodating 3,000 people, and Gough's meeting was such a triumph he returned a fortnight later. In Folkestone and Leeds, in Penzance and Edinburgh, in Jersey and Liverpool, the conquering hero conquered again. Five weeks after Gough's debut he was present at the start of a great temperance procession in Russell Square. 'Every description of vehicle which could be begged or borrowed', wrote *The Times*, 'was brought into requisition to convey the enthusiastic teetotallers and the procession was made up of omnibuses, cabs, clarences, broughams, gigs, etc., headed by bands of music, the vigour of which must have taken the aristocratic residents of Russell Square and its neighbourhood not a little by surprise.' Gough led this army of supporters through the West End and down Whitehall to the Surrey Gardens on the south bank, where he spoke to an audience of 17,000, the largest of his tour. But the excitement his name aroused did not wear off and eight months later, at Sadler's Wells, a plank bridge had to be laid from the pit to enable eager pledge-signers, stirred by his oratory, to reach the stage. 'He spoke and conquered', acknowledged the temperance historian, Dawson Burns. 'His voice . . . of organ-like richness and compass . . . his power of feeling . . . imparted to his appeals an electric energy which the least sympathetic of his hearers was for the moment unwilling to resist.'

Only in one place was the conquest incomplete. In June 1854 Gough appeared in Oxford, despite the forebodings of the local temperance society, which had refused to arrange the meeting, for a recent anti-smoking lecturer had been literally 'smoked out' by the undergraduates, with 'pipes and cigars in full blast'. The London League sent down a chairman of its own but when Gough walked on to the platform he found the room crowded with young men in cap and gown, who subjected him to 'a volley of questions . . . some of them ridiculously personal and some bordering on the profane', mixed up with Biblical texts in favour of wine and with shouts of 'Hats off!' 'Caps on!' 'Down in front!' and 'Hurrah!' An appeal by Gough to 'the Englishman's motto—Fair Play' led to ironic cheers and shouts and for twenty minutes of 'deafening cat-calls', 'he spoke in pantomime'. Finally, according to a newspaper report,

> he stepped forward . . . and offered to whip every one of the 500 students singly. His offer was loudly cheered and promptly accepted and a big six-foot athlete was sent up on the stage. Gough, who is a little man, backed off as the big fellow approached him, and explained, 'My friends, you evidently misunderstand me. This is to be an intellectual contest not a prize fight' . . . The college lad . . . reminded the plucky lecturer that it was one of the apostles who wrote to Timothy—a young man, too, like themselves—to take a little wine for the stomach's sake . . . Gough slowly examined the six-footer from top to toe and then said, 'My friends look at this athlete; this fellow with muscles like steel . . . who could knock down an ox . . . he is the personification of health and strength, but he thinks he needs a little wine for his stomach's sake' . . . The students fairly yelled with delight and their defeated champion retreated.

Although Gough claimed always to suffer from stage fright, when 'trembling seizes upon every nerve; my throat and tongue become dry and feverish; my voice hoarse or husky', he always overcame it, and any speech by him was an entertainment in itself. He exploited to the full his old gift for playing character parts and could bring vividly to life the drunks and negroes and Irishmen who featured in his stories. Many of his anecdotes were frankly designed to raise a laugh and were, to a pious mind, faintly and agreeably shocking. Gough had an American story of a man overcharged in a New York restaurant who remarked 'God will punish the proprietor in due time', to which his companion replied: 'God has punished him already; I've got my pocket full of his spoons.' He had a negro story, of a coloured man tempted to steal a pair of handsome boots who compromised by stealing a pair of cheap shoes. He had a temperance hotel story of the guest who said, 'If this is tea, I want coffee; if it is coffee, I want tea.' Above all he had a fund of drunk stories, like that of a man on his way home from the saloon who bumped into a pump and, pointing at the handle, threatened, 'Drop that stick and I'll knock you down.' Gough had, too, many cautionary anecdotes about clergymen who had fallen through drink, of whom he seemed to have known a remarkable number. These included a Doctor of Divinity from Edinburgh, who 'stood in a low dram shop, with his face blackened and . . . preached some of his old sermons for whisky' and 'one of the best Greek scholars of the United Kingdom', who, having been dragged half-naked 'from under the bench of a music hall . . . would steal postage stamps of his benefactor to get drink'. He claimed, too, to know a girl who had said 'No' instead of 'I will' at the altar, on smelling liquor on her intended husband's breath.

Gough was always ready to tell a story against himself and the begging letters and offers of marriage he received provided him with a useful source of material. He possessed, too, a great capacity to exploit local circumstances. If the hall where he spoke were under repair, Gough would weave into his speech a description of how one day all the scaffolding of temperance effort would fall away to reveal the glorious façade of a drink-free world. One incident at Exeter Hall deeply impressed a not uncritical Anglican clergyman:

> He moved a little to one side and took from the lap of a mother a bright, chubby-faced, curly-headed little fellow and, lifting him right up in front of the audience, with all the ring of his matchless voice he shouted, 'Men and women, fathers and mothers, is it not worthwhile to try and save a child like this?' I have seen an audience moved, but never moved like this. In a moment the tears stood thick as rain on every cheek and there was a huskiness in the 'Yes' which burst, it seemed, from every lip.

Gough's appeal was essentially to the emotions. 'The address was a succession of pictures', wrote one observer. 'He addressed himself to the fancy and to the heart.' Many of his speeches ended with a famous oratorical set-piece, his 'panegyric on water', which caused James Silk Buckingham to describe him as 'the American high priest of the pump'. While Gough held up a glass of water he would launch into his peroration:

> Here is our beautiful beverage, water, pure water . . . There is no necessity to drink, except to quench one's thirst . . . Did you never lift the goblet of pure water to your lips and feel it trickling over the tongue and gurgling down the throat? . . . Our beverage is beautiful and pure, for God brewed it, not in the distillery, but out of the earth . . . Beautiful water! See how it weaves a golden gauze for the setting sun and a silvery tissue for the midnight moon! Watch it descending in the feathery snow-flake, or painting with fairy pencil flowers and leaves upon the window pane . . . Look at it as it trickles down the mountain side, like silver ribands, mixing with the heather bloom . . . Beautiful water! . . . It never broke a mother's heart . . . Never did pale-faced wife or starving child . . . weep into it a bitter tear; never did drunkard howl back from his death-bed a fearful curse upon it.

There was only one unfortunate feature of this and many similar passages: Gough had appropriated them, without acknowledgment, from another speaker. The famous prose-poem on water had in fact been composed by Paul Denton, a Methodist missionary in Texas, who, in 1836, had invited a crowd of cowboys to an open-air barbecue and had bravely delivered it, pointing to a nearby spring, in response to shouts of 'Where's the liquor?' 'When you see . . . a glass of water placed upon the table', wrote one of Gough's critics caustically, 'you may be sure Paul Denton is coming.' Gough, however, brushed aside the charge of plagiarism; he had, he said, improved on a poorer original. Similar complaints about putting his name to temperance hymns written by others he simply ignored.

Gough's second visit to England, in 1857, started under even less happy auspices than his first. The trouble began in April when one of his British admirers published a letter from Gough reporting that 'The cause in this country is in a depressed state. The Maine Law is a dead letter everywhere.' This frank admission soon appeared in 'grog-shop windows throughout the land'

and, complained a temperance speaker, 'at Huddersfield, where I was lecturing on prohibition, the publicans placarded the town with it'. It caused consternation to the teetotallers, and revived all the old distrust of Gough, who, it was hinted, hoped thereby to ruin an English tour which his unpaid rival, Neal Dow, was just beginning. Twenty years later, the injury still rankled and a temperance historian wrote of the notorious letter that 'a modicum of caution, used in omitting statements clearly hyperbolical, would have averted a world of trouble'; the truth, being inconvenient, should have been suppressed.

On Gough's arrival in July 1857, while audiences everywhere succumbed to his magic as they had done three years before, the memory of the dagger plunged in the back of the United Kingdom Alliance still festered in the mind of one of its leading supporters, Dr. Frederick Lees. The result was to be, to quote an Alliance-minded temperance historian, 'years of discord and division, productive of much injury to the common cause'.

Lees was, in his own, very different, way, as big a fraud as Gough. His very title was undeserved, for though known as 'the doctor' he had no medical qualifications, but only a worthless honorary doctorate of philosophy from an obscure German university, awarded for some entirely spurious 'Biblical scholarship'. He was described at the age of thirty as 'gaunt, pale and hollow-cheeked... big headed in proportion to his stature and slight bulk', while another friend remembered him as 'a little thin-faced, thin-bodied man, volatile as water and as easily agitated', and a third remarked that 'had Lees been put on a white horse he might have passed for Death in the Revelations'. On the platform he had 'a... tendency to over-emphasis of words' and 'a slightly pedantic peculiarity in pronunciation'. 'In speaking', wrote *The North of England Advertiser* when Lees was forty, 'he moves about with a quick sharp motion; and when he has said anything which he thinks very clever, pushes forward and cocks up his head in a manner which... reminds one of a weasel looking out of a hole.' As an orator he was simply not in the Gough class, but it was said of him that 'any attempt to injure or impede the progress of the cause, or insult even the humblest of its real friends and supporters he . . . felt as an injury done to himself'.

Lees was the son of a Radical schoolmaster known as 'Orator' Lees and he was reared on Cobbett and *The Poor Man's Guardian*, later becoming a keen Chartist. Though apprenticed to a solicitor he inherited private means and never practised, and in 1835, aged twenty, he signed the pledge after listening to Joseph Livesey in the Leeds Music Hall and began to occupy his time travelling about the West Riding to preach teetotalism. Lees sprang to eminence in the temperance movement overnight a year later at a public debate in the same building, when he won back an audience which a leading Leeds physician had almost persuaded to vote against teetotalism. In the same year he routed a renegade teetotaller, a Baptist minister, and two years later he was cheered after speaking impromptu for an hour-and-a-half during a debate in Birmingham Town Hall. Similar triumphs in other places followed. These speeches, reprinted as pamphlets, helped to spread Lees's fame, as did his classic *Argument, Legal and Historical for the Prohibition of the Liquor Traffic*, already mentioned, and other works to be described later in which he 'proved' that the Bible condemned alcohol. Whenever the teetotallers were attacked in the press it was to Lees they turned as their champion and though to modern tastes his voluminous output seems intolerably prolix and tedious, an admirer described his books as 'the arsenal from which the artillery of their whole battle' came.

That robust anti-teetotaller, the Rev. Jonathan Turner of St. Ives, had taken Lees's measure as early as 1842. 'In the hands of Dr. Lees', he wrote, 'philosophy can reconcile the most palpable contradictions and prove that light and darkness are both one.' Turner's references to 'the wiliness, the dishonest trickery of this "philosopher"', were echoed seventeen years later by *The Weekly Record* which complained of 'a school of forward and impertinent zealots . . . impatient of all discussion . . . intolerant of all heresy. These persons', it concluded, 'disgust intelligent men and bring our cause into disrepute . . . Of this party Dr. Lees has been the creator and the idol.'

Lees's reputation was bound up with the success of the Maine Law, for he had visited America and reported in glowing terms on the achievements of local prohibition. In 1853 he had even written an address of welcome to Gough and later had dedicated to him part of his collected *Works*—a doubtful compliment, it might be felt. Now, however, Lees was desperate to discredit him. He wrote to America for suitable evidence, introduced Neal Dow on the platform with anti-Gough remarks and on Christmas Day 1857 sat down in his house, appropriately called Meanwood, to write a venomous letter to his friend William Wilson, a Nottinghamshire farmer.

> I have just returned from Scotland, where I have met with several persons who can speak to a fact of which I was previously cognisant, that your friend, 'Saint Bartholomew', has been often seen narcotically and helplessly intoxicated.[1] I should have announced that fact before . . . but out of fear of injuring the cause and out of pity for the 'Saint' himself I forbore . . . But he has been sinning even worse than before . . . 'St. Bartholomew' . . . I believe to be as rank a hypocrite and as wicked a man as breathes in the Queen's dominions.

An evasive reply from Wilson prompted a further outburst on 4th January 1858. '"The Saint"', declared Lees, 'has been *often* intoxicated with drugs (twice to my own certain knowledge), once insensibly so in the streets of London, many times in Glasgow, until he was helpless.'

Dr. Lees, to whom bad judgment came naturally, had made a poor choice of confidant. Soon the whole temperance world was buzzing with the story and Wilson even sent a copy of the famous letter to Gough himself. Gough not unnaturally demanded to know the author of this 'cowardly and unmitigated falsehood' and when the name was revealed immediately sued Lees for libel.

The case split the temperance movement down the centre. The issue was not Gough v. Lees but the National Temperance League versus the Alliance, moral suasion versus prohibition,

[1] Gough's second name was Bartholomew.

flamboyance versus pedantry. Gough's supporters cheered him louder than ever at every meeting; Lees's carried a resolution urging him not to apologise. The climax came on the 21st June 1858, in the Court of the Exchequer, where it soon became clear that Lees was hopelessly outclassed. Public performances were Gough's *métier* and in the witness box he made a powerful impression. He had, he readily admitted, been 'formerly addicted to intemperate habits', but swore that he had never taken drugs, except—a nice touch—sixpennyworth of laundanum as a boy. He said, quite truthfully, since there had already been talk of cancelling the profitable Exeter Hall meetings, that his £2,000 a year income from lecturing 'would be wholly paralysed by such attacks unless they were put down'. He did not, however, seek humiliating terms, but merely to clear his name. Lees's counsel could do no more than admit there was no justification for the libels and hope that his client would not suffer 'by reason of the bungling manner in which I have attempted to express myself'. The verdict went to the plaintiff, with costs, and a nominal five guineas damages.

Lees failed to realise that he had got off lightly. He blamed his counsel for the loss of the case, publicly repudiated the apology made in court, and two years later published an elaborate 150-page vindication of himself, *Final Words for History*, a wearisome wilderness of underlinings, exclamation marks and parentheses, which would have provided material for a score more libel actions. Even the dedication, to 'his quondam friend', William Wilson, 'as a lasting memento of violated honour and betrayed confidence', was probably actionable and though Lees reproved Gough for not behaving like a Christian, he showed remarkably little sign of a forgiving spirit himself. Wilson, he alleged, was behind a plot to discredit the Alliance, while 'the Goughites' had hired a 'bruiser' to break up Lees's recent meeting at Sheffield and were also responsible for the 'cat-calls, cock-crowing, songs, a dog-fight and now and then a few oaths' which had greeted him at the scene of his old triumphs, the Music Hall, Leeds. As for Gough, he claimed that he 'devoted himself to the cause for "the Lord's sake"...

while in reality he had fished and angled with the most consummate craftiness for the £.s.d.' In October 1854, said Lees, he had seen Gough stretched out on a sofa in Glasgow 'in a very helpless, stupid and incoherent condition', though a servant had, somewhat naïvely, said he could not be drunk as it was a temperance hotel. In London Gough had presented a 'singularly dull and stupid appearance' at the Crystal Palace one afternoon, but at a private tea-party afterwards had been '*talkative*, LIVELY, LARKING', playfully pushing the other guests about. 'Such you see', commented Lees caustically, 'is the effect of a good cup of TEA on a delicate, nervous constitution.' As for Gough's pipe, the innocent-sounding 'honey-dew tobacco' he smoked was actually steeped in laudanum.

Lees's supporters followed his lead. Edward Grubb delivered in a Bolton chapel a remarkably abusive sermon; taking Gough's *Autobiography* as his text, Grubb worked his way through it from the 'LIE on the title-page, for a commencement', since Gough was not the real author, up to his present career as a temperance lecturer, 'amusing the frivolous with old jokes' and indulging in a 'shameless gamble, carried on under the name of religion and philanthropy'. This, alleged Grubb, brought him in £30,000 a year but an American visitor had written, 'I never knew him to attend an anniversary, convention . . . or even a festival, without being assured beforehand of pecuniary reward.' 'How different', summed up Grubb, not without justice, 'was the character and circumstances of the old advocates . . . They lived by their own labour and not by their wits . . . The temperance cause was regarded by them as a sacred obligation; it had not then become a commercial speculation in the hands of needy adventurers.'

Other admirers of Lees expressed their support for him in a practical fashion. In 1859 a public meeting in Manchester presented him with a purse of sixty guineas, the contributors describing him as 'the great teacher of temperance doctrine', and in the following year another appeal raised 1,000 guineas, used to buy his house for him—the grounds became, after his death, a temperance tea garden.

Many, however, did not subscribe. Some leading teetotallers threatened to boycott any function Lees attended. One Scottish Doctor of Divinity, despite Gough's anecdotes about his colleagues, described attacking Lees as 'throwing water on a drowned rat', and another said that Lees deserved to be put in the pillory. Gough himself displayed an ostentatious magnanimity, ignoring all Lees's later libels, boasting to a triumphal meeting at Exeter Hall that 'He had never said a reviling word against his accuser' and, with much-publicised forbearance, refusing to have Lees made bankrupt or sent to jail for refusing to pay his legal costs. He would, said Gough generously, 'leave him alone', an announcement he publicly repeated some twenty times in the next two years.

This second British tour, which carried Gough as far as the Orkney Islands, proved as successful as the first. In August 1860 he made his farewell appearance at Exeter Hall and was presented with a Bible, subscribed for by those who had taken the pledge on one of the ninety-six occasions he had spoken there. His speech in reply was vintage Gough. He compared 'this splendid testimonial of your goodwill, rich in morocco and gilt', with 'another book, a little one, torn, ragged and imperfect' but even more precious to him, for 'on the brown, mildewed fly-leaf . . . are these words . . . "John Gough, the gift of his mother on his departure from England to America"'. As Gough, registering emotion as only he could, stammered out his final sentence, 'Two gifts and two departures', there was not a dry eye in the house, including Gough's, for when a man shouted 'God bless him, three cheers!' and the audience leaped to their feet waving their sodden handkerchiefs, 'that unsealed the fountain and I bowed my head and cried like a little boy'.

In 1878 Gough paid his third and last visit to England. By now he was showing signs of age, and eight years later, back in America, he collapsed from a stroke in mid-speech at the age of sixty-eight, dying a few days later. His last recorded words were, not inappropriately, 'Young man, make your record clean.' Lees survived until 1897 and his final remarks were more mundane: 'That red book—don't forget to take it back.' His later years had been wholly characteristic, for between 1860 and 1874 he four times stood for Parliament as a Radical, twice withdrawing at the last moment, twice splitting the anti-Tory vote, so that each election ended in bitter public recriminations. His death produced one final uproar for his coffin was virtually kidnapped *en route* to the Anglican cemetery for a long, emotional service in the Wesleyan chapel, followed by a 'somewhat noisy demonstration' at the graveside, when the local vicar refused to allow a nonconformist minister to deliver another 'impassioned address'. This unseemly affair made headlines in papers all over the country, and provided an excuse for press attacks on 'the selfishness of the clergy of the Establishment'. It was the sort of quarrelsome exit that Lees would have loved.

*Chapter Fifteen*

# FLAT BEER ON SUNDAY

'The assertion that if the public house is closed the beer must necessarily be flat is disproved by facts.'

— Rev. J. M. Morrell, *Reasons for a Sunday Closing Bill for Cornwall*, 1882

ALTHOUGH DIVIDED on many subjects, all sections of the temperance movement agreed on one: the opening of public houses on Sundays was an affront to God and a temptation to man. Even Bishop Wordsworth of Lincoln, no friend of the teetotallers, told a public meeting in 1870 that 'Sunday drinking . . . meant misery in this world and eternal shame and sorrow in the world to come . . . Publicans . . . knew that their souls were in peril so long as they continued to sell liquors on the Lord's day.'

Since 1828 the law had required public houses to close during the hours of divine service, but it was widely ignored and, even where the law was kept, respectable families on their way to church were often thrust off the pavement by early revellers staggering homeward from a breakfast-time drinking session. All proposals for Sunday closing, however, met strong opposition. It would, it was pointed out, endanger the sacred right of the working man to obtain his jug of 'dinner beer', while bottled beer deteriorated rapidly once opened. Equally insuperable was the problem of the traveller. In the 1830s, and for long after, railways were few and their carriages open. For men arriving, shivering or sweating, at an inn on foot, on horseback, or in carts or coaches, hot punch or cold beer seemed a vital necessity whatever the day.

The sabbatarians began with a victory. In 1839 the Metropolitan Police Act closed all public houses within a fifteen-mile radius of Charing Cross from midnight on Saturday till 1 p.m. on Sunday, and this was followed by similar laws affecting other cities and in 1848 by an extension of the law to the whole of England and Wales. Scotland already had Sunday closing, for English M.P.s, reluctant to interfere in a purely Scottish matter, had allowed through the Forbes-Mackenzie Act, which from June 1845 closed all Scottish licensed premises from 11 p.m. on Saturday till 8 a.m. on Monday, except for hotels catering for travellers. The success of this measure, like that of the Maine Law in America, was much debated. Three months after it had come into force, the Lord Provost of Edinburgh claimed in *The Times* that cases of Sunday drunkenness had been almost halved, and during several Sunday evening walks through the lowest quarters of the city, 'I saw no person drunk, heard no swearing or obscene language and saw no fighting or improper conduct'. Letters from Scottish readers, however, told a different story. One referred to 'the state of deceit at present practised in Glasgow on the Sabbath' while two men who asked for dinner at an inn, after travelling fourteen miles, had been told, 'Ye can carry butter and bread in yere pouches' and been given only a couple of biscuits, thrust at them through a window. But Sunday closing was soon too deeply entrenched in Scotland to be dislodged. A Royal Commission reported favourably on the working of the new law in 1860, and nearly forty years later an Edinburgh justice told the Royal Commission on Licensing that 'Not ten percent of the electorate in Scotland would oppose the continuation of the Act.'

The sabbatarian revival in England was less striking, though by 1855 church attendance was said to have risen by 50% in a generation. Many tradesmen, however, whose own shops were shut on Sunday saw no reason why the publican should not suffer likewise. If drinkers could buy beer, asked the Bishop of Lincoln a little later, 'Why should ladies be prevented from buying flowers and crinolines on the Lord's day? . . . Why should he be prevented from buying books or . . . butchers meat?' By the 1850s English M.P.s were being bombarded with petitions in favour of Sunday closing and many mayors called towns' meetings to carry similar resolutions, which often gave a false impression of public sentiment. 'The parties getting up the meeting', explained a Manchester witness to a Select Committee in 1855, 'were purely of the religious class and ministers of the gospel . . . who . . . can pack a meeting at any time.' At Leeds the Sunday drinkers turned up in force at a meeting and, since the uproar was soon too great for anyone to be heard, hoisted placards reading 'Hold up both hands' when the vote was taken, producing 'a mass of confusion'. Many such meetings were simply boycotted. After the Chartist fiasco in 1848, a Licensed Victuallers' spokesman told a Select Committee, people thought Parliament would ignore further petitions. They trusted, too, 'that the House of Commons . . . will not pass one law for the rich and another for the poor and whilst hotels and club houses are open at which the rich can get wine . . . will not shut the public houses and oblige the poor man to go without his pot of beer on Sunday'. A London wine and spirit merchant described what happened at the Sunday-closing meeting he attended. 'I got . . . into a corner of the room where I thought I should not be seen', he told M.P.s, 'but I had not been there long before somebody recognised me . . . Several women rushed at me and attempted to scratch my face; and the man who was lecturing said there was blood on my head, blood on my house, blood on my forehead and on my children and I should go to hell.' He prudently stayed away from the next meeting but two friends who went and laughed immoderately when the lecturer said, 'If you drink nothing but water you will be as strong as elephants', were arrested for causing a disturbance.

In 1853 the House of Commons appointed a Select Committee on the control of places of public entertainment, which was reappointed in the following year. Although a London City missionary complained that in Marylebone 20,000 patronised the public houses and only 18,000 the churches, the weight of the evidence was strongly in favour of a brighter Sunday. The

Committee uncovered little evidence of misconduct on Sunday, except in one Leeds beer-house, where teenage boys threw dice for the right to choose a girl and take her upstairs, and a Birmingham gin-shop to which customers were attracted by a 'man with his face painted black and a banjo'. It was plain, however, that the existing Sunday observance regulations were often evaded. At Cremorne Gardens admission was free, to comply with the law, but one had to buy a ticket 'for refreshments', while many people were driven 'to low tea gardens, where there is a system carried on of getting gin or brandy over the wall'. Sir Joseph Paxton, in charge of the grounds of the Duke of Devonshire's stately home at Chatsworth, described how 800 visitors from Sheffield visited them every Sunday without any trouble. 'The only disturbance we ever had', he remarked dryly, 'was with a party of teetotallers; they were so excited with the scene and with the speechifying ... that a number of them bolted up into the woods and broke down the evergreens to carry off a trophy of the day. We were obliged to send the police after them.'

The Committee's Report, in July 1854, recommended the opening of 'places of national recreation and instruction ... on Sunday after 2 p.m.' but favoured much shorter hours for public houses, from 1–2 p.m. and 5–9 p.m., or 6–10 p.m. The working man need not suffer, for already many publicans provided 'their customers with stone bottles and jars in which to take their beer home, well corked, on Saturday night for Sunday use ... If it is well corked down ... so as to keep it airtight the beer will drink equally well on the following day.'

The opponents of Sunday closing were taken by surprise when, on the very day the Report on Public Houses was presented to Parliament, Thursday, 13th July 1854, a Bill was introduced to give effect to its restrictive recommendations. Within ten days it was passed by the House almost without debate. Only one M.P. made a firm stand against it. Francis Berkeley, Liberal member for Bristol, was the son of an earl and best known for his annual motion in favour of the secret ballot which was 'looked on by the House rather as a good joke'.

'Was the piety of the age so extreme', he asked, 'that persons were not to be able to obtain needful refreshment on Sundays? If so, why did they not legislate for the rich as they did for the poor? Why did they not close the clubhouses of the rich on Sunday and prevent them going to Greenwich to eat whitebait or to Richmond to eat turtle and venison?' In the Lords the Bill was passed within a week, one peer admitting that he did not yet favour prohibition but 'perhaps it might come to that'. Thus on Monday, 7th August, virtually undebated, the Sale of Beer Act, 1854, received the royal assent.

The new law took the public unawares. 'The Beer Bill came so suddenly upon the people', said a Lambeth magistrate, 'that ... the first intimation that many a working man had was when he tapped at the door of a public house at 11 o'clock on Sunday night and found the Bill had passed to prevent his admission.' On this first day, Sunday, 13th August 1854, *The Times* reported next morning, 'A crowd of nearly 200 surrounded *The Hero of Waterloo* and claimed the right of being supplied with refreshments on the grounds of being travellers, but Mrs. Okey refused to serve them ... In the neighbourhood of the Eastern Counties Railway at Shoreditch a similar scene of disappointment took place ... In several places ... persons ... on being refused pretended that they were seized with the cholera', for which brandy was the traditional remedy, 'but ... none of those were served'.

In the evening 'most of the licensed victuallers had put the hands of their clock forward some few minutes',[1] but many customers refused to leave until 'turned out by the police'. That night many Londoners went to bed hungry, thirsty and angry, for as the last excursion trains rolled in 'from Hampton Court, Richmond, Windsor and Southampton ... some of the passengers ... having been refused any refreshments in the towns they had visited ... expected they would meet with every accommodation on reaching the metropolis'. As a leading article commented a few days later, 'excursionists ... cannot obtain refreshment in the country environs of London because

[1] Probably the origin of this now familiar custom.

it is too early, nor on their return to town because it is too late'.

Not only day trippers were inconvenienced. 'A Commercial Traveller' described in *The Times* his failure to obtain a glass of beer with his supper on reaching London after a weekend visit to his family. '"What!", exclaimed I, "after being shut up in a railway carriage upwards of four hours and arriving in the metropolis at . . . half-past ten I am told I cannot refresh myself with a glass of ale or spirits and this in a civilised and Christian country."'

Much of the trouble arose from varying interpretations of the words 'bona fide' inserted into the Act before the word 'traveller' to prevent evasion. At Gravesend, Kent, the magistrates allowed 85 out of 90 public houses to remain open throughout Sunday afternoon to cater for arrivals by rail or boat, while in Eccles, Lancashire, the police pounced on landlords serving the crowds who had come by road from Manchester and Salford to enjoy the traditional Wake Sunday. Three travellers who arrived one Sunday afternoon at *Jack Straw's Castle*, Hampstead, were all prosecuted, one having come by private brougham, one by public omnibus, and one on foot. The magistrate reluctantly dismissed the charges, but added that had the third walked from the East End to Piccadilly instead of from the West End to Hampstead he would not have qualified. Some landlords served all comers, some refused to serve anyone, some insisted on every customer recording his name and place of departure in a book, which soon contained 'many absurd addresses'. The landlord of *The White Hart*, Putney, who provocatively displayed a notice in a window facing the church, 'Refreshments furnished for travellers', was convicted for serving drinks too freely but the verdict was quashed on appeal.

By early September *The Times* was asking the question that exercised magistrates everywhere: 'Who is—who is not—a bona fide traveller? . . . What does a traveller look like? Is he a dirty man, with muddy or with dusty boots, according to the season? Surely nothing is simpler than for an impostor to step into a puddle or kick up a cloud of dust around him just as he makes application at the inn door? What if his waistcoat is too dandified, and he has not a carpet bag in his hands?' A landlord, said *The Times*, needed 'the gift of second sight' or 'a clairvoyant barmaid... Unless an available test can be suggested', it summed up, 'the restriction ought to be universally enforced or entirely abolished.'

Nearly half a million signatures to petitions against the new law were collected in less than a year, and by the summer of 1855 public discontent had reached boiling point. When a wealthy sabbatarian M.P., Lord Robert Grosvenor, introduced a Bill to prevent all Sunday trading in shops it produced an explosion. On 24th June 1855 thousands of working people converged on Hyde Park, apparently spontaneously, 'to see how the aristocrats kept the Sabbath'. Groups of demonstrators gathered outside the houses of M.P.s who had voted for the Bill 'and every carriage seen in the streets, especially if it chanced to be a bishop's, was chased with yells and cries along the road... As the carriages began to appear for the afternoon drive along the Serpentine... the occupants were saluted with hisses and yells and cries of "Go to church".' Several frightened horses bolted, though no one was hurt, but on the following Sunday there was a far more dangerous disturbance, when a crowd of 150,000 collected, 'a mile long and a quarter of a mile deep, extending from Apsley House to Kensington Gardens'. People driving in the park were pelted with clods and stones; a mob besieged Grosvenor's home, 'and the club-houses in Pall Mall ... were honoured with much attention... Towards the evening the riots had assumed so formidable a character, that large reinforcements of police were brought from distant quarters... The police used their staves with considerable freedom... Above 100 persons, some severely hurt, were lodged in the police cells.'

By the third Sunday detachments were roaming through the West End, 'smashing the windows in their progress, for which the macadamised roads furnished ready ammunition', attacking the homes of the Duke of Marlborough and Archbishop of

York, attempting 'to fire a long line of straw laid down before a house in which a person lay dying' and 'carrying scattered devastation into distant quarters'. Thereafter the disturbances gradually died away, although 'it was many weeks before the Park again became an agreeable or even safe place of recreation'.

The Hyde Park riots gave the upper and middle classes an unpleasant fright. Francis Berkeley seized his opportunity and, two days after the first outbreak, successfully moved for the appointment of a new Select Committee on Sunday closing, with himself as chairman. The Committee sat for only two weeks and made no secret of its sympathies. 'Do you think it desirable that the working classes should be compelled on their day of recreation... to carry knapsacks on their backs like common soldiers?' one magistrate was asked. Was a reduction of sixty cases of Sunday drunkenness a week in a population of two and a half million really 'a sufficient compensation for the inconvenience which the sober and industrious and well-conducted classes suffer?' demanded one member of the Chief Commissioner of Metropolitan Police. To the Chief Constable of Wiltshire, who reported a 20% drop in drunkenness, it was suggested that the real reason was that the Crimean War had drawn off the most disreputable part of the population into the Army. Thomas Wakley, the famous Middlesex coroner, even agreed that existing restrictions would encourage alcoholism, since beer kept standing all day 'would be a nauseating beverage', driving a man to spirits instead.

The Committee made great play with the absurd anomalies produced by the 'bona fide traveller' clause. Some magistrates, it established, held that a traveller must go by carriage and some that he must walk. Some thought a journey by a scheduled train qualified but not a cheap day excursion. Several took travel on business as the test, but others would allow a drink to an East Londoner who took his family for a walk in Victoria Park. Was 'a person... going to bury a relative three or four miles off' entitled to 'refreshments near the graveyard?' asked the Committee. And was it not ridiculous that only the parents and godparents at a christening could have a drink while friends who 'went merely as a matter of civility' must wait outside the inn door?

Many witnesses were only too happy to tell the Committee what it wanted to hear. Some readily blamed the Hyde Park outrages on the recent law and Thomas Wakley explained that when there was 'an unusual noise' in a public house on a Sunday it was probably 'made by a man who had been a teetotaller for two or three months and then for two or three days he has broken out and become like a madman'.

The Committee's Report, only seventeen lines long, dismissed the 1854 Act as 'attended with much inconvenience to the public', and the 'bona fide traveller' clause as useless. An immediate increase in Sunday licensed hours was recommended, to 1–3 p.m. and 5–11 p.m. Berkeley introduced a Bill on these lines on the following day, 27th July 1855, in a speech of only four sentences, and it passed through both Houses virtually undebated, becoming law on Tuesday, 14th August, exactly a year after its ill-fated predecessor.

The 1855 Sale of Beer Act was a major defeat for the teetotallers. Francis Berkeley was immediately subjected by *The Alliance News* to a series of such vicious attacks, which accused him of being hand in glove with the licensed trade, that he sued the paper for libel, collecting an apology and five guineas nominal damages. His admiring Bristol constituents, who had suffered much from Sunday closing, raised a subscription in his honour and, at a public ceremony, Berkeley was presented with a silver salver, 'given by Englishmen of all classes in recognition of his manly advocacy of the people's rights', and an oak casket, made from a beam from St. Mary Redcliffe church, containing 1,000 guineas.

Rebuffed in England, the teetotallers redoubled their efforts to ensure that 'the noble example' of Scotland should be followed by Ireland and Wales. In 1877 a Bill imposing Sunday closing on Ireland from the following year was pushed through Parliament, after the five principal towns had been exempted from it. The Act was renewed from year to year, the Chief

Secretary for Ireland declaring in 1889 that it had 'conferred vast benefits on the population', but attempts to include 'the five cities of refuge' were, however, consistently defeated.

After several abortive attempts, a Bill to impose Sunday closing on Wales reached third reading late in the session in August 1881. 'The suspense', wrote a supporter, 'was painful; day by day and all through the sleepy, dreamy hours of night, up to four and five o'clock in the morning, we remained at our post eager to catch the faintest ray of hope.' The Bill went through just before midnight one Saturday, after attempts to exclude Cardiff had failed, and came into force in 1882.

Even before the new law, obtaining drink out of hours had been a popular Welsh sport. A Carmarthenshire licensee described in 1877 how 'an old fox of a constable . . . on Sunday afternoon instead of going to chapel took a cross-country trip to a small public house where he found about a dozen topers . . . some darting up the big chimney, some into the cellar' and eventually seven of them and the publican appeared in court. In Glamorganshire breaches of the law were so numerous that the police formed a special 'flying squadron' to stamp them out. In the industrial south the law was everywhere evaded by the creation of licensed clubs and by the famous Sunday morning exodus from Cardiff across the Monmouthshire border. One witness told a Royal Commission on the working of the Act, in 1890, that 'he had seen on a Sunday morning on the road to Rumney fifty men in one mile all under the influence of drink', and another described the specially shaped spirit-flasks, known as 'belly cans', which were sold surreptitiously on Sunday for concealment under the clothes. The Commission finally favoured Sunday closing, though concerned at drinking clubs, the abuse of the 'bona fide traveller' clause and the contempt for the law being bred among those who saw no wrong in Sunday drinking.

To all evidence of the evasion of Sunday closing in Wales, the teetotallers' inevitable reaction was to demand the extension of Sunday closing to Monmouthshire or, better still, to the whole of England. A Central Association for Stopping the Sale of Intoxicating Liquors on Sunday, founded in the 1860s, claimed enormous support, but this mysteriously vanished whenever a Bill came before Parliament. In 1863 a Bill for total Sunday closing was beaten by 278 to 103, but a year later was reintroduced after amendment to allow an hour's opening in the morning and evening 'to enable the public to get their dinner and supper beer'. A Sheffield member, John Roebuck, clearly no Buckingham, said that the Sunday closing movement united 'those two muddy streams of sentiment', the sabbatarians and teetotallers, who now form 'one foaming, muddy river, which it was very difficult to stem and very disagreeable to see . . . and to smell'. The Bill was thrown out by 123 to 87, but in 1880 a Sunday closing resolution was actually carried, by 153 to 119, after an amendment that sufficient provision must be made for 'the inhabitants in the metropolitan districts . . . to secure public co-operation'; the lesson of 1855 had been well learned. A final Sunday Closing Bill, in 1914, was only beaten by 196 to 177, though nearly half the Sunday closers came from Scotland, Wales and Ireland.[1]

By now the temperance movement was deeply involved in the campaign for local prohibition and a by-product was a demand for Sunday closing in individual counties. Bills for Sunday closing in Lancashire, Staffordshire, the Isle of Wight and Yorkshire were drafted, but the most serious agitation was in Cornwall, where a supporting petition was said to have been signed by a majority of the adult population. 'We want', explained the Rev. J. M. Morrell of Penzance, in *Reasons for a Sunday Closing Bill for Cornwall* in 1882, 'to put Cornwall into the proud position of leading the van in this Holy War for rescuing God's day from the desecration of centuries.' The Bill received a second reading by 43 to 10, but got no further. Morrell also tackled a familiar problem. 'The assertion that if the public house is closed the beer must necessarily be flat', he wrote, 'is disproved by facts', unless 'the working man pulls

[1] While English M.P.s have tended to abstain from voting on licensing legislation affecting only Ireland, Scotland or Wales, members from those countries have felt no such inhibitions in regard to England.

the cork on Saturday nights . . . Is it worthwhile to keep thousands of persons at work on Sunday to accommodate gentlemen of such weak purpose as these?' The real answer, however, to the argument, 'There is nothing in the world so bad as flat beer', was: 'There is flat religion, which is caused by Sunday beer.'

The author of *The Drunkard's Plea for Sunday Closing*, in 1884, struck a more emotional note:

> The hour was late but the mild night was fair
> When the Rector rose up from his old study chair
> And, calling his dog, went to take a look round,
> Just to see all things right, in his pet garden ground.

Hearing 'a deep groan just outside of his gate', the Rector, being a temperance man, immediately identifies it correctly:

> Ha, ha, thought the Rector, here is no cause for fear,
> 'Tis the sad, sad old story of brains drowned in beer.

Sure enough he discovers a man who took 'just a pint . . . to settle the stomach' on Sunday and is shocked to find it is Wednesday. The vicar is deeply impressed by his advice:

> . . . Mind me parson; I tell you what's true
> Shut up the damned publics all Sunday; for you
> Can never do us the least good till you do.

*Sunday Closing* appeared in *The Western Temperance Herald* in 1899 and had perhaps more literary merit and a rousing chorus:

> Sunday closing is our watchword
> Right throughout the land,
> Sunday closing we will fight for,
> Firm and watchful stand . . .
>
> Sunday closing is a blessing
> To our sister lands,
> Earnestly we crave the boon may
> Rest in England hands.

Sunday closing! For it boldly
Plan and strive and pray.
Raise aloud imperious voices,
Vote on voting day.

Sunday closing! Sunday closing!
Be our battle cry.
Lift the banner, push the warfare,
Victory is nigh.

Victory was not, however, nigh. Victorian piety was past its peak and with the coming of the bicycle the bona fide traveller was everywhere multiplying. The growth of rail travel also helped the drinkers, the Rev. J. M. Morrell complaining that they were driving a train through the commandment about keeping the Sabbath day holy. Many bona fide travellers, he said, 'have gone a few miles by train and then demanded liquid refreshment to recruit their wasted energies. Three or four miles in a railway carriage was too much for them.'

Bona fide travellers were by now a national joke. In 1872 Parliament had laid down that one must travel at least three miles to qualify, and in 1893 a journey ceased to be 'bona fide' if refreshment was its main object, but evasion of the law had become a popular game. Sometimes travellers, after receiving 'reasonable refreshment' at a public house, walked to the corner and then came back for more, claiming to have made a fresh journey. Often a single day return railway ticket was passed from hand to hand, to justify each new applicant's claims to a drink. In his classic *Diary of a Nobody*, published in *Punch* in 1892, George Grossmith described how truthful Mr. Pooter was shut out of a Hampstead inn after a Sunday afternoon walk from Holloway, while his companions, claiming to come from Blackheath, spent an hour drinking brandy and soda. The Minority Report of the Royal Commission on Licensing in 1899 described the bona fide traveller as 'a fraud and a nuisance deserving of no consideration whatever', but the Majority Report considered that 'to enact complete Sunday closing in England would be a step too far in advance of public opinion'.

During the first world war, as will be mentioned later, opening hours on Sunday, as on other days, were drastically reduced, though only 'for the duration', and concessions to the bona fide traveller were withdrawn. It was not until a new, permanent Licensing Act was passed in 1921, however, that he finally made his last journey. This solved the problem of providing him with refreshments by laying down that a public house could open at any time—but that no drink could be served outside normal licensed hours.

*Chapter Sixteen*

# PRESCRIBING POISON

'The true nature of alcohol should be pointed out. It is a positive poison.'

— R. HICKS, surgeon, *The Injurious Effect of Alcohol upon the Human Frame*, 1841

NO OBSTACLE proved more troublesome to the teetotallers than the opposition of the medical profession. The early days of the temperance movement coincided with a positive craze for prescribing alcohol, started by Dr. Robert Todd around 1839, who would cheerfully prescribe two pints a day of his popular 'brandy and port wine' cure. His favourite precept, that 'it is far more dangerous to life to diminish or withdraw alcohol than to give too much', was one which most doctors enthusiastically followed and when Dr. Grindrod of Manchester signed the pledge in 1837 he found few imitators among his colleagues.

Many of the early attacks on alcohol on medical grounds were written by laymen. Robert Macnish in *The Anatomy of Drunkenness* in 1834 warned that 'persons addicted to malt liquors increase enormously in bulk. They become loaded with fat; their chin gets double or triple, the eye prominent and the whole face bloated and stupid'; spirit-drinkers 'become emaciated . . . spindle-shanked; their eyes are glazed and hollow; their cheeks fall in'. The Rev. W. R. Baker in *The Curse of Britain*, in 1838, quoted the case of a man 'advised to take brandy to keep away the cholera' who had followed this advice so enthusiastically that in six months he had delirium tremens, while another, having taken brandy and water to improve his digestion, had graduated to two bottles a day and 'died a driveller and a sot'.

Even where a doctor was not actually creating drunkards, alleged the teetotallers, he was making it easy for people to break their pledge. Joseph Livesey's *Temperance Almanack* in 1839 had warned, 'Teetotallers, Beware of "Except as Medicine".' Father Mathew also dropped the medicinal loophole from his pledge in 1841. 'When I introduced that clause,' he said, 'I had no idea that a man in perfect health would have a doctor's certificate in his pocket and then consider himself authorised to take wine and punch at dinner . . . My intention was that he should bring his prescription to an apothecary or druggist.' This was a frequent complaint. If, said the teetotallers, alcohol really *were* a medicine it should be labelled as such, and taken in small doses at fixed times, not swallowed by the quart pot whenever the patient felt like it.

The teetotallers' main quarrel with the doctors, however, was that the latter accepted alcohol as a useful everyday servant of man, instead of denouncing it as the product of corruption and decay, which far from curing disease, was more likely to produce or encourage it. The successive appearances of cholera from 1831 onwards, a then mysterious disease, whose effects were sordid, painful and often fatal, proved ideal for their purpose. 'One of the most awful pestilences . . . permitted to scourge the nations of the earth', wrote the Rev. W. R. Baker in 1838, 'was chiefly indebted to intemperance for its deadly violence.' Ironically enough it was a near-teetotaller, Dr. John Snow, who proved, in 1854, that it was water, not alcohol, which transmitted cholera, but his findings were simply ignored. Dr. Frederick Lees still declared that spirit merchants ought to exhibit a sign 'Cholera sold here', and as late as 1886 a temperance pamphlet asserted that 'when the cholera is bad people who drink rum are the first to fall ill'.

Not every doctor was a John Snow and many medical teetotallers were ready to lend their authority to the most outrageous and unscientific assertions. Thus Henry Mudge, a Bodmin surgeon, in 1839 defended bracketing moderate drinkers and drunkards together on the ground that 'in classifying mankind for temperance purposes, it is . . . sufficient to lay hold on the two prominent marks of drinking alcohol and abstaining from it'. 'The true nature of alcohol should be pointed out', agreed Surgeon Hicks of London in 1841. 'It is a positive poison.' 'Alcohol is poison' soon became one of the teetotallers' favourite battle-cries. It was in vain that the apostate teetotaller Thomas Smeeton pointed out in 1849 that 'Alcohol alone and, as such, is drunk by no one. It is modified by mixture and dilution', and that Democritus, about the same period, asked, 'Because common salt, when largely employed, produces sickness and vomiting, must you not use it as a condiment for food?'

The ultimate in exaggeration was surely reached when the teetotallers spread the rumour that a heavy drinker was liable to undergo spontaneous combustion. Since a solution of 40% alcohol in water will not burn, while any human being whose blood contained even 1% would die of alcoholic poisoning, the story was easily disproved. It achieved, however, a wide currency after the publication in England in 1810 of a book which recounted how an old Frenchwoman addicted to spirits had one day begun to smoulder in her chair, and an Italian nobleman with the curious habit of taking a daily bath in brandy had also gone up in smoke. A medical witness told Buckingham's Committee in 1834 that such cases were 'quite possible', and Charles Dickens in *Bleak House*, in 1853, described how a junk dealer quietly burned out, leaving a dark, greasy coating on the walls. When challenged, Dickens quoted thirty similar cases, all a century old, but contemporary examples came from Canada, where a heavy drinker was said to have glowed with a 'widely-extended, silver-coloured flame', and from Boston, where a man caught fire after belching near a lighted candle. A teetotal pamphlet graphically related what, it reported, had happened in San Francisco in 1877 when one toper 'turned to a gas jet to light his pipe. A second later there was a drunken moan, a flash of alcoholic flame and he fell heavily on the floor, his head and neck veiled in smoke, while blue jets of flame were issuing from his ears, mouth and nostrils.'

Many teetotallers, disclaiming the 'medicinal purposes' escape clause, took pride in their rigid fidelity to their pledge. When his nineteen-year-old son seemed to be dying of typhus, three doctors pleaded with Thomas Whittaker to let them give the young man wine. 'Had he died', recalled Whittaker, 'the town would have cursed me . . . Had my son taken the wine and lived, the wine would have got the credit of that life.' He refused, and his son lived. Joseph Livesey, at seventy-five, faced a similar choice, when dangerously ill with rheumatic fever. He asked to be raised in bed and given a mirror, remarking, after inspecting his reflection, 'Well, there is a look there I don't like. I believe, however, I shall get well again; but whether I do or not, I will not drink the stuff . . . Put me down again and if I am to die I will die now.' Livesey did not die, but survived for another fifteen years.

Suggestions that they might inadvertently be ingesting alcohol in their food particularly infuriated the teetotallers. They denied that alcohol was present in the yeast in bread, and were outraged when the Bishop of Norwich in 1841 challenged them to give up sugar, as it was chemically linked to alcohol. They rejected the findings of the famous German Professor Liebig, in the 1830s, that alcohol was converted into useful energy in the body, rejoiced in the subsequent 'discovery' by three French chemists that it passed out of the body unchanged, and only unwillingly acknowledged, after further research, published in 1864, that alcohol *was* retained by the system, long enough at least 'to do a great deal of mischief'.

Much ingenuity was devoted to trying to find alternatives to alcohol as a domestic remedy. The author of *Temperance Substitutes for Brandy*, in 1886, recommended 'young girls and women' to take ginger tea, essence of peppermint, camomile clove tea, and camphor water for relief for period pains in place of the traditional gin. In emergency, the family could safely turn to temperance brandy, consisting of 'a teaspoonful of compound cinnamon powder in a wineglassful of hot water', or a pinch of cayenne pepper in a tablespoonful of hot water. M.S.B. in *Something I want you Mothers to Know* in 1889 advised 'warm beef tea or an egg beaten up in milk' during labour, instead of 'hot wine, brandy or . . . gin'. Nor, as was commonly believed, did a nursing mother require stout, for M.S.B. had 'a very intimate friend' with thirteen children, 'and she tells me that the little ones she has nursed without beer did better than those she nursed when she was taking alcohol'.

With the medical profession the teetotallers had at first little success. *The Temperance Lancet*, launched in 1841, lasted only a few months, and the British Medical Temperance Association, restricted to teetotal doctors, founded in 1876, had by 1880 no more than 235 members. The therapeutic value of alcohol was by now, however, frequently debated in *The British Medical Journal* and *The Lancet*, which carried as early as 1862 a leading article declaring that 'The question now is between a very little alcohol and none at all.' The teetotallers regularly gave a well-attended breakfast during the annual conference of the British Medical Association, though the cynics said a 'dry' luncheon would have been a better test, and it was claimed as a victory when, in 1880, wines ceased to be included in the price of the ticket at the B.M.A. annual dinner.

The London Temperance Hospital opened in 1873, moving to its present premises in 1881. Though it admitted both drinkers and teetotallers virtually no alcohol was prescribed there, being provided in fact for only seventy-five cases in the first 25,000 treated. The hospital's mortality rate in its first five years, with only twenty-eight deaths out of nearly 600 in-patients, conclusively proved that alcohol was not essential as a drug, and during the last quarter of the nineteenth century it began to disappear from hospital dispensaries. The leading medical teetotaller, Sir Victor Horsley, recalled how when he entered University College Hospital as a student in 1878 drink was still a regular article of diet for all patients, but a graph later showed that this was the very year in which the line of rising expenditure on milk in seven leading London hospitals crossed the line of falling expenditure on alcohol. Salisbury Infirmary, which had spent £302 on wine, spirits and beer in 1865 and £217 in 1880, spent only £18 in 1905. Now, if you prescribed alcohol in hospital, declared Horsley, 'people would stare at you'. Another teetotal doctor pointed out in 1925 that since the beginning of the century the amount of alcohol prescribed in London hospitals had dropped by a further 85% and that instead of being ordered as routine, it was now prescribed only out of 'caprice' or 'idiosyncrasy'.

The teetotallers had long found it intolerable that alcohol should be provided out of the rates in workhouses and workhouse infirmaries. In 1842 the Guardians of the Poor at Luton actually dismissed their medical officer for refusing to prescribe alcohol and in the 1870s the Guardian responsible for banning beer at the workhouse was burned in effigy at Reigate. Meanwhile, the Workhouse Drink Reform League was producing pamphlets and wall charts which revealed the expenditure on alcohol in every workhouse in the country. The League's arch enemy was the East Preston, Sussex, Union, which spent 23s. 7d. per inmate per year on drink. 'More money is spent at East Preston with 149 inmates', complained the author, 'than at 202 Unions added together with 25,913 inmates.' The League's unwelcome enquiries uncovered many cherished perquisites, as at Stockwell Asylum, where the staff in one quarter of 1886 disposed of 3,379 pints of ale, while the patients received only twenty-nine pints, and the barrel of beer provided at Wolverhampton Workhouse for the Guardians, 'to refresh themselves' during their weekly meetings. Eventually the teetotallers obtained a ruling from the Local Government Board that the Master of any workhouse might be surcharged for all alcohol not supplied on medical advice, and at Islington in 1884 one found himself with a bill for nearly 900 quarts of porter drunk by his nurses. As a result of such tactics, and a general change of sentiment, between 1871 and 1885 one Union after another went 'dry' and the total expenditure on workhouse drink fell by nearly half.

Among many doctors, however, alcohol continued to enjoy

a unique reputation. 'The stimulus of alcohol,' wrote Dr. William Sharpe in 1882, 'when judiciously controlled, always leads to higher mental efforts . . . in which the mind . . . sweeps intuitively into the veiled and distant regions of universal truth.' Four years later, Mrs. R. D. Bolton, in *What we expect of our doctors: A lady's letter to her physician*, was still castigating an imaginary Dr. Blake for recommending alcohol despite such cases as a nineteen-year-old girl who had to have the sideboard locked against her since being ordered a medicinal glass of port. 'With some parents . . . at the present time', complained the physician to Rugby School in 1891, 'the question of proper feeding is comparatively secondary if the boy can obtain his wine or stout twice a day. This is their panacea for every ailment and for every constitutional delicacy.'

Meanwhile, that great enemy of alcohol, Sir Victor Horsley, was making his name as a surgeon, and in 1908 he published, with Dr. Mary Sturge, the definitive second edition of his classic, *Alcohol and the Human Body*. The title-page carried an uncompromising quotation from one of Queen Victoria's physicians: 'Alcohol is a poison—so is strychnine; so is arsenic . . . It ranks with these agents', and the sub-titles of the first chapter, *Alcohol as a Drug*, ranged encouragingly from 'tremulousness . . . hysteria and epilepsy . . . tissue degeneracy' to 'healing of wounds delayed . . . churning power of stomach delayed . . . alcohol as a cause of immorality in youth'. If alcohol had killed its human victims, as the authors claimed, they had slain many a harmless plant or animal in the same way. Geraniums, potatoes, petunias, watercress and nettles had all speedily succumbed to solutions of diluted alcohol; whole batteries of dogs, kittens, guinea-pigs and sparrows had had their constitutions fatally undermined, while lesser breeds like amoeba and earthworms had perished by the score from unwanted drinks. A one in a thousand solution of pure alcohol, the authors proudly reported, had killed a freshwater jellyfish in five minutes, while water fleas showed an even worse head for liquor and succumbed to one part in 4,000. Crayfish were made of sterner stuff, surviving up to a day, but nature's toughest

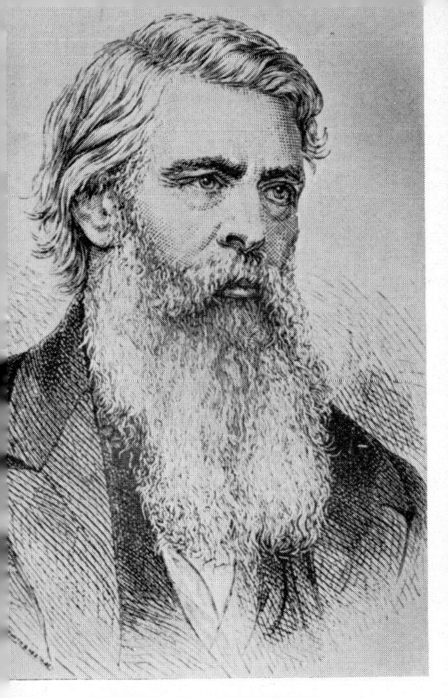

JOHN B. GOUGH

DR. FREDERICK LEES

E AUDIENCE CROWD ON TO THE PLATFORM TO SIGN THE
LEDGE AT GOUGH'S MEETING AT SADLER'S WELLS, 1854.
(DRAWN BY CRUIKSHANK.)

GOUGH'S BIRTHPLACE AT SANDGATE, KENT

GOUGH'S HOUSE, HILLSIDE, MASSACHUSETTS, BOUGHT FRO
HIS EARNINGS AS A TEMPERANCE LECTURER

drinkers were perch, which after falling drunk to the bottom of the tank rapidly recovered when placed in fresh water. Drinking rabbits had, of course, proved less able to resist cholera than sober bunnies, the offspring of alcoholic guinea-pigs showed 'marked stunting of growth and weight', and hens which had been at the bottle hatched out feeble and mentally retarded chicks. Two American professors, recorded Horsley and Sturge, had compared the performance of dogs fed on alcohol with those given water. Two sober dogs had retrieved 922 balls of 1,400 thrown 100 feet away, while two drinking dogs had fetched only 478. Even more striking were the effects of alcohol on another group of puppies, Tipsy, Frisky, Winnie, Berry II and Bum. 'The least thing out of the ordinary', it was reported, 'caused all the alcoholic dogs to exhibit fear, where the others evinced only curiosity or interest. Whistles and bells never ceased to throw them into a panic, in which they howled and yelped, while the normal dogs simply barked.' Poor Bum apparently got d.t.s, for 'He had a number of paroxysms of causeless fear with some evidence of hallucinations. He would . . . start at some imaginary object and go into a fit of howling.' However he had learned his lesson, for when at death's door from distemper he recovered after refusing to touch any food containing drink. Winnie, less abstemious, died, and Frisky, another drinker, was dangerously ill for a week.

*Alcohol and the Human Body* was soon under heavy attack. Dr. C. A. Mercier, a mental specialist, was particularly scathing:

> To do the authors justice they make no pretence of impartiality. They set out with the intention of showing that alcohol in any form or in any quantity is wholly, unmitigatedly and irredeemably vile. I find from their book that vegetables, when they are watered with alcohol . . . wither and die; and I resolved at once that never in future will I water my cabbages with Château Mouton Rothschild . . . or '47 port . . . The perusal of this book has decided me to find some other destination for these pernicious . . . beverages; and my cabbages will have to put up with some less expensive . . . form of moisture—with dilute sewage, for instance . . . If we are

to abjure alcohol because it is injurious to cabbages, it would be a good plan to drink diluted sewage, which is so beneficial to them.

A fellow medical knight, Sir James Crichton Browne, pointed out that 'aseptic and antiseptic surgery were the direct outcome of Pasteur's brewery work'. As another doctor had remarked, had Pasteur been British, 'cannot we imagine the fanatical outcry which would have been raised had the words "wine" and "beer" appeared on his monument?' as they did in France.

To convince the layman, the teetotallers frequently appealed to the example of waterdrinking athletes and other public figures. When Blondin crossed Niagara Falls on a tightrope in 1859, they pointed out that 'his only beverage was chocolate'; when a teetotal soldier carried off the Queen's prize for rifle-shooting in 1866 it was remarked that he asked for his health to be drunk in ginger-beer; when the polar exploration ships *Alert* and *Discovery* returned prematurely due to scurvy, in 1876, it was said the three teetotallers aboard suffered least from disease. The movement's most often-quoted hero was the 'famous pedestrian', E. P. Weston, who in the same year walked fifty-five miles round a Nottingham cricket ground between 7 a.m. and 7 p.m., on beef tea, gruel and grapes, playing cornet solos in the band in a spare half-hour at the end. Weston became in every sense a walking advertisement for temperance. In 1883 he walked 5,000 miles in 100 days, starting out from the Westminster offices of the Church of England Temperance Society and ending up on a Saturday night at a music hall in Waterloo Road, warning the crowds who turned out to greet him against 'the use of artificial stimulants'.

Soon the trade's defenders were counter-attacking on the same front, the holder of the London to Brighton walking record obligingly testifying that 'my chief beverage has been beer'. One rowing man reported that when his doctor, the ex-stroke of the Cambridge eight, prescribed beer, 'The result was magical', and he carried off the Diamond Sculls at Henley in 1905 and later an Olympic championship. (Cambridge remained faithful to alcohol into the nineteen-thirties. 'I, like other members of the crew, drink beer and port', the Cambridge cox reported in 1931. 'When we feel run down we have champagne. We often feel run down.') Even more convincing, the great cricketer Jack Hobbs, it was revealed, liked 'a glass of champagne and perhaps a liqueur at night', while an ex-captain of the Surrey eleven posed the clinching question: 'What individual ever deserved or enjoyed his glass of wine more . . . than . . . W. G. Grace?'

*Chapter Seventeen*

# WINE FOR THY STOMACH'S SAKE

'Drink no longer water but use a little wine for thy stomach's sake and thine often infirmities.'

— St. Paul, I Timothy v, 23

'St. Paul did not set up for physician-general to the Christian world in all ages, nor did he prescribe wine as a panacea for all the ills the flesh is heir to.'

— F. R. Lees and J. Dawson Burns, *The Temperance Bible Commentary*, 1868

WHEN THE teetotal movement began no major Christian body regarded alcohol as sinful, although some small sects, and some individual Quakers, abstained from it as a luxury. Drinking customs were common in many churches, especially among the Presbyterian clergy, who were so often the subject of John B. Gough's cautionary anecdotes. A Presbyterian minister 'sealed the gown' with drink when he graduated, and was 'fined' a bottle of wine on moving into a new manse, publishing a sermon, or even, in Edinburgh, preaching in his own pulpit during May. The Presbyterian General Assembly traditionally sent the magistrates two guineas to toast its deliberations, while the beadle who carried the kirk Bible back to the manse after service was automatically rewarded with a glass of spirits.

The first attempts to convert the churches to teetotalism provoked violent opposition. When Thomas Whittaker was entertained to dinner by a vicar at Yeovil, who prayed for the success of his meeting, the curate rose from his knees and rushed out of the house, denouncing 'the blasphemy of asking God to bless anything . . . so contrary to his word as teetotalism'. In South Shields around 1839 the nonconformist clergy, in alliance with the doctors, were said to have hired gangs of roughs to break up teetotal meetings, and leading Wesleyans would heckle the speakers, Bible in hand, with shouts of 'Wine maketh glad the heart of man.' A rumour that teetotallers were atheists led to the use of the Baptist chapel being refused, and they had to retreat to the Primitive Methodist meeting house, which was also used by the Catholic Total Abstinence Society, at two pounds a meeting and 'find your own candles'. In the 1860s in the same town a famous Wesleyan minister was locked out of his own church after preaching teetotalism there and caused such a disturbance he was arrested and fined for brawling. Ten years later it was believed in Northampton that the teetotallers were part of a Papist plot, after which 'the Catholics will have their day again in England'. As late as 1877 one Welshman was complaining of 'our vicar . . . receiving the tithes of the parish at a public house and . . . distributing tickets amongst his parishioners which would entitle them to so much ale or liquor depending on the amount of the tithes paid . . . Some of them required a great deal of assistance to pack them in their saddles.'

Probably the most effective argument used to change opinion in the churches was the value of total abstinence to the weaker brother. This was the plea which had won over Father Mathew, while Cardinal Manning signed the pledge in 1872 when invited to preach temperance to drunken Irish labourers in Southwark, since he realised that only teetotalism could help them. Both insisted, however, that moderate drinking was morally permissible. 'I repeat distinctly', said Manning in 1872, 'that any man who should say that the use of wine . . . is sinful when it does not lead to drunkenness, that man is a heretic condemned by the Catholic Church.' A teetotal Jesuit writer in 1914 endorsed this view. Teetotallers who said that alcohol was 'intrinsically evil' fell into the fifth-century Manichean heresy that all matter was bad.

Much of the religious opposition to the teetotallers was based on what now seems a curiously minor issue, that the teetotallers' pledge was a rival to the baptismal vow. Father Mathew always insisted that the pledge was 'merely a resolution in favour of total abstinence expressed aloud', but some priests refused absolution to pledge-breakers for committing the mortal sin of 'telling lies to the Holy Ghost'[1] and an enquiry by *The Tablet* revealed fourteen different opinions among Catholic clergy as to the pledge's true meaning. Many non-Catholics were highly critical of the pledge, particularly the Bishop of Lincoln, who in a famous sermon in 1873 protested that the pledge was 'often almost forced upon young children', who later broke it. 'What is this, but in the name of . . . temperance to teach indifference to truth . . . Thus Satan gets the better of us . . . He professes to be an advocate of sobriety, but beguiles us into sins which are quite as bad as drunkenness.'

Soon a hail of angry pamphlets and sermons was being launched around the episcopal ears and Dr. Frederick Lees arrived in Lincoln to denounce him from the platform of the Corn Exchange. Referring to the Bishop's text, 'Every creature of God is good', Lees demanded, amid cheers, 'Is gunpowder a creature of God? Is a filthy book or an obscene picture such a creature?' As for the pledge being given to children, did not the Bishop confirm them? Yet if capable of 'judging of the whole question of salvation . . . they must be able to understand the simple matter of the evils of drink'.

Even the pledge controversy, however, did less to alienate the teetotallers from moderate opinion in the churches than their campaign against communion wine. This began on purely pragmatic grounds. John B. Gough said that on first receiving communion after signing the pledge 'the small draught . . . of . . . wine brought back to me vividly the old sensations', and an Anglican clergyman acknowledged 'sad relapses into sin from this very cause'. Many teetotallers were also troubled by

[1] Such penitents were, however, often offered absolution if Father Mathew himself released them from their pledge. Hence the eager crowds who returned their medals in person or by post.

the inconsistency, as one put it, of banishing wine from their homes while regarding it 'as suitable for the Lord's Table. Until it is driven out from the shelter of the church . . . we cannot expect it to be banished from the world.'

Several nonconformist associations to promote the use of non-alcoholic communion wine were formed, and some chapels, as at St. Ives, founded largely for this reason. Where their clergy remained unsympathetic, some individuals took independent action. One Northamptonshire Baptist regularly remained in his pew at communion time 'to administer the sacred ordinance to himself' from an innocuous bottle, while a Catholic writer recorded with horror, 'We have heard of fanatics celebrating the communion with tea.'

The objections to communion wine on practical grounds were soon overshadowed by the campaign against all alcohol as innately evil. The fact that the Bible contained several hundred references to alcohol might have seemed an insuperable obstacle in an age when men took Scripture literally. One text in particular might have daunted the stoutest waterdrinker's heart, Deuteronomy xiv, 25–26, which, after describing the turning of tithes into money, went on: 'And thou shalt bestow that money for whatsoever thy soul lusteth after, for oxen, or for sheep, or for wine, or for strong drink, or for whatsoever thy soul desireth.' The temperance movement met the challenge by its favourite device of a competition, and in 1842 two Scotsmen offered a prize for the best essay on this notorious passage. Eighteen competitors bravely undertook the task of proving that it meant the reverse of what it said, the prize going to that irrepressible campaigner Dr. Frederick Lees. There were, said Lees, three different words for wine and strong drink in the original Hebrew, 'yayin', 'tirosh' and 'shechar', but all clearly meant 'good', i.e., non-intoxicating, wine, in places where drink was referred to approvingly, and 'bad', i.e., alcoholic, wine, where it was mentioned critically. The wine used by Christ in the Last Supper was clearly of the innocuous kind; 'the wine of the drunkard' could not have been served, since 'the supposition offends our sense of moral propriety'.

Although in many quarters Lees's name became a joke, the more extreme teetotallers hailed the 'two wines' theory with delight, for it explained away every difficulty from Christ's first miracle at Cana, where, it now appeared, He had turned water into grape-juice, to Paul's advice to Timothy to use an innocent digestive tonic. In 1844, Lees, never the man to leave well alone, published a long *Prize Essay on the Nature, Elements and Rites of the Christian Eucharist*, which followed up his debunking of wine by some special pleading on behalf of water. 'If', he suggested, 'we recollect . . . the servile condition of the Hebrews in Egypt and the excellent quality of the Nile water . . . it will seem most probable that WATER was the general drink at the original institution of the Passover.'

In 1872, his health worn down by incessant writing, Lees combined a foreign holiday with a search for the legendary non-alcoholic wine, which he had now persuaded himself had for centuries been the normal drink in Mediterranean countries. It proved singularly elusive, but was finally run to earth at a Benedictine convent in Sicily, where Lees was 'able to taste the boiled-down grape juice, a thick sugary liquid of rich hue and delicious flavour, perfectly free from alcohol'. Others proved less impressed and by 1876 Lees's almost annual publication on the subject had risen to 160 pages in *The Answer to the Unanswerable or an Exposure of the Fallacies of Three Irish Advocates and Eleven Syrian Witnesses.* The 'Irish advocates' were professors who had shown Lees to be hopelessly unscholarly, while the eleven Syrian witnesses had, in May 1875, signed a declaration, based on forty years' residence in the Middle East, which proved him a liar. 'During the whole time of our residence and travelling in Syria and the Holy Land', they stated categorically, 'we have never seen, nor heard of, any unfermented wine, nor have we found among Jews, Christians or Mohammedans, any tradition of such a wine having ever existed in the country.' Faced with such evidence, Lees could only bluster about 'tapsters' and tipplers' criticism', and point out that the Syrians were 'a simple un-intellectual people' who could not be relied on.

Lees's masterpiece was *The Temperance Bible Commentary*, written in collaboration with the Rev. Dawson Burns. In this 450-page volume, published in 1868, the authors worked their way through 493 references to drink in the Old Testament and 144 in the New, rewriting each to make it favourable to teetotalism. 'Stay me with flagons', in the Song of Solomon, became 'Sustain me with a cake of grapes', and 'A feast of wine on the lees', in Isaiah, was amended to 'A feast of preserves, well clarified'. 'Wine', which it was said in Zechariah 'shall make the young maidens flourish', was altered to 'vine-fruit', since 'in all ages ... where alcoholic liquor is freely used, its employment to make young females "thrive" would not be ventured upon'. The authors failed, however, to pluck out that Biblical thorn in the waterdrinking flesh, St. Paul's advice to his disciple Timothy, in I Timothy v, 23: 'Drink no longer water, but use a little wine for thy stomach's sake and thine often infirmities.' The best they could suggest was that Timothy 'would feel at liberty to take ... any species that was most salutary, preferring, we may be sure, those kinds that ... ministered least to sensualism and to public vice', and that even if the saint had been so misguided as to choose the alcoholic variety, 'This advice was meant for Timothy alone and ... St. Paul did not set up for physician-general to the Christian world in all ages.'

The Bible Wine Controversy, as it was known, called forth some curious examples of Biblical scholarship. One writer calculated that 'fresh grape juice' used at the Passover must have been fermented as it was six months since the last vintage. As for the marriage at Cana, 'for our Lord to have pointed to the water when told there was no wine would have been very different from His wonted sympathy with the wants of man'. 'Wine', argued another anti-teetotaller, in 1884, was 'emblematic of the spiritual joy which God keeps for His servant in heaven.' Why should it only be Timothy who had been entitled to a drink, asked one Hyde Park orator, 'as if all of us, more or less, had not aching or infirm stomachs, which required soothing and refreshing by an occasional imbibing of beer, wine or strong drink'? To such critics the teetotallers replied with books like *The Waterdrinkers of the Bible*, published in 1885, which claimed Christ as a teetotaller because He had refused wine on the cross, and even, remarkably, Timothy himself, on the ingenious grounds that St. Paul's advice to him implied that he normally drank only water. The same author opened up a promising new area of controversy in pointing out that the Bible mentioned 'several kinds of water... some of them... anything but innocent' such as the 'waters of bitterness' and 'the bitter water which causeth a curse'. It was 'therefore... important even in using such a simple thing as water to... drink only that kind which is fit and proper'.

The teetotallers never did achieve much success in the Church of England. A survey in 1873 claimed 4,000 of the 34,000 Protestant clergy in the British Isles as total abstainers, but this included only 660 out of 23,000 Anglicans, or about one in thirty-five. The waterdrinkers had, however, made substantial inroads into other denominations. More than half the Presbyterian clergy were now abstainers, in public at least, and among the nonconformists the tide was now set strongly towards teetotalism. By 1877 a third of all Wesleyan ministers were abstainers and by 1880 a majority of all nonconformist theological students. In 1901 a temperance propagandist claimed that most dissenting ministers were now teetotallers and, though this seems more doubtful, a quarter of all Anglican clergy.

By now many nonconformist churches were celebrating communion in grape juice but in 1877 the teetotallers' old Anglican enemy Bishop Wordsworth of Lincoln formally forbade one of his rectors to use unfermented wine. The teetotallers sought legal advice, but counsel would only say, unhelpfully, that all depended on the meaning of the word 'wine'. Sometimes an incumbent found himself at odds with extremist parishioners. One anguished vicar wrote to his bishop for advice, protesting that 'we clergy have no right, so far as I can see, to consecrate unfermented wine'. His bishop agreed and issued a Charge to his clergy warning against a 'spirit of fanaticism', which in turn prompted fresh outbursts from the teetotallers, including an attack on *The Church Times*, which 'like the Bird of Darkness dreads the daylight of truth', because it refused to print their letters and advertisements.

Another stalwart adversary of the teetotallers was Dr. S. R. Hole, Dean of Rochester, an impressive figure who stood six feet four high and weighed seventeen stone. In 1889 his defence of moderate drinkers provoked an open *Letter of Remonstrance* from a fellow Anglican priest, who accused him of resembling the American clergy who had justified slavery as a 'divine institution', thus 'trifling with a national sin'.[1] The Dean was unabashed and three years later at a Church Congress attacked those who 'would have us read that the Good Samaritan poured in oil and water and took the poor wounded Jew to a temperance hotel'. The teetotallers hit back with *The Dean and the Drink*, which recalled that many an ecclesiastical dignitary had taken to the bottle, but by 1912 even the prohibitionist Bishop Hicks of Lincoln (a successor to Christopher Wordsworth) was declaring that the 'two wines' theory 'is steadily repudiated by the best Biblical scholars and has... seriously hindered the acceptance of our principles by the thoughtful Christian public'. As for communion wine, 'I for one am content with a mixed chalice of weak wine and water.'

Although the Church of England as a whole stood firm against teetotalism it did much to promote temperance measures in the 'moderation' sense. In 1869 and 1874 respectively its two 'Parliaments', the Convocations of Canterbury and of York, issued massive reports, based on impartial and widespread enquiries over the whole country, which recommended practical remedies for the drink problem, ranging from earlier closing to better housing. 'The discomforts of the cottage drive men to the public house', the York report said bluntly. The Church of England Temperance Society, which in 1873 replaced various earlier organisations, succeeded in embracing both moderation men and teetotallers. Every member undertook 'to exert myself for the suppression of intemperance', but there was a separate

[1] This was a popular and effective parallel; the early teetotallers had been strongly anti-slavery.

pledge for those wishing also to join the Total Abstinence section.

The split in the churches on the teetotal issue delighted the growing rationalist movement—Charles Bradlaugh, an avowed atheist, had been elected to Parliament in 1880. 'During the recent General Election the Christian forces were fairly divided', gloated G. W. Foote in *The Bible and Beer* in 1895. 'The parsons joined the publicans in supporting the Tories, while the dissenting ministers joined the teetotallers in supporting the Liberals.' He dismissed 'the contention that Bible wines were non-intoxicating', remarking provocatively that 'Jesus Christ was no more a teetotaller than Paul. There is no evidence that he ever drank water when there was anything better going.' The real remedy for intemperance was to ban the Bible, which 'reeks with wine . . . There will always be temptations enough to indulgence in drink, without placing unexpurgated editions of such a book into the hands of boys and girls as the veritable Word of God.'

The other long-term beneficiaries of the 'Bible Wine' controversy were the manufacturers of grape juice. Ever since the 1830s the teetotallers had been attempting to produce that 'natural' liquid of pressed fresh grapes which, they asserted, had been an everyday drink for thousands of years. When, however, a Manchester Baptist minister did succeed in taming the rebellious grape, 'so much fidgetting care', commented the lapsed teetotaller Thomas Smeeton in 1849, 'had to be taken to keep the perverse juice from fermenting and its use to any extent was so suggestive of colic and diarrhoea that very few . . . needed any apostolic warning to keep quite clear of the sickening mixture for the future'. There was universal relief when, in 1863, a Kensington teetotaller, Frank Wright, succeeded in producing unfermented wine that stayed non-alcoholic. The Scottish temperance reformer, John Hope, optimistically presented every Presbyterian minister in Edinburgh with a bottle and distributed 2,000 more free samples at a lecture, but the wine seems to have been an acquired taste for an Anglican clergyman warned in 1894 that one was found to feel 'a sense of disappointment' and 'conclude that what you are tasting is in no sense wine, but probably cider or other juice, with wine flavouring'.

Frank Wright's business prospered, however, and an advertisement in 1883 offered 'new wines direct from the vineyards, guaranteed to be . . . unfermented and unintoxicating' at 3s. 6d. a bottle or 40s. a dozen, for 'Madeira, Muscat, Marsala'. 'Port wine with bark' was, said Mr. Wright, 'most valuable as a tonic and stomachic in cases of exhaustion from overwork'. What a pity, many teetotallers must have reflected, that it had not been available for troublesome, dyspeptic Timothy.

*Chapter Eighteen*

# THE TEMPERANCE INDUSTRY

'Pledge cards, fifty and upwards, half-price. A large variety of chaste designs... When ordering state whether for Band of Hope, Temperance Society, Total Abstinence Society or "Temperance Pledge". Cash with order.'

— Advertisement in temperance pamphlet, 1916

IF, MIRACULOUSLY, the campaign for prohibition had succeeded, not only the publicans would have suffered financially, for at its peak the temperance movement provided a living, directly or indirectly, for a substantial number of people. The first to profit were the printers. *The Preston Temperance Advocate* and its early imitators only escaped stamp duty by printing no news less than a month old, but the abolition of stamp duty in 1855 and of the duty on paper in 1861 opened the flood-gates. By 1880 a temperance history could list more than 200 periodicals from *The Abstainers' Journal*, published in Edinburgh, to *The York Temperance Visitor*, as well as nearly 900 books and pamphlets, many titles covering a whole series of tracts. Some authors published fifty or sixty books in a few years.

The range of temperance literature was remarkable. An anonymous 20-page pamphlet, *An Earnest Appeal from the Furnace by a Bottle Hand to his Fellow Workmen*, in 1856, described the night shift in a glass works, and the mishaps of drunken, unpunctual 'Harry Behind, who . . . has slept his call', and who 'cannot cast a true ring . . . and . . . begins to be a little ashamed of telling the *taker-in* to throw so many into the pot'. *A Dog's Protest Against Intemperance*, in 1885, sang the praises of a dead drunkard's 'big black dog', Keeper, who 'the moment John went into a public house . . . put his tail between his legs and trotted home'. Mrs. R. D. Bolton, in 1886, in *And so we bury our dead*, addressed herself to undertakers. 'I have heard that if it's . . . anything catching, we're much safer from the infection if we take . . . coffee than if we're excited by wine, one pall-bearer tells another.'

The favourite target for such appeals was, however, the farm labourer. 'If total abstinence were universal', confidently advised a country rector, the Rev. George Pope, in *Thought Food for Farmers, Labourers and Artisans* in 1883, 'political and social discontent . . . would, to a great extent, be unknown . . . Every man could then have his pig, cow, plot of ground.' The way to bring 'this desirable condition of things' closer, farmer John Abbey told the Northamptonshire Chamber of Agriculture in 1892, in *Temperance in the Hay and Harvest Field*, was to cease serving free beer during harvesting. It was the farmer's plain duty to abandon this harmful tradition—and thus save his labourers from 'intemperance and unthrifty habits' and himself from £20–£80 a year. Lime juice and 'stokos', made of oatmeal, sugar and sliced lemon, were far cheaper, or they could copy the Berkshire farmer who had built a copper in his fields and served hot tea.

Clearly intended for a middle-class audience was *Country Walks and Temperance Talks*, a 200-page book by the Rev. Dawson Burns, published in 1901 at a shilling and recounting the conversation of a group of tourists visiting Devonshire. With Mrs. Mansfield, widow of a distinguished doctor, travel her 'graceful and dignified' elder daughter Constance, her younger daughter Rosalind, whose 'vivacity and lightheartedness appeared inexhaustible', and their respective boy friends, Roland, a rising young barrister who enjoyed an occasional 'glass with a friend', and solid Leonard, 'the son of a London banker', a teetotaller. On a trip to a lighthouse at Mortehoe Leonard asserts, with all the assurance of a comfortably off man, that 'tens of thousands . . . might visit the seaside if they did not frequent the gin shop'. During a steamer trip to Minehead,

Leonard sadly recalls the number of people employed in the drink trade; while the moonlight shines down on the sea at Clovelly, he is busy warning his companion of 'the danger of contracting a craving for alcohol by . . . moderate potation'. Through excursions to Plymouth Hoe, Tavistock and Exeter the unequal contest continues, reaching its climax after a final walk on the hills around Bristol, when Mrs. Mansfield reveals that her husband, having boasted of his moderation, died of drink. At this, Constance, forgetting her dignity, weeps aloud, while Leonard, with a banker's eye to the main chance, has his pledge book out in a flash and persuades Rosalind and Roland to sign on the dotted line.

Aimed nominally at middle-class women, but perhaps catering for the market for curious literature was *Intemperance and Tight Lacing*, published in Manchester in 1898. In the United States the campaign against women's stays was intimately linked with the prohibition movement and the American author of this pamphlet explained the connection. 'Alcoholic drinks powerfully excite amativeness . . . obscenity and licentiousness . . . Tight-lacing around the waist keeps the blood from returning to the heart and thereby inflames all the organs of the abdomen.' After apologising for feeling compelled to mention the subject, 'although I know it will injure the popularity and sale of this work', this public-spirited writer appealed 'to every patriot, to every Christian . . . Let the finger of scorn be pointed at every tight-laced woman.' His final plea was to the culprits themselves: 'Do you think', he asked, 'our Saviour thinks any more of you for being corseted? . . . Tight lacing is incompatible with Christianity.'

Perhaps the oddest tract of all was *Tippling and Temperance*, published in May 1890, 'a treatise in 1,289 words each commencing with the letter T . . . the first edition of 455 words . . . being too . . . incomplete as an exponent of the evils of intemperance'. 'Thoughtless thousands turn to the too tempting tap', it began. 'Thriving tradesmen taste tipple timidly . . . time-wasters tipple tremendously . . . thereby turpitude thrives, turmoil triumphs.' Worst of all was 'the trivial, time-serving toss-pot' who became a 'truculent tyrant throwing toast, tea-cake ... table-knives, tea-cups ... trays, tongs, then tearing the table-cloth', all in marked contrast to the behaviour of the 'tolerant temperance theorist'.

The most successful propagandist work of all was *Danesbury House*, the first novel of Mrs. Henry Wood, which won a prize of £100 offered by the Scottish Temperance League in 1860, and after achieving an unprecedented circulation was still in print at the end of the century. The plot revolves round the Danesbury family, owners of an engineering works forty miles from London, whose misfortunes begin when 'little William Danesbury, a lovely child of nine months old', narrowly escapes being poisoned by his drunken nurse, Glisson, who is later dismissed. Mrs. Danesbury, called home to care for him, is killed in a carriage accident caused by a drunken turnpike keeper, but her husband soon consoles himself with a new wife, who presses wine upon her stepchildren. The older two, Arthur and Isobel, refuse out of loyalty to their teetotal mother's memory; young William takes an occasional glass; while Mrs. Danesbury's own sons, Lionel and Robert, accept eagerly. Inevitably, therefore, when the family grow up, Arthur inherits the family business, Isobel marries well, while William only narrowly escapes a drunkard's grave. Lionel dies raving from delirium tremens, and Robert kills himself. The nurse Glisson, whose drinking started the chain of disasters, turns up again, 'a bundle of rags, bent as if with age', lamenting those glasses of gin and water with cook in the kitchen of Danesbury House long ago. Eventually Arthur opens a 'coffee public house' and makes the village 'dry', leaving the survivors to look forward to happier days, and Mrs. Wood, incidentally, to even greater success in the following year, with *East Lynne*.

*Danesbury House* was soon adapted for the stage, for temperance dramas were now in vogue. Many were imported from the United States where they were popular with managers, since they attracted a new, puritanical, clientele who normally boycotted the theatre. Often theatre-owners sought the best of both worlds, by putting on a 'straight' temperance play one week and a farce mocking temperance the next, like that in which John B. Gough first appeared.

Two temperance plays were particular hits. *The Drunkard*, 'a moral domestic drama of American life', opened in Boston in 1844, being backed by the great showman, P. T. Barnum, who was himself a temperance lecturer and kept a huge pledge in the foyer for audiences to sign. He was probably part-author of the play, which was widely performed on both sides of the Atlantic. The plot can be deduced from the stage directions. Act One, Scene One begins with 'Interior of a pretty rural cottage, flowers, painting, etc.', but is soon followed by a wretched garret . . . Mary in miserable apparel . . . Julia sleeping on a straw bed on the floor'. Before long in 'A . . . shed, supposed to be near a tavern . . . Edward discovered lying on ground . . . clothes torn . . . appearance horrible etc.' By Act Three, Scene Five, however, we are back in the original setting with 'everything denoting domestic peace and tranquil happiness . . . with roses, myrtles, etc., under windows' and Julia leading a chorus of villagers in *Home Sweet Home*. In between, honest Edward has been first degraded by and then rescued from drink, to be reunited with his wife Mary and child Julia, who promises in her final speech to pray for temperance reformers.

*The Drunkard* was soon rivalled in popularity by *Seven Nights in a Bar-room*, based on a famous tract, *Ten Nights in a Bar-room*, first published in the United States in 1854 and in Great Britain in the following year. The play was a great favourite of local repertory companies and contains several classic scenes. In one, little Mary is struck by a glass thrown in a tavern while singing *Father dear Father, Come Home with Me Now*, which became a national hit. Later Mary dies on stage, from this blow, while her grief-stricken parent renounces drink for ever. In the finale the whole cast resolve to destroy all the liquor in the town and to vote for the Maine Law.[1]

[1] *Ten Nights in a Bar-room* enjoyed a further brief boom in 1943, when a retired Pennsylvania teacher left 25,000 dollars to the local high school on condition it always kept ten copies of the book in its library.

Many similar plays were intended for amateur production at temperance meetings, like *An Awkward Half Hour*, by A. J. Foxwell, published around 1889. This required only six characters and one set, and its simple plot revolved round a man, dropped at the wrong house by a drunken cab driver on Christmas Eve, being mistaken for a thief. After some knock-about farce, child carol singers arrive and are given coffee, as being 'better than beer or wine this cold night'.

Mock-trials were another popular Victorian entertainment. In *The Trial of John Barleycorn alias Strong Drink*, published in Manchester about 1879, John Barleycorn is charged on twelve counts, from 'causing good and wholesome grain to be destroyed' to being 'a common corrupter of our youth'. Despite defence evidence from Judas Moderation and Mr. Lovedrink, a surgeon whose patients have deserted him for Mr. Drink-water, the accused is found guilty and banished, his property being divided among temperance societies and ruined families. *The Trial of John and Jane Temperance*, in 1882, gave a new twist to the same theme by putting the usual heroes in the dock. A comic Irishman testifies that thanks to Jane Temperance's work, his wife 'calls me anything but respectable names', and Mr. Muchprofit, a brewer, complains of losing his seat in Parliament to a teetotaller, who used 'most underhanded, paltry and sly means ... He spent very little money in electioneering expenses.' John and Jane are, inevitably, acquitted.

Magic lantern lectures on temperance were also very common, the best-known, *The Trial of Sir Jasper*, being based on a 'temperance tale in verse', published in 1873. The slides were of greater artistic merit, being prepared from contemporary drawings by Doré, Cruikshank, Tenniel and others. First the wicked Sir Jasper appears:

> He, THE DISTILLER, makes and vends the gin!
> Arraign him as the chiefest source of sin.

He is followed by a procession of his victims.

> God's minister ... who skulks along,
> Humming the loose air of a tawdry song,

makes an early appearance but is followed by such unfamiliar figures as Lady Deign, who 'beat her small maid, who said she liked champagne', and 'Sir Augustus Hugh Fitznought', who 'Home in a costermonger's cart was brought'. Finally, with the court inflamed against him,

> Sir Jasper left the scene of grief and crime
> And sought a back-door exit—just in time.

George Cruikshank, the most famous of teetotal artists, had originally been a 'moderation man' but the immense success of his set of eight anti-drink engravings, *The Bottle*, in 1847, led to strong and successful pressure on him to sign the pledge. He celebrated his conversion with *The Drunkard's Children* in the following year, and in 1862 produced his temperance masterpiece, *The Worship of Bacchus*, an enormous picture showing how men had worshipped wine through the ages and containing more than a thousand separate figures. Every self-respecting teetotaller soon owned a reproduction, it became the standard present for retiring temperance society officers, and on public exhibition, in London and on tour, it attracted large crowds. In 1863 Cruikshank personally exhibited the picture to the Queen at Windsor Castle and it was eventually presented by the temperance movement to the nation.[1] Cruikshank remained active in the temperance movement until his death at the age of eighty-six. He liked to compare advocates of moderation to jackdaws hopping round a dish, but afraid to eat, and would skip about the platform imitating them until 'the meeting was convulsed'. At eighty he could still dance a creditable hornpipe and would do so on the platform as proof of the vigour conferred by abstinence.

Despite Queen Victoria's interest, the teetotallers remained uneasy about the royal family's attitude. In 1848 they had been outraged when the royal family visited a distillery near Balmoral, though hastily spreading the story that all but foreign Albert had either refused to taste the whisky samples offered to

[1] The nation has not proved very grateful. *The Worship of Bacchus* is still owned by the Tate Gallery, but not exhibited.

them or had spluttered them out. The Queen herself, it was claimed, had put her glass to her lips without drinking, and had called her husband sharply to order as he was about to take a second mouthful. Even after the Prince Consort's death a bottle of whisky continued, however, to be placed in his room each night, and his son, the future Edward VII, presided in 1877 as Prince of Wales at a dinner in aid of the Licensed Victuallers' Asylum. This provoked further public criticism although the temperance movement agreed that the prince was not wholly lost, since no licensed premises were allowed on his estate at Sandringham.

In addition to the innumerable amateur entertainers, who made this their particular contribution to the cause, there were also many professionals working the temperance circuit. Sometimes a parent society provided each branch with one performer a month in return for its subscription, one society's handbook in 1890 classifying the available talent as 'clerical, lay, lady, and working men'. Mr. Alfred Harding offered 'Illustrated Temperance and Sanitary Lectures with numerous experiments and diagrams at the fixed charge of one guinea'. One versatile London Entertainment Society—'Full of good taste', according to the Rev. Bickersteth of Belvedere, Kent—provided 'conjuring, ventriloquism, merry midgets, punch and judy, dissolving views, magical clowns, negro comedians and handbell ringers'. The Palmerston Mission Working Men's Choir asked, in return for their 'songs, musical dialogues, recitations and short address', only 'third class travelling expenses and light refreshments', but Mrs. E. M. Story, of East Ham, knew what was due to a lady. Her lecture on 'The Newgate Philanthropists' merited 'second class railway fare and a collection'.

Many publishers also catered for temperance societies with 'do it yourself' entertainments, like *The Young Nurse*, 'a dialogue for six girls', or *The Temperance Lifeboat*, 'a concerted piece for seven boys', and innumerable temperance songbooks. One advertisement alone listed 150 titles at threepence each. For the soprano there was *Don't Marry a Man if he Drinks*; for the mezzo-soprano, *Katy's Mishap* and *Quite Embarrassing*;

for the tenor, *Pledge me, Love, In Sparkling Water*, while many songs had rousing refrains like

> For I've drunk my last glass boys,
> I've drunk my last glass,

or, more selfishly,

> Oh I am safe, am safe! No danger can I see;
> The wine will ruin you, perhaps, but cannot injure me.

Teetotallers unable to sing could always oblige with a recitation. The numerous temperance reciters on the market were packed with anecdotes of drunken engine drivers who ran down their own children, noble brides who delivered temperance lectures at their wedding breakfasts, and moderate drinking clergy who caroused in the vestry, while their ruined daughters, who had learned to drink at the rectory table, expired unrecognised in the snow outside with nameless infants in their arms. Few authors were guilty of understatement. Every shriek is agonising, every brow is fevered, every bed has its drunkard raving in it or child kneeling beside it, it is always Christmas Eve, and usually midnight. The only light relief comes from well-worn teetotallers' jokes like 'I always say the best side of a public house is the outside', and gruesome puns about drinking habits bringing a man to his bier.

Such catch-phrases were also a feature of temperance almanacks, the first of which had been published by Joseph Livesey and in. An 1859 pamphlet, *The Turkish Bath: An Antidote for* every day of the year: 'Cold water will cure a purpled nose'; 'Up and be doing—stop all this brewing'; and 'Brewers' horses are fatter than their customers'. By the 1850s *Temperance Placards*, large posters costing sixpence each, were also on sale. A typical one, '*Bitter' Beer*, showed that scene dear to every teetotaller's imagination, a brutal drunkard dragging his wife by the hair through the wreckage of their home. For two shillings one could also buy from the National Temperance Publications Depot, the leading publisher in this field, a whole book of *Temperance Mottoes*, consisting of 'illuminated floral cards for rewards, wall decorations, etc.' and bearing such quotations as 'Honest water ne'er left man in the mire, Shakespeare'. It was also possible to buy temperance wafers, each carrying a suitable reminder, to seal letters to drinking friends, and temperance mugs, inscribed inside the bottom, 'Remember the Reckoning'. One confectionery firm added to its range of 'conversation lozenges', large, flat sweets usually printed with such exhortations as 'Give me your heart' and 'Spare my blushes', some less flirtatious observations: 'Intemperate habits are sooner acquired than cast off' and 'Misery, poverty, sickness and untimely death are the effect of drunkenness'. Supplying the day-to-day paraphernalia of the movement made many printers prosperous. Pledge cards '50 and upwards half price' were offered in 'a large variety of chaste designs'; a sample packet cost sixpence. For excursions one could obtain for 'two and sixpence, postage fivepence, 1,000 Railway Tickets... with announcements of meetings, etc., printed on one side', while the best buy was clearly '175 Temperance Proverbs, Quotations and Maxims' at twopence. The real enthusiast could even decorate his home with temperance wallpaper, in a design incorporating drawings of Father Mathew and his famous medal.

The teetotal agitation also benefited bath manufacturers, for a regular craze developed in mid-century for hydropathy, a system of treatment involving hot or cold water, both outside and in. An 1859 pamphlet, *The Turkish Bath: An antidote for the Cravings of the Drunkard*, tactfully acknowledged that 'notwithstanding the number that have been rescued by Total Abstinence Societies, there is a large class unreached by them among the higher orders... The remedy proposed offers to *them* a means of escape which does not hurt their self-esteem.' By prolonged soakings in hot water, it was claimed, followed by a rub down with cold, 'the blood is so purified... that... the craving appetite for strong drink ceases... In no country has drunkenness been found coexistent with The Bath.'

A chemist in the Mile End Road offered a cheaper remedy, Temperance Pills, to prevent 'that uneasiness and sinking at the stomach' the new teetotaller would otherwise feel. The former drinker must 'immediately upon signing the pledge, commence . . . taking the first night two pills, the next night three and the following night four pills . . . This should be continued for at least a fortnight or three weeks.' If the results were alarming the patient was 'particularly cautioned against supposing that it is his having taken too large a dose which is the cause of his suffering as . . . even a stronger dose is required in those cases'. If any pills (costing 7½d. or 4s. 6d. for the family size) were left when the craving had gone, they would come in useful as 'the most efficacious remedy for . . . sickness, acidity or heartburn, spasms and flatulent distensions, giddiness, headache, drowsiness, dimness of sight'.

For those whom neither The Bath nor Temperance Pills could cure there was always an alcoholics' asylum. An advertisement for one Home for Inebriate Women in 1890, which charged from seven-and-sixpence to three guineas a week according to status, neatly reflected the social divisions of the time. '*Lady* inmates have meals in dining-room . . . and their own drawing-room. Work-room inmates have their meals apart and sit in work-room. Servant inmates have their meals in the kitchen and do the work of the house.'

*Chapter Nineteen*

## COFFEE AT THE PUB

'Give the working man a public house... where good coffee and tea... take the place of beer and gin.'

— *The Coffee Public House, How to Establish and Manage It*, 1878

THE CAMPAIGN against drink had begun as part of a general movement to improve social conditions and two books were particularly influential in helping to identify temperance and social reform in the public mind. In *Ragged Homes and How to Mend Them*, published in 1860, Mrs. Mary Bayly described how as a child in Wiltshire, her father, a teetotaller, had sent her out to visit the sick. She soon realised that 'The nice soup sent for the sick man was spoiled by being smoked in the warming up... The sago intended for the infant was burnt or only half cooked... Medicine and food alike failed to be efficacious in the absence of cleanliness.' As a married woman she resolved to try to bring about some more permanent improvement in the way the poor lived, bravely choosing for the experiment one of the toughest areas in all London, the Kensington Potteries.

The Potteries, which, said Mrs. Bayly, resembled 'a village, not picturesque', was the refuge of several thousand people driven together because their trades were too anti-social for ordinary neighbourhoods, even in mid-Victorian England. In the Potteries chimney-sweeping ranked as a clean occupation. Rubbish-scavengers, pig-keepers, people who boiled offal down for fat, men who made bow-strings from animals' intestines, these were the main occupational groups. Living conditions were squalid; sometimes a family occupied an upstairs room and pigs, poultry and a donkey the ground floor. Life was coarse, the adults, 'sallow and aged', amusing themselves with rat-killing or illegal cock-fighting and bull-baiting, the children 'ragged, neglected . . . pale and flabby' killing time by pelting passers-by and throwing stones at windows. Yet poverty was not ultimately to blame. In the summer a brickmaker and his family, working all hours, might earn three pounds a week, but 'the effect of an increased income', noted Mrs. Bayly, 'is that more money goes to the public house', and by December the same man's 'wife and children were shivering at my door . . . begging for food and clothing'.

Severe cholera epidemics in 1849 and 1854 had already brought the Potteries to public notice and Mrs. Bayly took her readers behind the scenes. She related how instead of giving them cast-off clothing, she supplied cloth, free patterns and needlework lessons to the members of the Mothers' Society she founded in 1853. Instead of doling out soup, she lent a saucepan and a recipe explaining how to make six quarts for sixpence. Instead of lecturing on the dangers of dirt, she loaned out a whitewash brush. Instead of preaching thrift, she started a savings bank. Soon men were coming to ask her to teach them to read and write, while their wives were turning up clean and tidy where once 'a clean face would have been as great a rarity as snow in harvest' and even planting flowers and putting up curtains.

Mrs. Bayly was flattered when one man said of her, 'She is one of the right sort; she doesn't bring us any tracts or any twaddle', and she never pressed her teetotal views upon her hearers. If a visiting speaker were praised, she would let slip that he was a waterdrinker. If cleanliness was discussed, she would casually recall how one local man's only shirt had been pawned for drink by the laundress. Nor was she slow to point out how twopence spent on vegetables or barley would have kept the baby quiet far more effectively than twopennyworth of gin.

Mrs. Bayly's book, and its successor, *Mended Homes and*

*What Repaired Them*, had an immense impact and undoubtedly helped its author's three pet causes of 'Education, Temperance and Sanitary Science'. An even greater impression, particularly within the Church of England, was achieved by *Haste to the Rescue* by Mrs. Charles Wightman, the wife of a Shrewsbury vicar, who also aimed 'to stir up ... the educated classes' and who admitted she had been influenced by *Ragged Homes*. Mrs. Wightman's book, published in 1862, was in the form of letters to her sister, recounting eighteen months' work by her husband Charles and herself among forty-three families in Butchers Row, 'The Potteries' of Shrewsbury. From her first-hand knowledge, Mrs. Wightman confidently denied that 'the working class are so ungrateful, they only care for what they can get from you', and that contact with them involved 'laying aside distinctions of rank'. She pointed out that her loans to men to get their clothes out of pawn to attend church or to pay off their debts at the public house had always been repaid, and that the poor even possessed table manners. After supper at the vicarage of 'cold meats, mashed potato, bread and butter, cake' for twelve men who had regularly attended her weekly meeting, 'we were amazed to find the cloth unsullied by a single spot'. Mrs. Wightman was obviously a woman of rare courage. She tackled alone 'a tall, strong, powerful husband', notorious as 'a very great drinker and fighter', whose wife fled in terror before the mention of temperance could rouse his fury. Confronted with a drunken brute, covered 'in clotted blood and dirt', who had beaten up his wife and almost murdered his baby, Mrs. Wightman fetched a sponge and cleaned him up. When some of her best members got drunk at a dinner to celebrate the completion of their work on a new reservoir, she tolerantly accepted that on such an occasion anyone might be 'laughed out of' keeping his pledge. Against such defeats she could set an attendance of 150 at her weekly meetings; twenty-five middle-aged men learning to read and write; and a savings bank in which 230 blacksmiths, iron-moulders, fishmongers, bricklayers and barbers—hard-drinking occupations all—saved £100 a week.

Discovering that before the chief local holiday, Shrewsbury Show, some men had formerly pawned their furniture to finance a debauch lasting ten weeks, Mrs. Wightman organised a counter-attraction, a train and waggon trip to the Wrekin, following this up with an even more ambitious trip, to Liverpool. Here her flock delighted her by taking tea at a temperance café and going on a steamer trip, while the men from Butchers Row took a busmen's holiday by visiting a slaughter-house. Finally, 'we all slaked our thirst at the public drinking fountain' and 'many were the longings expressed for the like boon in Shrewsbury'.

Liverpool had in fact 'the honour of initiating this species of public benefaction' in March 1854, the first London fountain not being opened until the following month. In 1859 the Metropolitan Free Drinking Fountain Association[1] was founded and was soon spending more than £3,000 a year. Most fountains consisted of a simple tap or open pipe let into the wall of a churchyard or other public place, but in others Victorian taste ran rampant. The most ornate were often erected as memorials to famous waterdrinkers; one cost £800 and involved a block of granite second only to Cleopatra's Needle in size. By 1879, 437 fountains had been opened in London alone, one fewer than the number of horse troughs. Equally revealing of mid-Victorian sentiment, when fountains were at last provided in Shrewsbury they were at first locked up on Sunday. Soon afterwards Shrewsbury's M.P., the sanitary reformer R. A. Slaney, offered to provide five more as soon as the water company could supply them—an example of the way in which the campaign for drinking fountains helped to attract public health reformers to the temperance cause.

Other reformers specialised in providing practical alternatives to the public house. The most famous worker in this field was Elizabeth Cotton, later Lady Hope, of 'the little old-fashioned town of D——' in Surrey. Her highly successful book, *Our Coffee Room*, appeared in 1876, being followed two years later by *More About Our Coffee Room*. Miss Cotton was

[1] Still in existence today.

moved to action on hearing a man boast, 'I don't hold with church, nor with parsons neither ... I goes to the public house almost every night—and Sunday, too ... and nobody cares', words which 'sank into my heart ... like lead'. Miss Cotton soon found premises, in a former ragged school, where there were two empty rooms, each about thirty feet by twenty.

> The lower room was furnished with two bars at one end, one ... for the display of provisions and sale of coffee, the other containing two sloping locked desks, for the reception of account books, etc., connected with the Savings Bank and Shoe Club, which we intended to start ... Five tables were then placed in the room, round which were put backed forms of corresponding sizes ... covered with long crimson cushions. Pictures were hung on the walls and things generally began to wear a cheerful aspect. But ... by far the most important item of our establishment was lacking. We had no MAN.

Miss Cotton prayed that a man would be forthcoming and sure enough one was. Soon 'A red lamp was placed at the gate ... inscribed ... in white letters, The Beckenham Rooms'; Miss Cotton's titled father made a somewhat pompous speech—'You may come in and out of the place as freely as a public house', a notice was put up announcing 'Coffee, tea, cocoa or any other drink served EXCEPT beer, wine or spirits, Coffee 1d a cup, Tea 1½d, bread and butter, two slices 1d, No bad language allowed' and the coffee room was launched.

By opening at 5 a.m., before the public houses, it caught men on their way to work, and was soon so crowded in the evenings also—it closed at 10 p.m.—that an extension had to be built for a boys' room and further premises opened in the centre of Dorking, close to several public houses. By this time Miss Cotton was also running a night school, teaching part-singing, arranging entertainments with 'double stereoscope, graphiscope, microscope, musical boxes' and tramping through mud over her ankles to publicise the coffee room to the workers at the local lime pits, who, black all over and wreathed in smoke, listened politely as they munched their bread and cheese and drank their beer. On Whit Monday she laid on an excursion to the seaside for many men who had never been there before, and when thousands of Scotch and Irish militia came into camp nearby during the summer manœuvres, Miss Cotton opened a tented version of her coffee room, with the co-operation of the military authorities. The first request she had was for whisky, but, characteristically, she soon had the men queuing up to buy halfpenny glasses of ginger beer and penny slices of currant pudding.

Demand from her customers compelled Miss Cotton to start a Total Abstinence Society but she had no sympathy with 'young ladies', who 'pledge book in hand... persecute the unfortunate tired guests of the coffee room' until the latter signed for the sake of peace and then retired to the public house. She was clearly motivated by a real respect for the working classes, pointing out that her rooms gave an opportunity to middle-class people 'to show some little attention to the railway-men, policemen and postmen' from whom they normally received 'such useful and faithful service without in return expressing the slightest appreciation of their labours'.

The coffee public house movement even benefited the agricultural labourers, the most neglected section of the whole Victorian working population. As the Duchess of Rutland pointed out in 1893, a country clergyman who exhorted 'a sturdy labouring man for his own good to avoid the alehouse' was likely to be asked, 'Well, maester, where be I to go? The missus, she don't want me of an evening when she is putting the little 'uns to bed.' Some vicars, explained the duchess, hired a room in a cottage for the use of their parishioners and paid 'some respectable woman . . . to keep a good fire in the evening'; one philanthropist even 'admitted women to his reading room'. Village halls were also valuable, but the real answer was a village library, 'one of the best means of combating the intense boredom which drives many to the alehouses'. One at Woodstock in Oxfordshire had eventually grown into a village institute and it was found that 'Men would tramp long distances in all weather on a Sunday afternoon' to borrow 'Lives of Nelson, Wellington and Gordon', and 'the numerous books about Her

Majesty . . . most of all, the Queen's *Journal of Our Life in the Highlands*'.

Many variants on the coffee-room idea were tried, some reformers feeling that the more the teetotal establishment resembled the public house in atmosphere the better, others that anything, like dominoes, which reminded the customers of their former haunts, should be discouraged. As with temperance hotels, the best coffee-rooms were often those run on commercial rather than purely philanthropic lines, like Lockhart's Cocoa Rooms, which now became a familiar sight in many places and made their founder's fortune. Another enduring, though non-teetotal, rival to the public house, was the chain of Yates's Wine Lodges, started by a Lancashire man to provide the working classes with good, cheap wine in respectable surroundings. Instead of advertisements, the walls carried reminders that 'Wine is a good servant but a bad master'.

The 1860s and 1870s were the great period of expansion. The first 'dry' public house, *The British Workman*, was opened in Leeds in 1867 and in 1874 a similar establishment was started in Liverpool, 'the black spot on the Mersey', where 20,000 dock workers had nowhere to eat or shelter except licensed premises. In five years British Workman public houses were said to have diverted at least £50,000 from the licensed trade and by 1890 there were sixty-five in the city. Similar successes were claimed elsewhere and some houses even offered the equivalent of saloon and public bars, while a few provided much-needed bedroom accommodation at ninepence or a shilling a night. It was claimed in 1883 that, 'It is no rare circumstance for a toper to find his way into a coffee tavern in the sweet delusion that it is a gin-palace and call loudly for a pint of "half and half".'

By 1867 coffee-houses were common enough to be mentioned in a privately-printed pornographic novel, *Rosa Fielding or A Victim of Lust*. In this somewhat crude story a hypocritical nonconformist, the Rev. Stiggins, is tarred and feathered by some officers of Dragoons, who deposit him in a wheelbarrow at the door of Miss Larcher's Temperance Coffee House. The ringleader, a major, then strikes up an acquaintance with the proprietress, soon leaving her 'to take what pride she could in the idea that if she were not a married woman she was at any rate no longer an old maid'.

The coffee-house movement also interested many noblemen. In 1874 Lord Shaftesbury became president of the newly-founded People's Café Company and in 1877 the Duke of Westminster took the chair at the inaugural meeting of the Coffee Public House Association, which issued a thoroughly practical pamphlet, *The Coffee Public House, How to Establish and Manage it*. 'Give the working man a public house where he may meet his friends and talk and smoke . . . and where good coffee and tea . . . take the place of beer and gin', it urged, stressing that the premises must offer the customers 'a warm and cheerful room and a comfortable seat . . . a boon they rarely enjoy'. The Association recommended providing cheap and solid food, with plates of ham at twopence, sausage and potato at threepence, and chops at sevenpence or eightpence. It was, however, troubled by allegations that 'temperance drinks' contained acetic acid, copper and lead, which 'were thought to stimulate rather than counteract the craving for intoxicating liquor', finally recommending fizzy lemonade at three-halfpence a glass and soda water at a penny.

To carry the war into the enemy's country the teetotallers favoured coffee stalls, which could be set up near public houses or wherever working men gathered together. They soon discovered, what Mrs. Bayly had learned in the Potteries, that intending customers were rapidly repelled by any mention of religion or even temperance. When Miss Cotton at Dorking acquired a pony-drawn coffee-stall, several men refused the job of stall-keeper because it was prominently labelled 'Church Temperance Society', and they 'did not like to be chaffed'. Miss Cotton sensibly removed the offending inscription, painted her stall an attractive crimson, with white borders, in place of its former dingy yellow, and put in charge an ex-coal-heaver who 'arrayed himself in a new suit of entire white'. When a publican offered him alternative work in his garden he indignantly refused, replying to all invitations to come and have a drink, 'I've had enough of that... You try half a pint of coffee, nothing like it.'

Such paragons were rare. The anonymous author of *Practical Hints on Coffee Stall Management*, in 1886, complained that 'clergymen and district ladies seem to... hold the curious belief that reformed drunkards must... make the best possible stall-keepers'. In fact they often retained their slovenly habits, and certainly their bad reputation. 'You will find it hard enough to get... a really good stall-keeper, without... confining yourself to the professing total abstainer class', advised the writer. Ex-butlers, footmen and army pensioners were all likely candidates, but 'there is no training school for coffee-stall keepers that can compete with the Royal Navy... My sailor could wash and do needlework as well as any woman; mend his fire and make his tea, coffee and cocoa better than most cooks; he painted, papered and varnished the stall inside and out; mended the windows, cleaned the lock... He was the best salesman I ever had.' He helped to make up for one man who got the stall a bad name by getting drunk every night, and others who thought that 'honesty to customers is folly', and rapidly returned in change any foreign coins they accepted. The writer provided a useful list of essential equipment and a comprehensive index from 'habits, bad (e.g. smoking)' to 'stoves, how to manage fire in'. He or she advised, too, if the business prospered and one acquired permanent premises, displaying cycling magazines to tempt in the swelling army of 'bicyclists'. It was important, however, to secure the site on a long lease or the brewers would be sure to buy it and turn you out.

This was not the only evidence that the campaign against the trade was having some success, for a temperance publication in 1883 claimed a marked drop in the revenue from liquor taxation due to 'the increase of coffee taverns and similar institutions'. Coffee itself had not in fact proved very popular; the amount consumed per head of population actually dropped by more than 40% between 1852 and 1890. The amount of cocoa consumed, however, rose nearly fivefold in the same period, and tea consumption increased by about 300%, so that nearly six pounds of it were being drunk every year for every man, woman and child in the population.

Miss Cotton's coffee-tent for the militia was only one of many attempts to provide harmless drinks for soldiers on manœuvres. The most famous worker in this field was Miss Sarah Robinson, whose activities were at first hampered by the fear that water-drinking soldiers might be lacking in martial ardour and by an order, issued in 1864, forbidding the formation of regimental temperance societies, as sectarian organisations, destructive of comradeship and discipline. In 1871 the order was virtually rescinded and by 1873 Miss Robinson was providing recreation tents, with a 'dry' canteen, during the great autumn manœuvres on Dartmoor, so that that year only five or six pledges were broken instead of the usual 1,000. In 1876 her *Christianity and Teetotalism, a Voice from the Army* claimed societies in nearly every regiment and an increase in the past year from 3,400 military teetotallers to 10,000—one in thirteen of the whole Army. Some of Miss Robinson's stories, however, seem too good to be true. One could believe in the soldier who 'when in liquor tried to kill the sergeant major' and even in the drunken clerk, who, with rare ingratitude, borrowed a teetotaller's great-coat to lie on while he cut his throat, but most ex-servicemen will find it hard to recognise the 'barrack room with nearly all the men abstainers, their pledge cards in neat frames on the wall, religious and temperance papers on the table'. She considered, with scant Christian charity, that 'military flogging was much too gentle a punishment' for officers who derided teetotalism.

In the Navy the temperance movement had won a famous victory in 1847 when the Admiralty agreed to provide a money allowance, or tea and sugar, in place of the rum ration. Miss Robinson's opposite number was Miss Agnes Weston of Bath, 'the sailor-boy's friend', who had begun to correspond with seamen in 1870, later opening temperance institutes in many ports.[1] By 1875, 7,000 of the 60,000 sailors in the Navy had

[1] Many 'Aggie Weston' clubs still flourish today.

signed the pledge, and most warships contained a 'floating branch' of the National Temperance League, including H.M.S. *Bellerophon* where the branch secretary had formerly boasted 'My chapel is the grog-shop.'

Miss Weston was clearly a worthier, if less colourful, figure than her notorious predecessor, George 'Bosun' Smith, a half-crazed crank who first appeared on the temperance scene in 1830, as secretary of an organisation for founding temperance societies in 'the chief seaports and garrison towns'. This was the beginning of what was charitably described as 'a long life of laborious benevolence, marked by some eccentricities'. Among these was Smith's award to himself of the title 'Reverend', though he also referred to himself as B.B.U., short for 'Burning Bush Unconsumed'. After some much-publicised temperance work among seamen in the London Docks, the Bosun took the lead in the 'anti-Popery' riots in the Anglo-Catholic church of St. George's in the East in 1859. His 'short rotund figure', in its invariable navy blue suit, and his escort of 'orphan children of both sexes', the boys dressed as soldiers and sailors, was also well known outside London, but the Bosun was rarely a popular visitor for he maintained that as he was doing the Lord's work it was impious to enquire what happened to all the money he collected. There was probably little regret when in 1863 Burning Bush was finally consumed by death in Penzance at the age of eighty-one.

*Chapter Twenty*

## BETTER FREE THAN SOBER

'If I must take my choice . . . whether England shall be free or sober . . . I should say it would be better that England should be free than that England should be compulsorily sober.'
— Dr. William Magee, Bishop of Peterborough, 2nd May 1872

THE ORIGINAL inspiration of the Prohibition campaign had been American and during the succeeding half-century other developments in the United States also influenced the British temperance movement. In 1868 the Independent Order of Good Templars was introduced into England by Joseph Malins, an Englishman who had joined it in the United States. The Templars, apart from being teetotallers, bore a marked resemblance to the freemasons with their secrecy, elaborate ritual and costumes, honorific titles and tradition of mutual help. The Order met an obvious need; within six years there were nearly 4,000 Lodges, with more than 200,000 members, in England alone, and it supported its own Templar and Temperance Orphanage. The link with America seemed likely at one time to prove a source of weakness for a split in the parent society over the treatment of negroes spread to Great Britain. The litigious Dr. Lees thereupon formed a breakaway organisation, had himself appointed its Grand Worthy Chief Templar, and in 1878 went to law to obtain a declaration that his was the true British branch. The result was a repetition of the Gough fiasco, for his rival Chief Templar, Joseph Malins, was triumphantly vindicated by the court.

The coming of the Good Templars struck a death-blow to a

similar, but ailing, British movement, the Temperance Lifeboat Crews, which aimed to translate into practical terms that favourite metaphor about 'launching the temperance lifeboat'. The movement became linked, rather strangely, with Garibaldi's struggles to liberate and unify Italy. In 1861 the expenditure by a Staffordshire publican of £300 on improving his premises inflamed a group of local working men into forming the first Temperance Lifeboat Crew. 'Shall Garibaldi fight for the freedom of Italy and shall we not do something to save our country from ruin?' cried one teetotaller, and a 'Garibaldian lifeboat crew' was duly formed, dressed, in honour of their hero, in 'red flannel blouses, white duck trousers and a gold band round their caps or glazed straw hats'. In this strange outfit the crews paraded the streets, demonstrated outside public houses, and held ceremonial meetings with mysterious rituals involving various ranks from 'admiral' to 'cabin boy'. By 1864 there were some forty crews in Staffordshire, all 'throwing out lifelines' to reclaim drunkards, and the movement then spread to the rest of the country.

Among its leaders was Peter Winskill, one of the two chief temperance historians, whose father had been an alcoholic.[1] As 'Admiral of the Havelock Crew', he took part on Easter Monday, 1867, in a great demonstration in Sunderland, in which a model lifeboat was carried in procession to the Town Moor, escorted by a Wesleyan minister and 'a number of his trophies, reformed drunkards'. Like most metaphors carried too far, the lifeboat parallel proved troublesome. 'In some districts', admitted Winskill, 'considerable sums were spent on uniforms, model boats, etc., to add to the attractions . . . Many of the members were put to an expense their limited means would not allow and the spirit of rivalry, instead of being directed . . . to good works was too often devoted to display, thus engendering jealousy, envy, etc.' The Good Templar Order completed the movement's decline for 'the novelty of its regalia, its signs, passwords and other attractions . . . better

[1] The father of the other historian was, like his son, a Baptist minister, thus illustrating two major sources of teetotal support.

organisation and financial arrangements . . . made it more acceptable and popular'. By 1870 most of the lifeboats had foundered without trace, although songs about rowing to the rescue—Winskill himself published a book of *Lifeboat Crew Melodies*—remained popular at temperance rallies. The Good Templars later subscribed not for a model but for an actual lifeboat, *The Good Templar*, which saved many lives.

A campaign to recruit more women as militant temperance campaigners also spread to Great Britain from the United States, and a successful tour by a famous American militant, Mrs. Eliza 'Mother' Stewart, in 1876, led to the founding two years later of the British Women's Temperance Association. The members failed, however, to follow the lead of their American sisters, 'the praying women', who knelt outside saloons loudly imploring the Almighty to strike the saloon-keeper dead, and 'the axe-women' who attacked the bars and bottles within with hatchets. The B.W.T.A. remained unshakeably respectable; it needed the suffragette campaign to goad British women into violence.

In 1879 the Blue Ribbon movement also reached Britain after sweeping America. Its members were ardent teetotallers who wore a blue, or sometimes a red or white, ribbon to advertise their opinions, and held fervent, evangelistic meetings. Soon blue ribbons were sprouting on jackets and dresses all over the country and even appearing on postmen's uniforms, the Postmaster-General having ruled, when appealed to, that his staff could 'wear . . . all the colours of the rainbow so long as they were kept from the drink'.

In 1857 the United Kingdom Alliance, seeing the millennium of national prohibition unaccountably delayed, reluctantly decided to support a policy of local prohibition. It now aimed to carry through Parliament a Permissive Bill to empower each district to vote, if it wished, to suppress all licences within its borders. In the same year the Bill's best-known supporter, Wilfrid Lawson, entered the House of Commons. Lawson—he became Sir Wilfrid on his father's death in 1867—was born in 1829, the son of a Radical, nonconformist and, later, teetotal baronet with vast estates in Northumberland. His father had progressive opinions and in 1830 startled a public dinner by proposing the unusual toast 'May the heads of Don Miguel and King Ferdinand be severed from their bodies and rolled in the dust and the sooner the better.' Young Wilfrid was educated at home, imbibing his father's views along with the water served at his table.[1] He grew up a 'tall, well-shaped and vigorous lad', notable for his 'beauty of character . . . and generosity of heart', who 'had he not been a teetotaller . . . would have been known as "a jolly good fellow"'. He enjoyed riding, tennis, and shooting, and became Master of the Northumberland Foxhounds, a position which made him aware of another local recreation, hard drinking, for when a fox was killed his neighbour, John Peel, the original of the famous song, would often say 'It munna be a dry one' and the hunt would gallop off to the nearest inn and sometimes stay there drinking for days. Lawson remained fond of hunting and of hunting metaphors throughout his life, later predicting that if the temperance pack did not split up it would 'be in at the death of the liquor traffic'.

In 1859, at the age of twenty-eight, he was elected for Carlisle. 'I was from the beginning to the end', he recalled, 'a fanatic, a faddist and an "extreme man" in the House of Commons.' He made his maiden speech as seconder to Francis Berkeley's unpopular annual motion in favour of the ballot when the House was waiting to hear Lord Palmerston, and was forced to sit down by 'a regular storm of groans . . . cheers . . . laughter and indescribable noise'. His reputation as a champion of unpopular causes was confirmed when in 1872 he supported Sir Charles Dilke's motion to enquire into the Queen's expenditure,[2] and in 1878 attacked the expedition to Afghanistan, as yielding 'nothing but rocks and ruffians, stones and savages'. During the South African war he became a prominent pro-Boer and was involved in a riotous anti-war meeting in Exeter

[1] The conversion of Sir Wilfrid senior to teetotalism is described in Chapter Eight.

[2] Dilke ungratefully described Lawson to his friends as 'the wit of the public platforms but a dismal man . . . in private'.

Hall, subsequently losing his seat, though he later regained it.

Besides the imperialists, the chief target for what Disraeli called Lawson's 'gay wisdom' was the licensed trade. The country, he alleged, was governed by two heathen deities, 'Bacchus and Mars . . . the god of battles and the god of bottles'. His third great enemy was the House of Lords, 'that most absurd and mischievous of all institutions', full of 'thick-headed fellows'. 'Who', he asked, 'would be fool enough to employ an hereditary bootmaker?' Peers of first creation he dismissed as 'men who had killed a lot of people in some battle . . . or . . . had brewed a lot of beer', referring to the latter in a famous phrase as 'the beerage'.

The Bill which Lawson moved on 8th June 1864 was designed 'to enable owners and occupiers of property in certain districts to prevent the common sale of intoxicating liquors' by a two-thirds majority, but his fear that it would be killed by the Upper House proved premature, for it was promptly thrown out by the House of Commons by 292 to 35, every influential member of both parties voting against it. One M.P. described his 'misfortune' of spending five months in Maine, where 'instead of the people going to a bar to drink they popped down a cellar', wine was sipped furtively behind closed shutters and hints were dropped to guests about bottles of spirits hidden in cupboards. The Radical John Roebuck said that 'he had never heard a more mischievous Bill proposed . . . The House was called upon to abdicate its functions . . . The Bill, if passed, would . . . render England no place for a peaceable man to live in.' It was 'directed against the poor man' who 'could not lay in a stock of wine or spirits' or 'go for his beer to the next parish' and if Westminster voted for prohibition members might even find their own bars locked against them.

Lawson became overnight 'the best abused man in England', and in the following year narrowly lost his seat, *The Times* predicting that no other constituency would dare take him on. He spent the next three years stumping the country and by 1868, when he got back to Westminster, was a national figure.

In 1869 and regularly thereafter, he introduced his Bill again. Support gradually increased, but by 1873 the Bill's opponents were still able to quash it by 321 to 81.

The Bill's most famous enemy was probably Dr. William Magee, Bishop of Peterborough and later Archbishop of York. Magee favoured local licensing boards combining elected members and non-elected magistrates and on the government's great licensing Bill of 1872 he made the speech which, wrote a temperance historian, 'may possibly be the means of transmitting his memory to posterity'. 'If I must take my choice,' the Bishop told their lordships, 'and such it seems to me is the alternative offered by the Permissive Bill, whether England shall be free or sober, I declare, strange as such declaration may sound coming from one of my profession, that I should say it would be better that England should be free, than that England should be compulsorily sober.' To rub salt in the teetotallers' wounds, Dr. Magee then left the House to preside at the annual meeting of the Church of England Temperance Reformation Society, where he described drunkenness as 'the canker eating into the very heart of our nation'. Soon 'Better free than sober!' was being shouted by every heckler at temperance meetings and goading the teetotallers from every public house wall.

Four years later the Bishop returned to the charge in a debate on a motion by the Archbishop of Canterbury to set up a Select Committee on Intemperance, the result of a Memorial sent to him by 10,000 Anglican clergy, including eleven Bishops. After pointing out that 'he was not altogether that apologist of intemperance and defender of abandoned publicans which had been described', Magee stressed the basic inconsistency in the local option case: 'The liquor traffic was either right or wrong. If it were right they should allow it everywhere, if wrong they should forbid it everywhere.' It was 'decidedly unconstitutional that men should be governed not by a representative government but by a plebiscite and a vote of the streets', and would mean 'incessant quarrelling . . . in every town in the kingdom'. If a two-thirds majority were to decide local policy, many places would vote to expel the Roman Catholics rather than the publicans. It would be far better to campaign for sanitary reform, since 'The advocates of teetotalism told ... men to drink water but ... in many places for water they were given diluted sewage.'

To all this Lawson replied with wit rather than argument. 'Unconstitutional', he said, was 'a capital word, because nobody knows what it means', while 'The Bishop of Peterborough went into convulsions' at the proposal 'to refer the question to the streets' because 'he believes only in people who live in squares'. As for the 'incessant quarrelling' argument, 'It would be far better to have the fighting once a year than the public house rows every night.'

Perhaps the most weighty protest against the Bishop's remarks came from a fellow Anglican clergyman, the Rev. R. M. Grier, who had organised the great Memorial to the Archbishop of Canterbury. Was it 'government by a vote of the streets' when the ratepayers decided whether to set up a free library in a town, asked Grier, or chose the members for a School Board? Would the Bishop's demand for better amenities for the working class instead of prohibition really solve the problem? 'We have started clubs and recreation rooms and mechanics institutes ... the people are drinking and drunken still.' Nor was it only the poor who suffered. 'Even as I write, my Lord, a dear relative of my own is suffering intense pain from a fearful blow inflicted by an educated man in a state of intoxication.' But Bishop Magee was not impressed and four years later again infuriated the teetotallers by vetoing a proposal from the Church of England Temperance Society for a day of humiliation and prayer against drunkenness, on the grounds that it 'was a vice of a small minority'.

The teetotallers were also irritated by the argument that prohibition would wreck the national economy by cutting off overnight the £30 million a year from licence fees and liquor taxation, almost a third of the total budget. The Inland Revenue, complained Sir Wilfrid Lawson, seemed to think that 'the great object for which a man was sent into the world was to consume duty-paid liquor'. The lost money would easily be made up by savings on workhouses and prisons or, better still, by abandoning foreign wars and disbanding the Army and Navy.

More convincing was the fact, which the prohibitionists constantly pointed out, that many landlords who regularly voted against the Permissive Bill kept their own estates 'dry'. The Report on Intemperance of the Convocation of Canterbury in 1868 had noted that 'there are ... within the province of Canterbury, upwards of one thousand parishes in which there is neither public house nor beershop' and in 1874 the 'dry' Shaftesbury Park Estate was opened near Clapham Junction in South London, by Lord Shaftesbury with Lawson and the Prime Minister, Disraeli, in attendance. The estate had been built by a teetotal company to provide better working-class housing and to strike a blow against the trade, and by 1890 contained 1,200 houses, with a population of 6,000, while two similar estates had been built elsewhere. Although Disraeli had spoken of 'the triumph of an interesting effort for the moral elevation of the great body of the people', within a few years the residents were signing petitions for local off-licences, and there was a regular trek to the nearest public houses. The soap-producing 'model' village of Port Sunlight, Cheshire, provided a similar disappointment. Two years after the residents had been presented, in 1900, with an inn serving only temperance drinks, 80% of them voted in favour of it selling beer as well.

The most often quoted example of prohibition was the linen-manufacturing town of Bessbrook, near Newry in Northern Ireland, built by a Quaker on a 6,000-acre site in 1857, with well-ventilated mills, 'superior houses' and a school, to which all employees had to send their children. 'There is a dispensary and its medical club, a temperance hotel, with club and news-room', rhapsodised a teetotal writer, but 'no pawnshop ... lodging-house for tramps, nor ... police station'. Sunday morning found all its 4,000 inhabitants at church, noted another observer, so 'You don't see ... the intelligent and independent operative hanging about ... ragged, unshaven, unwashed, a short pipe in his mouth, the penny Radical newspaper in his pocket, waiting for the "public" to open.' The 'model town' seems, however, to have deteriorated rapidly for in 1908 its Rector reported that 'Bessbrook is ... the reverse of a "teetotal paradise". Drunkenness is very common ... There is a fair amount of crime ... much poverty ... and disease.' He was, he said, 'amused at the notion' that he 'had come from the most exemplary place in the British Islands'.

Inconvenient facts, like opposition, merely made Sir Wilfrid Lawson more obstinate. 'The "practical" men tell me,' he said in 1874, '"Oh, you will never carry it." "Never" is not a word in my dictionary.' By now he had become a licensed parliamentary humorist. When a fellow Liberal M.P., the brewer Michael Bass, jocularly offered him a pint of beer a day for life to drop his Bill, Lawson replied, 'I couldn't do it under a barrel', and he was the first to enjoy the joke when the manufacturer of a tea- and coffee-making machine for publicans named it 'The Wilfrid'. Why, he was fond of asking, if alcohol was a harmless food, did witnesses so often explain in court that a man had 'been drinking' and never that he had 'been eating'; and why were people always said to be 'the worse for drink' and never the better for it?

The trade retorted by describing Lawson as 'the pop bottle pump orator', 'the apostle of slops', 'the peregrinating pump handle', 'a confiscatory molly coddle', and 'that old cracked teapot'. When the Lord Mayor called a public meeting at Guildhall in 1871 to debate the Permissive Bill, Lawson was shouted down, and at a similar meeting in Exeter in the following year a man's ribs were broken, and Lawson and the Bishop of Exeter, Dr. Temple, were pelted with bags of flour so that 'at the close of the meeting', Lawson remarked, 'we looked like two sporting men returning from the Derby'.[1]

More serious, however, was the opposition of Joseph Livesey. In 1862 he told the Scottish Temperance League that the prohibition agitation was 'a terrible mistake. I found that many of my friends, as soon as this Permissive Bill was launched, slid

[1] Dr. Temple's statement at this meeting that he was a teetotaller was responsible for a famous newspaper headline: 'Bishop's strange confession'. He later became Archbishop of Canterbury.

away from our meetings . . . as everything would be done by a coup d'etat.' 'The buyers of drink are a majority', he pointed out in a pamphlet in 1873. 'Are they a likely lot to vote for clearing away all the public houses in their district?' The Alliance retorted with a letter to Livesey, now aged seventy-six, urging him to 'make some atonement' for his opposition before he died, so that 'the record of this mischief will not go down to posterity'.

Long before this the Permissive Bill had been replaced by a new policy, 'local veto' or 'local option', a phrase possibly coined by Mr. Gladstone. The local optionists proposed that a tenth of the local electors in any district could sign a requisition for a poll and if this in turn produced a two-thirds majority for 'No licence' all licences in the area would, after three years' warning, be withdrawn, though inns, hotels, restaurants and railway refreshment rooms would be exempt. A later version also allowed for 'limitation', with a quarter of the local licences being suppressed after each successful poll. Lawson, too, had changed his tactics, introducing in 1879 not a Bill but a Resolution, which was beaten by 252 to 164, a remarkable increase in support. The following year, after a Liberal victory in the general election, the tide turned. On 18th June 1880, a red-letter day in temperance history, Lawson's Resolution was carried by 229 to 203. 'The announcement', wrote a temperance historian, 'was received with loud applause from both the ministerial benches and the strangers gallery. The outer lobbies were crowded with excited and jubilant friends of the movement.'

Although the Prime Minister promised early action on the 'reform . . . so loudly called for',[1] licensing was not even mentioned in the Queen's speech in 1881 or 1882 and in 1883 Lawson hopefully introduced his Resolution again. This time the Prime Minister himself spoke in its support and the 'Ayes' swelled to 228 while the 'Noes' shrank to 141. Two years later, however, when the government fell, no Bill had yet appeared. 'The patience of numbers of temperance workers was

[1] Not, however, by English M.P.s, the majority of whom voted against the Resolution.

exhausted', wrote a disillusioned teetotaller, 'and they resolved no longer to pin their faith to any ministry or ally themselves with any political party.'

This bitterness was understandable for in recent years much effort had been expended in gaining support in Parliament. The Alliance had resolved in 1862 that it was 'absolutely necessary that the friends of temperance in every constituency organise their electoral influence' and a paper on 'Electoral Action' had advised local committees to organise lectures, launch petitions, write letters to the press and, above all, oppose at Registration Courts the claims of publicans and other known opponents to appear on the voters' list. A 'Vote for Vote' policy was recommended in which support was given only to candidates who promised to vote, if elected, for local option and members of the Good Templars were also told 'under no circumstances vote for those who are hostile'; if no candidate replied satisfactorily to the test question, the voter should stay at home. As Lawson told the Alliance annual meeting in 1875, they would succeed only when the Conservative or Liberal Whips warned the party leaders that the voters were in earnest. Then, he predicted, 'You will see them all rushing to support the Permissive Bill' and one might even find 'the sacred names of Bass and Allsop transferred from the backs of bottles to the back of the . . . Bill'.

But the great change of heart never came and in 1887 the refusal of the Prime Minister, Lord Salisbury, to receive a prohibition deputation led to the foundation of an independent National Prohibition Party. It proved a total failure. At its first 'mass meeting' in the Memorial Hall, Farringdon Street, where thirteen years later the Labour Party was born, only fifty people turned up and they were soon divided on whether the Party should always put up its own candidates, while an ultramontane minority objected even to local option. The new Party existed thereafter only on paper, finally fading away, as will be mentioned later, after the first world war. A separate Scottish Prohibition Party, founded in 1901, had, as will be seen, slightly more success.

Some teetotallers now looked hopefully towards the Conservative government which had taken office in 1885, and in 1888 its Local Government Bill unexpectedly conceded the principle of local control over the number of public houses. The Bill, which created County Councils, empowered them to set up local Licensing Authorities, of representatives from both the district concerned and from other parts of the county, with the power to suppress licences. Because, however, the Bill provided for compensation from the rates for displaced licensees, the Alliance violently opposed it, Lawson describing it as 'This scheme for the confiscation of public money to enrich brewers and publicans'. The whole licensing plan was therefore dropped and a further local option Bill, introduced by Lord Randolph Churchill in 1890, also foundered on the principle of compensation, which Lawson insisted must be fought to the death. On this issue the short-lived alliance between teetotallers and Conservatives finally split and after much badgering, local option was finally accepted as official party policy by the Liberals in the Newcastle Programme of 1890, on which two years later they came back to power.

What followed was all too familiar. In 1893 the Chancellor of the Exchequer, Sir William Harcourt, duly introduced the government's Liquor Traffic (Local Control) Bill, but owing to Parliament's absorption in Home Rule, it never achieved a second reading and two years later a milder Bill was also abandoned. Its only result was to turn into a rout the Liberal defeat in the subsequent election in which Harcourt and 100 others lost their seats.

The beaten Liberals blamed the prohibitionists for 'the catastrophe' and many repudiated local option; the prohibitionists blamed the trade. 'King Beer threw himself into the contest', said Lawson. 'Drink swept the country more thoroughly than it had ever done before.' There were dark hints that Gladstone's successor, Lord Rosebery, had shares in an Edinburgh brewery and was half-hearted about local option, like other 'Liberal liquor men'.

Perhaps the most effective argument in favour of local option was its appeal to local patriotism. 'The people of England are striving to get back again that local freedom when a knot of English farmers used to meet in "moot" around the village tree', wrote one Cornishman in 1883. 'Let the voice of the people decide', pleaded the local optionists' campaign song.

This will put the thing to rout,
Vote it out!

urged another temperance hymn. The scheme's opponents meanwhile invoked the claims of freedom. The Permissive Bill, said one, was 'a Bill to permit you to prevent me doing what you don't like and I do'. 'The text of the local optionists is "Give the people the power"', one St. Ives nonconformist minister, a worthy successor to Jonathan Turner, bravely told his congregation in 1885. 'Our reply is, *the people have the power* ... There is not a man in St. Ives need taste a drop of strong drink unless he wishes ... but ... my feeling is that my neighbour has the same right ... to a house in which to drink his beer undisturbed by me, as I have to a house in which to pray undisturbed by him.'

The local option campaign never recovered from the successive defeats the Liberals suffered in championing it and was further discredited when only five of the twenty-four members of the Royal Commission on Licensing in 1899 felt it even deserved a trial. In the same year one Liberal M.P., goaded beyond endurance by teetotallers on his constituency executive, resigned his seat, 'appealing to the electors to confirm his opposition to the Veto Bill'. The lesson of the resulting Osgoldcross, Yorkshire, by-election, was clear. In a straight fight with a Radical temperance reformer, the anti-veto member was returned by a majority of two to one. The teetotallers, mysteriously, claimed this crushing defeat as a victory, *The Western Temperance Herald* expressing the hope that it would put an end to the 'tendency to belittle local veto in certain Liberal circles' and would silence 'the senseless chatter about dropping this measure out of the Liberal programme', and to the 'very foolish articles and letters' attacking it which often appeared in the chief Liberal organs, *The Daily News* and *The Westminster Gazette*.

In 1906 Sir Wilfrid Lawson died, of bronchitis and old age. Although England and Wales still stood firm against local option, his followers scored a belated victory when in 1913 a Bill imposing it upon Scotland was forced through the House of Lords under the Parliament Act, although the first polls under the new law were not to be held until 1920. Their results are described in a later chapter. In 1930 the Scottish Licensing Commission concluded that experience had not 'justified this experiment', but despite the efforts of Scottish licensees, as their trade paper put it, 'to achieve freedom', local option still remained in force in 1968—a monument which Sir Wilfrid would no doubt have preferred to the statue which his admirers raised to his memory on the Embankment.

*Chapter Twenty-one*

## A LICENCE TO DO HARM

'The licence of a man to do harm to his fellow subjects.'

— Sir Wilfrid Lawson, 12th December 1881

WHILE THE local option campaign was making—or failing to make—progress, other temperance reformers were pressing forward their favourite remedies for drunkenness. Although there were fewer drunks in the streets—drunk and disorderly cases per 1,000 population in London in 1860 numbered only half the figure for 1834—the temperance campaign had made people more aware of those which remained, and the teetotallers were therefore incensed when between 1860 and 1863 the Chancellor of the Exchequer, Mr. Gladstone, introduced a series of measures making drinking easier and cheaper. These followed a Commercial Treaty with France abolishing or lowering numerous customs duties, for Gladstone hoped to recoup by increased sales the resulting loss in revenue. In 1860 his Refreshment Houses Act gave restaurants the right to sell wine, and in 1861 he created the 'grocers' licence', which enabled virtually any shopkeeper to obtain a licence to sell wines or spirits for 'off' consumption, beer being added in 1863. Gladstone's aims were, he explained to the Commons, to assist sobriety by placing 'wine within the reach . . . of the lowest order of the middle classes and . . . the better portion of the working classes', and to encourage people to drink 'in conjunction with meals'. Sir Wilfrid Lawson commented caustically that the Chancellor 'suggested that an additional supply of wine would make people sober' while even the Tory Marquess of Salisbury gibed that Gladstone's 'specific for the cure of intemperance . . . was . . . of a somewhat recondite and subtle character—namely allowing brandy to be sold by grocers'.

Complaints about 'gin from the grocers' became a feature of temperance propaganda. In 1872 it was said in the House of Commons that in Ipswich one grocer's shop sold 100 bottles of gin a week to women shopping, while in Salford female customers were given a free drink and then told that further orders could go down on the bill as 'groceries'. In 1877 the editor of *The Lancet*, then going through one of its anti-alcohol phases, collected nearly 1,000 signatures from doctors to a petition against the grocers' licence by which, it was said, 'female domestic servants are often enabled to obtain bottles of spirits, wine and beer . . . as "commission" on the household bills' and 'women . . . and children of respectable households' had been introduced to drinking. The Rev. J. M. Morrell's speaker's handbook in 1883 quoted an actual example: 'A lady, the wife of a respectable man' who, thanks to 'the wine obtained at the grocer's next door . . . was found wandering about the streets by night, scantily clad, begging brandy for a sick child—of course, it was for herself.'

Objections to the grocers' licence, though for different reasons, briefly united teetotallers and licensees, an alliance seen again in 1882 when another Liberal government agreed to drink being served on trains. Sir Wilfrid Lawson even quoted approvingly a publican who had called it 'a scheme for making people drunk at the rate of sixty miles an hour', while the Rev. J. M. Morrell had his usual cautionary tale ready, this time of a girl whose downfall began when ' "my mother gave me a bottle of diluted brandy to keep me warm on my journey to London" '.

The 1860s also saw, however, much legislation of which the temperance movement approved, including an Act forbidding the payment of miners' wages near licensed premises—a principle extended in 1883 to cover all trades—laws making small debts for drink irrecoverable at law and, in 1864, a Public House

Closing Act which shut all public houses in London on weekdays between 1 a.m. and 4 a.m. and was later extended to many other towns. All this seemed to the teetotallers, however, to be merely nibbling at the problem and the return of a Liberal government in the election of 1868, the first in which most working men in the towns had a vote, failed to lead to that immediate reckoning with the trade for which they had hoped. The new Prime Minister was not, his Home Secretary, Henry Bruce, complained, really interested in licensing reform. Gladstone's panacea was free trade, 'which the House won't have'.

The new restrictions on beer-houses, already mentioned, imposed in 1869, originated in a private member's Bill. It was not till April 1871 that Bruce at last introduced the government's own Intoxicating Liquors (Licensing) Bill, an enormous 177-clause document designed to reshape the existing law. It proposed, among much else, higher licence duties, a corps of special public house inspectors, and far shorter hours. Outside London closing at 10 p.m. would be compulsory and the justices would be empowered to impose even shorter hours if they wished, including all-day closing on Sunday. Most important of all, the Bill laid down a fixed scale of the number of licences in relation to population throughout the country. In ten years' time any licences above the permitted maximum might be suppressed without compensation, the granting of additional licences being subject to local option. Even licences which did survive would, a typical Gladstonian touch, be auctioned to the highest bidder.

Like many later Liberal governments, Gladstone's first ministry had greatly underestimated the nation's devotion to its beer. Within three weeks there were posters everywhere denouncing the Bill as 'based upon the principles of injustice and spoilation' and violating 'every known principle of English freedom'. A conference of publicans described it as 'vicious in its character, indefensible in its confiscation of the right of property' and the trade paper, *The Morning Advertiser*, called it 'a cold, calm, deliberate plan to rob the licensed victuallers of the fruits of their industry'. Eight hundred thousand people signed hastily organised petitions against the Bill and at by-elections later in the year the Liberals lost seat after seat.

While the trade thundered against the Bill's violence, the temperance movement sneered at its feebleness. The Alliance had warned that if the government's plan did not include local veto on old licences, as well as new ones, 'Thank you, sir, for nothing, we shall say' and it was as good as its word, contemptuously dismissing the Bill as 'deserving of utter condemnation by every temperance reformer'. Soon the moderates were pleading with the extremists. 'We should commit an imprudence of the first character were we to risk this Bill', warned Cardinal Manning. 'It would be cruel after having stirred Mr. Bruce to take this step to leave him in the lurch', pleaded an M.P. Reluctantly, a national conference of leading temperance organisations decided to support the Bill, but it was too late. Only five weeks after its introduction it was dropped.

In May 1872 the government tried again with a much milder measure, though not with much enthusiasm, the government spokesman explaining candidly that 'if the promised Bill was not introduced we should have lain under the imputation of having no plan upon the subject'. The Bill, with little opposition, became law in the following month. The Intoxicating Liquor (Licensing) Act, 1872, besides generally tightening up the law, forbade the sale of spirits for 'on' drinking to children under sixteen, and laid down new opening hours—5 a.m. to midnight in London, an hour less, at the justices' discretion, elsewhere. But it was what the Liberals had threatened, rather than what they had done, which was remembered and when, in 1874, the government went to the country, it was decisively beaten. Gladstone dramatically, though with some exaggeration, exclaimed in a letter to his brother, 'We have been borne down in a torrent of gin and beer.'

The new House of Commons was nicknamed 'The Publicans' Parliament' and when the government prolonged opening hours by half-an-hour the teetotallers said that this was the trade's reward for winning the election for the Conservatives, although modern research has shown that many publicans still supported the Liberals. The 150 Liberal candidates who were local optionists had, however, done particularly badly and the trade as a whole was beginning to identify itself with the Conservatives. By the end of the century it probably *was* contributing heavily to Conservative Party funds and nearly every public house *had* become an unofficial Conservative committee-room[1] for after 1872 a positive mania for licensing reform seized all sections of the Liberal Party. 'Everybody has now a licensing Bill', commented Sir Wilfrid Lawson in 1883. 'A man is looked upon as rather an inferior sort of fellow if he has not a licensing scheme.' A few years earlier only one such Bill appeared every two or three sessions; now each year there were twenty or more. Lawson despised them all. Any licence was, he said, 'the licence of a man to do harm to his fellow subjects', but 'every temperance reformer has to go through the licence epidemic (like the distemper with dogs) before he becomes a vigorous and valiant soldier'. His fellow members were not discouraged; in 1890 twenty-five more licensing Bills were introduced, fourteen of them on a single day.

Some Bills were thinly veiled attempts to secure prohibition while many schemes were based on the myth of the 'drink-pushing publican' and its corollary, that drunkenness could be ended by removing the profit motive from the sale of alcohol. The most popular, the Gothenburg System, took its name from a Swedish port, which in size and character roughly resembled Cardiff. All the spirit licences in Gothenburg had in 1875 been handed over to a trust company, or Bolag, run by unpaid directors. The company received only a tiny fixed return on its capital, all other profits going to the town treasury and local agricultural society. It made every effort to discourage customers through higher prices, shorter hours, which ended at 7 or 8 p.m., and strict rules against the manager, who received the profits from the food sold but not from the drink, giving

[1] Only unofficial, however. The use of public houses as committee rooms during national and local elections was made illegal in 1883 and 1884.

credit or serving several glasses to the same person. Soon no licensing reformer's education was complete until he had visited Gothenburg to inspect for himself the Bolag's somewhat grim houses, identified only by a black signboard, their all-male, all-adult clientele, which marched in, swallowed a single drink at a gulp and marched out again, and their drinking mugs appropriately shaped like medicine glasses. An early visitor was Joseph Chamberlain, who in 1876, at the age of forty, became a Liberal M.P. To the local 'gas and water socialism' which he had long advocated, Chamberlain now added a plan for 'beer and spirit socialism', to harness municipal enterprise to the cause of temperance reform. Local authorities, he pointed out to Birmingham Corporation in January 1877, already controlled the workhouses, the jails, the asylums and the police force. Why not also give them control of the trade which kept all these institutions busy, and which led to 1,000 disorderly citizens being jailed every year and a quarter of the police force being hauled before the Watch Committee for being drunk on duty? Municipal ownership would mean, too, 'a profit to the ratepayers' and better beer. To support his argument Chamberlain produced samples of ordinary beer tested by the public analyst, 'all very dark in colour, of a harsh disagreeable taste and unusually bitter', and a fine, sparkling specimen of the proposed municipal brew. By forty-six votes to ten his colleagues, impressed, voted for municipalising the drink trade, but at Westminster the Chamberlain name counted for less and a few months later his fellow M.P.s rejected the scheme by an overwhelming majority. Municipal ownership remained, however, a popular remedy, the Bishop of Chester in 1893 producing a particularly neat scheme, under which the profits of publicly-owned taverns would be used to build 'bright and attractive temperance houses' to drive them out of business.

As Parliament steadfastly refused to pass the necessary enabling legislation no local authority ever did take over its public houses, but there were many experiments by private individuals in what was called 'disinterested management'. In these the clergy took a leading part. The first 'parish pub' was opened in the Warwickshire village of Hampton Lucy by the rector, the Rev. Osbert Mordaunt, in 1876. His predecessor had bequeathed to his parish of 450 people its only public house, *The Boar's Head*, and Mordaunt, resisting teetotal demands to close it down, decided to run it on 'model' or 'improved' lines. The previous unsatisfactory tenant was dismissed and one of the rectory servants installed as salaried manager. The villagers accepted a ban on credit and much shorter opening hours, but when Mordaunt stopped the sale of spirits he was warned that the winter death rate was bound to soar. Fortunately only one adult death occurred in the village that year, and the persistent demands of women for 'medicinal' gin and brandy were 'met by adding spirits to the store of simple medicines kept for the use of the villagers at the Rectory'. Mordaunt's greatest problem was obtaining drinkable beer, only solved after a long struggle against poor quality and short measure, and he had constantly to change his brewer to keep the standard high. Protected from competition by the squire, who promised to prevent any rival inn opening, *The Boar's Head* soon had a modest turnover of about £300, of which about £50 was profit, £25 of this being earmarked for the organist's salary and the rest being spent on public purposes like the choir treat, a better water supply and a reading-room.

Although Mordaunt's experience helped to correct the teetotal illusion that the publican's licence was automatically a licence to print money, he insisted, in pamphlets and to the Royal Commission on Licensing, that the experiment was a success.[1] The teetotallers, however, constantly criticised *The Boar's Head* and steadfastly opposed all similar ventures. As one explained, 'If ... public houses are made so respectable, people will go there who would not think of using the present public house.' Diverting the profits to the poor, said another, was 'philanthropy through the pot-house'. Joseph Malins, head of the Good Templars, was a particularly implacable enemy of

[1] *The Boar's Head* has since 1950 been run by a local brewery. The income from the lease is used for parochial purposes, like financing the church music.

'disinterested management' and related with relish in 1902 what happened to one apostate member, who was persuaded by its new owner to run *The Anchor* at Scaynes Hill in Sussex. 'The Christian Good Templar left the Lodge to become the praying manager of the clerical public house. In about a year the clergyman turned him out as a drunkard.' At *The Fox and Pelican*, 'opened under clerical and titled auspices' in one Hampshire village, alleged Malins, 'in a few weeks drunkenness is palpable; one of its enthusiastic patrons and supporters has to be conveyed in a wheelbarrow by a policeman'.

The teetotallers also maintained that a council eager for municipal improvements might 'push' the sale of drink even harder than an ordinary publican. The president of the National British Women's Temperance Association suggested that a visitor to such a town might be told 'We have . . . drunk ourselves into the electric light and now we are going to drink ourselves into a new cricket ground and pavilion.' Joseph Malins even insisted that it would become impossible to get a licence suppressed, since 'a town council will defend its own public houses', and that 'police supineness' would be replaced by 'police paralysis'.

The failure of the movement for municipal ownership led to a search for other ways of taking the profit motive out of the drink trade. The resulting schemes, often based on a rural parish and with an aura of paternalism, made a particular appeal to the clergy and to members of the House of Lords. In 1896 the Bishop of Chester launched the People's Refreshment Houses Association, financed by £1 shares on which the maximum return was 5%—later 7½%—though to prevent infiltration by brewers or teetotallers every shareholder had only one vote. The P.R.H.A. opened, or bought up and improved, public houses all over England and Wales, but especially in the south, and by 1901 had eighteen, where one could buy 'tea, coffee, temperance drinks or light refreshments, just as easily as beer or spirits'. But not all managers showed the right attitude. The manageress of *The Red Lion* at Broad Clyst, Devon, was criticised in a report for showing 'an evident desire . . . for "trade"', unlike the landlord of *The Plymstock Inn*, Devon, where, noted the local vicar, 'many of those who sat and drank by the hour under the old régime... now think it too respectable for them and stay at home'. The manager of *The Plume of Feathers*, at Sherborne in Dorset, too, 'was... careful from the first to discourage loafing', so that 'at first the old customers left and others were slow to take their place'. The P.R.H.A. achieved none the less a modest profit of £1,100, from which £5 or £10 donations were made to various good causes in the villages concerned, from the fund for providing street lamps to the local flower show.

Many trusts were owned by the villagers themselves, like the Grayshott and District Refreshment Association in Hampshire, which built *The Fox and Pelican*. This had already incurred Joseph Malins's wrath and two other observers who visited it around 1901 were not favourably impressed, for it provided draughts, dominoes and newspapers for its customers, and 'the association of games and other recreations with the sale of intoxicants is surely to be... discouraged'. They strongly approved, however, of the weak beer and the manager's attempts to close on Sunday at 8 p.m., and to refuse service to known drunks. So far his efforts had failed, for 'the district appears to contain a somewhat unusual proportion of lawless spirits'—the same desperadoes, no doubt, who liked to play dominoes over their beer. The authors admitted that Sunday closing and shorter hours would be 'probably suicidal' unless the trust enjoyed a local monopoly. This was indeed the fatal weakness of many trusts—the tendency, instead of providing a superior public house, to make it the thin end of the teetotal wedge. This probably did more harm to the movement than all Joseph Malins's denunciations.

The most successful trust of all was never really part of the temperance movement. In 1901 Earl Grey, a future Governor-General of Canada, began a campaign for restoring country inns, many of which had degenerated with the coming of railways into mere drinking dens. 'We do not', he said, 'ask the legislature to come to our assistance. We are content to make the best use of the opportunities which the law allows us.' Grey's plan was for every county to form its own trust to buy up and restore suitable properties and to run them on 'improved' lines, and he pressed his plan upon the lords-lieutenant of various counties and at public meetings throughout 1902 and 1903. Several county trusts were formed, but the most enduring proved the Hertfordshire Trust, which in 1904 took over and improved its first inn, *The Waggon and Horses* at Ridge Hill, near St. Albans, installing a former London policeman as manager. The inn, which also provided three comfortable bedrooms, proved a great success. Its tea-garden was so great an attraction to cyclists that soon the demand for tea was draining the garden well dry and extra barrels of water had to be delivered by the brewery which supplied the beer. Within twelve months the inn's takings from non-alcoholic sales made up 68% of its turnover. The Hertfordshire Trust acquired further properties with equal success and after absorbing several other county trusts became in 1919 a public company, Trust Houses Ltd., controlling 100 hotels and inns.[1]

In a debate in the House of Lords in 1904 many peers boasted of the success of their local trusts. In one hotel the non-drink income had risen from a few pence a day to three pounds. At another, a brewer's drayman had been seen drinking a cup of coffee. Many working men, though still ashamed to order non-alcoholic drinks when the bar was full, often did so when it was empty and the new houses were much less willing to serve half-drunk customers than the old. The Chairman of one Trust described how an 'improved' house near Goodwood had turned away dozens of racing men for this reason. Finding suitable property, particularly in the back-streets of the cities where the need was greatest, was the real problem. The Bishop of London, when running a social work settlement in the East End, had offered £10,000 for one well-sited house; it had gone to a brewer for £50,000.

[1] The company now owns nearly 200 hotels and the income from some shares is still used for charitable purposes. *The Waggon and Horses*, victim of a new trunk road, was given up in 1958.

Public houses run by trusts often refused to serve children and their action encouraged a nation-wide agitation for the imposition of a legal minimum age-limit. Although *The Morning Advertiser* bravely asked, 'Where is the harm in children being sent to the public house for their parents' beer, or being taken into the public house by their parents?' most temperance reformers believed that such contact inevitably involved corruption. Indignant teetotallers could often be seen ostentatiously counting children leaving the public house and collections of slides showing ragged little mites anxiously clutching foaming jugs of beer could be borrowed for magic-lantern shows. The physical danger to 'child messengers', as they were known, was even more apparent than the moral risk. 'In the course of a year', reported *The Birmingham Daily Mail*, 'hundreds of accidents occur to young children . . . engaged in fetching beer for . . . their parents. Sometimes they are knocked down in crossing the horse-roads, but generally the accident is caused by the youngsters falling with jugs and bottles in their hands.' One six-year-old girl, according to a teetotal pamphlet, was crippled for life by a tram because she dared not hurry across the tramlines for fear of being beaten for spilling her father's beer.

If brutal parents were driving their innocent offspring to the public house, unscrupulous publicans, according to the teetotallers, were busily enticing them in. 'On a recent Sunday morning', wrote a police court missionary in *The Wigan Observer* in 1897, 'from 12.30 to one o'clock I saw 164 children ranging from eight down to three years of age, go in a licensed house and come out with beer and sweets. Some of these went round the corner, looked at the sweets and sipped some of the beer.' The Chief of Police at Manchester revealed in the same year that 'of 2,992 houses in the city . . . 1,112 houses give sweets or other small inducements to children', and there were many complaints about publicans who distributed penny whistles, sticks of rock bearing the brewer's name and even cheap cigarettes, known as 'halfpenny puffs', to child customers. Some, it was said, installed special steps leading up to the bar for children too small to see over the top. Although the trade insisted that free gifts merely caused a child to buy father's beer from one house rather than another, and some bold apologists argued that sweets were an aid to temperance since no child sucking a toffee could sip beer as well, the 'drinking children' campaign did the publicans' image considerable harm. Some began to display notices reading 'No children under 13 served here', and unofficial pressure to stop children being served was often put on licensees by the police and the licensing justices.

The controversy produced some ingenious arguments on both sides. To the trade's contention that it was a father's right to have his beer fetched for him, the teetotallers replied that this was unfair to bachelors. The temperance argument about protecting children was countered by the suggestion that 'an intelligent boy of eleven or twelve' was less likely to get into trouble at the public house than a sixteen-year-old, 'the age at which boys and girls begin to sow their wild oats'. On the teetotallers' side there was undoubtedly much exaggeration, but grim fact, colourful falsehood, and, above all, persistence, yielded their reward. In 1901 the 'Anti-Sipping Act' was passed, forbidding the sale of drink for 'off' consumption to anyone under fourteen except in sealed vessels, the origin of the paper seals still seen on some beer bottles. 1908 brought a greater victory, the Children's Act, which made it illegal for anyone under fourteen to enter a bar, thus excluding women with infants and young children, and causing the construction of separate 'jug and bottle departments'. It also became illegal to give alcohol to a child under five except as medicine; no longer could crying babies be plied with gin in the street. The minimum age for 'on' drinking was raised to eighteen in 1923 by Lady Astor's Act, the same limit being extended to 'off' sales in 1953.

What, apart from 'saving the children', had the teetotallers achieved during Queen Victoria's reign? Dr. Lees had estimated in 1888 that there were five million teetotallers in a population of thirty-seven million but this was obviously an exaggeration, unless children were included. It was in fact the vast armies of the Band of Hope which explained the discrepancy between the teetotallers' impressive strength on paper and their poor performance at elections. The Church of England Temperance Society advanced a more realistic figure, 222,000 active temperance society members, and these, according to one 'moderation' expert in 1903, were 'earnest persons belonging to the middle and lower-middle classes, eminently respectable, and never in any danger whatever of falling victims to drunkenness'.

A survey of *The Present Position of the Temperance Movement*, in *The Western Temperance Herald* in 1898, struck a careful balance sheet. 'We are not so successful as we used to be in getting public meetings', complained the author. 'We print the bills but the benches are empty . . . We have no Gough nor Father Mathew.' On the other hand, 'The old class of medical prescribers is dying out . . . Everywhere the abstainer is one point ahead of his rival in applying for a situation . . . Two-thirds at least of nonconformist ministers and one-third of the clergy are pledged abstainers; not three in a hundred of students in the colleges take wine . . . To apply for a licence at a Church bazaar now raises a howl of execration.'

The secretary of the Western Temperance League contrasted in the same year 'the good old days when . . . there used to be an . . . influential temperance society in every town or village' with the present position, when 'the one society if it exists at all is . . . weak and ineffective because every church and chapel has a . . . temperance organisation of its own and . . . the Templars, Rechabites and Sons of Temperance and the British Women's Temperance Association have each a branch'. The remedy was joint action for 'aggressive work' through local United Temperance Councils. But it would be a struggle, for 'there are now thousands of shareholders in brewery and distillery companies and many of these are Members of Parliament'.

This last subject had been a particularly sore point since 1886 when Guinness's Brewery had become a public company. 'The eagerness to secure the bare chance of an allotment', it was said, 'recalled the wild excitement of the railway mania' and the £6 million issue had been fifty times oversubscribed. The tee-totallers were shocked to find temperance reformers and non-conformist clergy among the applicants. From the pulpit once occupied by Gough the great evangelical preacher, the Rev. Charles Spurgeon, thundered his denunciation of fellow Christians who accepted brewery dividends. 'What', he demanded, 'did they wash ... such leprous and defiling gold ... in ... before they took it?'

The same decade brought another, very different, problem for the temperance movement. 'Let wine prevail at public banquets during this year of Jubilee', warned one writer in 1887, 'and thousands will never live a decent life again ... Does loyalty demand that they—reformed drunkards—shall rouse again the demon taste for drink? ... The total abstainers of the British Empire are perfectly loyal to their country and queen', but 'We cannot drink the queen's health without promoting national intemperance'. There were, concluded the author, four alternatives: singing the national anthem instead of drinking the loyal toast; declaiming 'Long live the queen!' over an empty glass; substituting Frank Wright's 'admirable unfermented wine'; or drinking to Her Majesty in that noblest of beverages, water.

No such dilemma had presented itself when the teetotallers had held their own jubilee five years earlier. The British Temperance League had celebrated the fiftieth anniversary of the signing of the original pledge by holding its annual meeting at Preston, where Joseph Livesey, frail, white-haired and silent, made a brief appearance before being driven round the town in triumph with the only other survivor of the original 'seven men', John King. In London the National Temperance League's Jubilee Fete had packed the Crystal Palace with 43,000 enthusiastic non-drinkers, while the famous massed Band of Hope choirs, 4,500 strong, made it echo with temperance songs, 'the condition of taking part ... being firstly abstinence and secondly a capacity for singing.'

*Chapter Twenty-two*

## A FIGHT TO THE DEATH

'The temperance party ... are engaged in a strife to the death with ... the trade.'

— LORD ROSEBERY, House of Lords, 26th November 1908

THE GROWTH in the numbers of those with a financial interest in the drink trade was one reason why between 1900 and 1914 the temperance movement was dominated by the great controversy over whether compensation should be paid to brewers and licensees whose premises were compulsorily shut down. The issue had already a long and complicated history. Bruce's ill-fated Licensing Bill of 1871, which did not provide for compensation, had been killed by opposition from the trade. The licensing sections of Ritchie's Local Government Bill of 1888, which provided for compensation from licence-revenue and the rates, had been wrecked by the teetotallers. The Conservative Chancellor, George Goschen, who in 1890 had formed a fund to buy up licences by agreement from an increased duty on beer and spirits, had been forced to divert the 'whisky-money' to technical education instead. Finally, Sir William Harcourt's unsuccessful Bill for local option, without compensation, in 1893 had merely helped to bring down the Liberal government and make permanent the alliance between the trade and the Tories. A mock-trial—a device borrowed from the temperance movement—published in 1892, reflected trade opinion clearly enough. The Rt. Hon. E. W. Goldstone, M.P., and Sir Gwillium Harecaught, M.P., arraigned before the High Court of Public Conscience, are confronted in cross-examination by Mr. Consistency, Q.C., with their past remarks

JOSEPH MALINS IN HIS ROBES AS RIGHT WORTHY GRAND TEMPLAR, 1880

*Blackie and Son Ltd.*

SIR WILFRED LAWSON

*Blackie and Son Ltd.*

NATHANIEL CARD

GEORGE CRUIKSHANK

A TEMPERANCE RALLY NEAR CHESTER, 1858

*Radio Times Hulton Picture I*

ARCHBISHOP (LATER CARDINAL) MANNING ADMINISTERIN
THE PLEDGE ON CLERKENWELL GREEN, 1872

in favour of compensation, defending themselves with the somewhat lame explanation that 'The teetotal vote is now a large one and we cannot afford to ignore it.' It needs only supporting evidence from Sir Wilful Dawson that his sole knowledge of the trade comes from a single night in a public house, which compared favourably with any temperance hotel, to ensure that Barons Equity, Right and Justice uphold the trade's claim for 'fair consideration'.

In 1896 Lord Salisbury's government had appointed a Royal Commission on Licensing and though Thomas P. Whittaker, one of its members, scornfully dismissed it as 'merely a device for staving off the evil day' of effective legislation, in the following three years it carried out the most thorough inquest into the drink problem ever undertaken. The twenty-four members divided in roughly equal proportions into brewers, teetotallers and 'neutrals' so it was not surprising that, although the Commission heard nearly 300 witnesses, most sessions ended in disagreement, often only resolved by the casting vote of the chairman, Lord Peel. The Commission's final report, in July 1899, appeared in two parts, and contained reservations by no fewer than fifteen members. The Majority Report, signed by seventeen members, recommended stricter control over licensed premises, harsher punishment for drunkards, and various minor reforms, including shorter hours on Sundays. The Minority Report signed by nine members—two had also signed the Majority Report—demanded shorter weekday hours, total Sunday closing at the justices' discretion, and a drastic reduction in facilities for the sale of drink. Although the whole Commission agreed that 'A gigantic evil remains to be remedied', on compensation it was hopelessly split. The Majority Report favoured it, on generous terms; the Minority Report signatories, including Lord Peel, the Archbishop of Canterbury and Thomas P. Whittaker, considered that on this basis it could not 'for a moment be entertained'.

The argument about the principle of compensation was now tending to obscure the real question of whether fewer public houses meant fewer drunks. As the author of one pamphlet rightly complained, 'both parties . . . seem to have rather hastily accepted the notion that if you reduce the number of licences you promote temperance . . . Shut up one house and you send its customers to another. This other house becomes more valuable and will be able to increase its attractions . . . There will be more drinking in one large attractive house than in three or four smaller, ill-appointed ones.' The results of a careful correlation of the number of licensed houses per thousand population and the statistics for drunkenness convictions over the whole country during a ten-year period, revealed the 'remarkable fact that as a rule the districts with least convictions have the most licensed houses; the places with most convictions have the fewest . . . In the two districts where drunkenness has increased there has been a decided decrease in the number of licensed houses.'

Such evidence was, inevitably, ignored. Most teetotallers who sat on a licensing bench—some would not do so on principle—seized every opportunity to refuse a new licence or to renew an old one, or to impose the most onerous conditions the law allowed. As any citizen could oppose an application for a licence,[1] local United Temperance Councils, armed with guides like *How to Shut Up a Public House*, carried on such a successful warfare against the trade at the annual brewster sessions that many licence holders failed even to appeal to the higher court of quarter sessions. *The United Temperance Gazette* for December 1898 printed a typical, gleeful report, *In the Licensing Courts*:

> Blackburn was the centre of excitement on the 25th August. The temperance party of the town had determined to . . . oppose the renewal of every licensed house which was within fifty yards of another . . . After a long and fierce fight the justices refused to renew two of the licences objected to . . . September 5th, the Licensing Justices at Devonport held their annual meeting. Mr. George Blaiklock . . . opposed six new applications on behalf of residents and the Royal Naval Temperance Society . . . All six applications . . . were refused.

[1] The right still exists, though now rarely exercised.

The teetotallers sometimes joined forces with the trade. At Reading, 'a city which could afford to part with a few licensed premises, there being one to 220 of the population ... the Reading Temperance Council agreed with the Beer Retailers in wishing no increase, and the combined entreaty was so effectual that the magistrates hardened their hearts to all newcomers, except one'. Elsewhere, as in 'the prosperous and clean little town of Hitchin', Hertfordshire, which already had thirteen public houses 'in one street and in one case three actually side by side', it was unrelenting war. Here the United Temperance Council forced fifteen publicans to apply for licences to sell beer alone, instead of full licences also covering wine and spirits. 'The result', gloated the reporter, 'is a depreciation of the value of the property.'

The slogan of this campaign of direct action had a distinctly unmartial ring: 'Remember Sharp v. Wakefield'. In 1887 Miss Sharp had sued the chairman of the Kendal, Westmorland, licensing bench, named Wakefield, after its refusal to renew the licence of a public house she owned. The grounds were not mismanagement, but merely that it was surplus to local requirements and in an isolated situation which made it difficult to supervise, and after four years of litigation the House of Lords, in 1891, decided they were reasonable. 'The grant of a licence', ruled the Lord Chancellor in an often-quoted pronouncement, 'is expressly within the discretion of the magistrates.' After 1899 many justices who had held their hand while the Royal Commission was sitting recalled this famous dictum. Often pressure was put on brewers and publicans to surrender some licences as the price of being granted others. 'The Farnham case', in Surrey in 1902, which involved the forced closure of six public houses, became another *cause célèbre* as did events in Birmingham where the brewers were coerced into surrendering fifty licences and arranging compensation among themselves. Temperance reformers began hopefully to issue lists of places they considered over-stocked with inns and taverns. Did their county, the author of *The Licensing Question in Hampshire* asked his fellow magistrates, in 1902, really need more public houses than other rural areas? Why did the 260 people of Appleshaw need four inns and the 743 inhabitants of Hurstbourne Tarrant six? If a pleasure resort like Bournemouth could manage with one licence to every 1,600 people, why did a sleepy cathedral city like Winchester need more than ten times as many? It was the threats implied in such pamphlets, rather than what was actually done, that alarmed the trade. Belatedly it realised that planned suppression, with compensation, was better than arbitrary closure overnight and petitions poured into Parliament for a change in the law.

The Conservative Party, returned to power in 1900, was not the feeble tool of the brewers the teetotallers often alleged. There were many Tory temperance reformers and in 1902 the government greatly tightened up the law on drunkenness. In introducing its major Licensing Bill in 1904 the Home Secretary, Aretas Akers Douglas, even admitted that 'according to the strict letter of the law . . . licences are held for a year only'. He argued, however, that as they had been 'yearly renewed . . . almost as a matter of course' and the state had collected death duties on their full value, compensation ought to be paid, particularly as the present uncertainty was driving 'many men of good . . . character' out of the trade. The government therefore proposed that whenever a licence was suppressed, except for misconduct, the owner should be compensated from a fund financed by a levy on the trade of from £1 a year on the humblest beer-house to £150 on a prosperous hotel, which would yield up to £1 million a year.

Although one Conservative back-bencher called the Bill 'an effort to settle the question of compensation on reasonable lines which . . . moderate men would support', this was an issue on which moderate men were few. The extreme teetotallers argued that the natural state of the trade was to be prohibited. If the state, in its unwisdom, did grant exemptions from this law to a few men, the 'monopoly value' of this right belonged to the public and had been stolen from them, a view summed up in the slogan, 'Why compensate a thief?' Even more serious, the Bill acknowledged the right of the publican to have his licence renewed so that, in Sir Wilfrid Lawson's phrase, it 'established the public house for ever'. T. P. Whittaker was equally critical of ministers, declaring that 'It was the hangman's whip of the publican's vote that brought them to the brewers' heel.' The Bill, however, went through the Commons by 217 votes to 129 and became law barely two weeks after reaching the House of Lords. A protest from the noble chairman of one Public House Trust at 'being asked to consider in forty-eight hours a measure that entirely changes the history of licensing legislation for 300 or 400 years', and Lord Peel's warning that 'every rotten beer-house... will be stimulated into prolonged existence by... this potent drug of compensation', were ignored. So, too, were some striking speeches from the Bishops, determined, as one said, to prove that the Church of England was not 'comparatively lukewarm' about temperance. The Bishop of London described how he had seen three East End children playing 'Home'—one child, 'the father', hit 'the mother' until dragged away by 'the policeman'. The Archbishop of Canterbury urged the government to impose a time-limit for compensation, after which any licence could be suppressed at will. When the government refused, Dr. Davidson professed himself 'disappointed'. In the restrained language of the Upper House this was a declaration of war.

In 1906 the Liberals had their revenge and in the new House of Commons, with Labour and Irish support, they outnumbered the routed Tories by nearly 360. The return of thirty Labour M.P.s, or fifty-three if one included miners' representatives, added a new factor to temperance politics. Most of the Labour members elected in 1906 were non-drinkers, including their leader, Keir Hardie, who forbade his followers to drink in the House, and Philip Snowden, a future Chancellor. His *Socialism and the Drink Question*, published in 1908, rejected the 'wild exaggeration' that drink was the chief cause of poverty; it was 'The Socialist contention that poverty is the main cause of drinking... The drunkenness of the upper classes... set the example to the masses, while the temperance movement began among the poor and spread to the rich.'

Although the new Prime Minister, Sir Henry Campbell-Bannerman, was not a prominent temperance man and his Chancellor of the Exchequer, Herbert Henry Asquith, had a supposed weakness for the bottle, they believed that a strong Licensing Bill would make a tactically sound issue for the inevitable fight with the Lords. The need for legislation had, too, become urgent since the recent 'Kennedy Judgment', which had established the right of a brewer to be compensated not merely for the loss of a 'tied' licence, but for the resulting drop in the sales of his beer. It was clear, also, that the lion's share of compensation under the 1904 Act was going to the wealthy brewery company, not to the poor, dispossessed tenant of the tied house, the very name of which was an affront to Liberal principles.

'All manner of legislation for the encouragement of temperance is in the wind', reported *The Mineral Water Trade Review* in 1907, 'and this should be good news for the aerator.' Its expectations were fulfilled in the following year. The immensely long and detailed speech in which on Thursday, 27th February 1908, Asquith, who six weeks later became Prime Minister, at last unveiled the government's proposals, was a parliamentary triumph, though when asked for his notes he produced only a scrap of paper with 'Too many pubs' scrawled on it. This was the heart of his case. Under the 1904 Act suppression of licences was going far too slowly. The government therefore proposed to get rid of more than a third of the 100,000 public houses in England and Wales by imposing a sliding scale which allowed from one licence per 1,000 people in crowded cities, to 1 per 400 in the depth of the country. All additional licences would gradually be suppressed over the next fourteen years, with compensation, raised from the trade, being shared out by a central Licensing Commission. The local licensing authority would decide which public houses to close down and, after the fourteen years' transitional period, all licences would be treated as new and could be refused without compensation. Local option would come into force immediately for the issue of new licences and might, if Parliament then agreed, be extended in fourteen years' time to all licences, and any area could then vote itself 'dry'. The government proposed, too, many minor changes, including stricter control of clubs, shorter Sunday opening hours and a great increase in the power of the justices, who could shut down additional public houses by negotiation, and make stringent conditions before granting any licence. These might include total Sunday closing, a ban on sales to children or on the employment of women, and —a vital provision—refusal of a licence to a tied house.

The Licensing Bill of 1908 contained something to delight every section of the temperance movement. 'Ministers . . . have upon their side', declared Philip Snowden, 'such a combination as I think has never supported a measure before', while even Sir Thomas Whittaker, newly-knighted, admitted that 'taking the Bill as a whole it satisfies me'. From the Conservative benches there arose an outburst of indignation. A. J. Balfour accused the government of building 'upon a foundation of injustice' and F. E. Smith said ministers proposed to 'treat the working classes as children or savages'. Other honourable members warned that the Bill would cost 160,000 people their jobs, ruin brewery shareholders by the score, deprive Kidderminster of seventy-four of its 124 public houses, and was so dangerously 'socialistic' that it would provide a precedent for nationalising the railways, the mines and even the banks. It was all very well the Bishops supporting the Bill, remarked one Tory, but they were more at home in the Athenaeum than a village inn.

The storm which burst around the government's head as soon as details of 'the robbery Bill' became known brought back memories of the early days of the temperance movement. The mayor of Burton-on-Trent told a public meeting that he 'had been compelled to leave the Liberal Party because it would not let them alone'. If this 'measure of flagrant national dishonesty' were passed, 'Burton . . . would be ruined and sink to a small and insignificant place'. The Liberal brewer M.P. for Huntingdon, Samuel Whitbread, offered to resign his seat so that he could oppose the Bill but, significantly, his constituents refused. Posters in public house windows warned that fewer inns meant higher rates and showed the working man having to pay 4d. for the glass of beer which now cost him 2½d., while barmaids pleaded piteously with their customers, 'Save my job.'

Some companies favoured more direct methods. *The Manchester Guardian* reported in March that breweries in Surrey had 'decided to withdraw all subscriptions to local and charitable institutions, including hospitals and convalescent homes', and a Watford brewery ostentatiously cancelled a half-guinea subscription to a fund to provide holidays for Ragged School children which it had paid for thirty years. Many firms tried to enlist the support of their own employees and tradesmen. The Managing Director of Watneys, recalling the Liberals' 1906 slogan 'The Big Loaf', warned 1,000 of his workpeople that 'the next election would be fought on the big pot or no pot at all'. Another brewery warned all its suppliers that 'the Licensing Bill means the ultimate extermination of our trade when orders from brewers must cease'. Harold Smith, brother of F. E., urged his audience at the Queen's Hall in March 'not to pay one farthing to any tradesman who is in favour of this Bill' but to tell him 'I must change my tradesman, for I can only deal with an honest man.' At a Midlands meeting, noted *The Northampton Daily Reporter*, one speaker urged similar sanctions by wives 'before they bought a new hat or bonnet . . . The next speaker, Mr. Wilson . . . told how he had recently declined to allow a teetotaller to tune his pianoforte.'

At Stockton-on-Tees one 'reverend champion of the trade' held a special, crowded service for publicans, abusing the government from the pulpit and pleading with the Almighty to move its heart. 'If the devil himself had put up at the last election he would have got in', said a speaker at Salford, 'but . . . the old gentleman would not have given us such a devil of a time as this government.' The prize for abuse was, however, probably won by *The Daily Telegraph*, which in one leading article described the Bill as 'utter iniquity', 'sheer brigandage', 'socialistic confiscation', 'despotic plunder', 'a measure of fraud' and 'a raiding expedition of partisan blackmailers', finally apologising for 'the utter inadequacy of words to convey ... the magnitude of this issue'.

The Liberals were unfortunate in that just at this moment the marginal seat of Peckham fell vacant, for this had been Conservative-held until 1906. Soon the streets of Peckham were almost impassable for the throng of eager campaigners with, pushing their way through them, waggon-loads of bedraggled children, 'The victims of drink', and brakes full of apprehensive old folk, brewery shareholders about to be ruined. Even the high-Tory *Morning Post* felt that 'the protest of the publicans' might be 'doing more harm than good. Van loads of hoarse-voiced men shout up and down the streets about their beer; whisky distillers' wagons ostentatiously parade the borough ... and paid orators make wild statements.' The Conservative candidate prudently returned a fifty-guinea cheque from a brewery director, but the local publicans' banner across the High Street uncompromisingly proclaimed: 'Thou shalt not steal. There is no time limit to this.' Some Tories tied jackets around their dogs inscribed 'Gooch for Peckham' and soon every self-respecting Liberal mongrel had a 'Vote for Gautrey' placard round its neck. Both sides poured speakers and canvassers into the constituency, but by polling day, 25th March, *The Times* was noting an ominous sign: 'The Unionist colour was red and Peckham appeared to be almost all red. Even small boys who sold election favours only stocked ... red.' Later that night, while 'the whole of Peckham ... presented the appearance of a huge fair ... a red magnesium light and the firing of rockets of a similar hue gave the first intimation to the waiting thousands ... as to the way the victory had gone ... The cheer could be heard for upwards of a mile away.'

A few minutes later the news reached the House of Commons: a Liberal majority of 2,300 had been turned into a Conservative one of nearly 2,500. Lloyd George, who was speaking on unemployment, was 'interrupted by an extraordinary commotion', and his reference to 'figures' produced a shout of 'Look at tonight's!' and a chorus of 'Resign!' The Liberals consoled themselves by later greeting the victorious Gooch with cries of 'The voice of beer!' although, ironically, he was in fact an abstainer.

During the next few months seat after seat turned against the Liberals and the newspapers were full of stories about the fall in brewery shares—although, appropriately, government stocks had fallen more—and the real or threatened increase in unemployment among cork-makers, coopers and beer-pump manufacturers. Besides the predictable opposition of such bodies as the Middle Classes Defence Organisation and the Liberty and Property Defence League, the Liberals were soon under fire from less familiar quarters, such as the Cambridgeshire Public House Trust, whose chairman called the Bill 'a death blow to the trust movement', and the Rural Labourers League, which wanted to know where, if half the pubs were closed, farmers and labourers could shelter from the rain on market day. Perhaps most ominous of all, a leading member of the Club and Institutes Union, 'a Radical all his life' who had 'endeavoured to end the House of Lords', pointed out that 'now he had to depend on that body to defend his clubs'.

In May, Lord Robert Cecil introduced into the House of Commons a monster petition against the Licensing Bill bearing 600,000 signatures, twelve attendants being needed to pile the huge bundles of forms in front of the table. Counter-petitions followed as the Liberal Publication Department poured forth a stream of pamphlets and leaflets, attacking brewers' excessive profits and exorbitant claims for compensation—*The Golden Fleece*, Bermondsey, with a rateable value of £67 a year, had been valued at £9,000 when closed down. Barmen were assured that even if they lost their jobs 'a slump in drink means a boom in every other trade' and publicans reminded that the Bill might provide them with a free Sunday and abolish 'ties', a point underlined by a cartoon showing a weary 'tied' tenant dragging a brewers' barrel behind him.

The most remarkable feature of the temperance agitation which occurred all over the country throughout the summer of

1908 was its unprecedented unity. At Preston, birthplace of 'moral suasion', 10,000 people drawn from all the churches, friendly societies and temperance organisations marched together in procession. In Manchester, where the British prohibition movement had been founded, a similar force, 50,000 strong, marched to Heaton Park to hear the chairman of the Alliance, a Liberal M.P., declare that 'the Bill was the greatest step forward in temperance ... during the lifetime of any man living'. To be nearer the fight, the Alliance offices were moved to Westminster, symbolising, perhaps, the extent to which London, rather than the industrial north, was now the centre of the British temperance world.[1]

In the spring the Bishop of London made a famous 'midnight march' through the East End, encountering in one mile on a Saturday evening nearly 200 men the worse for liquor, among them a group who, when invited to join in *Lead Kindly Light*, insisted on singing *For he's a Jolly Good Fellow*. On a later Saturday, in May, 9,000 Liberals crowded into the Albert Hall—40,000 had applied for tickets—to cheer the Bishop, who urged that 'Every Christian body in England ought to rally shoulder to shoulder', to sing 'Britons never, never shall be slaves' and to shout 'No surrender!' Six weeks later, when it was the trade's turn, the Albert Hall was equally crowded and it was Balfour who was cheered, while banners proclaimed 'We fight for right', and 'The writing on the wall—Mid-Devon, Hereford, Worcester, Leeds, Hastings, Peckham, Dewsbury, Manchester, Pudsey'—the by-elections lost by the Liberals. The Albert Hall was also hired by another of the Bill's opponents, Horatio Bottomley, who made the only speech, moved a vote of thanks to himself and declared it carried unanimously. The indoor meetings were followed by even greater demonstrations in Hyde Park. On a sunny Saturday in July, contingents of Liberals marched from all over London to

[1] These were great years for the Alliance. In 1908 Lloyd George, whose vice was not drinking, and in 1907, even more improbably, Winston Churchill, presided over its Annual Meeting — the only two future prime ministers to do so.

hear Sir Thomas Whittaker and fifty other M.P.s speak from several impromptu platforms. 'There was a tone of robust conviction', reported *The Times*, 'in such banner mottoes as "The Big D Alliance—Drink, Disease and the Devil"' and the only opposition came from 'half-a-dozen . . . rather merry working men' who held up 'a baby's milk bottle . . . from which they had obviously not been drinking' while 'singing . . . "Beer, beer, glorious, glorious beer".' Young Winston Churchill, arriving on foot, drew such a crowd that 'the police had great difficulty in rescuing him and setting him, red and smiling, upon the unhorsed waggon'. To the 15,000 people who swarmed round it he made a characteristic speech—'They have told us they will give us no quarter. Whoever asked for quarter?'—and prompt at 6.30 p.m. a Resolution supporting the Bill was put from every platform and carried with a roar of acclamation.

On Sunday, 27th September, the Bill's opponents took over the Park. Public houses all over England and Wales were stripped of their staff as 100 special trains carried them to London, where, in seven processions, they marched through the streets behind banners bearing the names of their towns. Many wore 'Honesty and Liberty' buttons on their lapels or carried bunches of hops or 'diminutive soda water bottles suspended on . . . sticks'. Although a Liberal minister dismissed the demonstrators as 'imported inebriates', and the teetotallers made much of the fact that many had been provided with free tickets and food by their employers, *The Times* considered 'A finer body of men, respectable, well-dressed and with an unmistakable air of sturdy independence has perhaps never before taken part in a meeting in Hyde Park.' The Liberal *Westminster Gazette*, on the other hand, thought that some of the demonstrators appeared 'specially chosen to illustrate the ravages of drink on the human frame'; no doubt among a crowd estimated at from 100,000 to half a million one could see what one wanted. This time there were 'twenty platforms ranged round the "Reformers' Tree" in a great semi-circle' until, at 5.15, bugles sounded and a Resolution condemning the Bill was greeted with 'a mighty shout of approval'.

Meanwhile, aided by the guillotine, and hindered by nearly 1,000 tabled amendments, the Licensing Bill had been making its weary way through the House of Commons, and at 5.15 p.m. on Friday, 20th November, amid cries of 'Robbery! Robbery!', the third reading was carried by 350 votes to 113. All now depended on Lord Lansdowne, leader of the Conservative peers, and King Edward VII, the very antithesis of a teetotaller, urged Lansdowne to try to amend it rather than reject it out of hand. But the Tory peers were made of sterner stuff. On the following Tuesday, 250 of them, including six dukes, crowded into the ballroom of Lansdowne House in Berkeley Square and here, as a Liberal writer later complained, 'between noon and the hour for luncheon' the fate of the Bill was settled. Only about thirty peers favoured amendment; the rest were solid for rejection. Next day Lord Crewe, the Lord Privy Seal, moving the second reading in the Lords, referred to 'a novel stage of this Bill . . . a sitting . . . not in this Chamber, but in a famous house in a famous square'. The rejection of the Bill would not, he warned, be popular with 'serious citizens' or with the clergy. The Archbishop of Canterbury, Dr. Tait, agreed. Among the 'simple people who perseveringly work in the back streets of our great towns . . . schoolmasters, schoolmistresses, the nurses, the rescue workers . . . there will', he said, 'be heavy hearts and weary disappointment today'. The renegade Liberal, Lord Rosebery, also stressed that though 'the temperance party are engaged in a strife to the death with "the trade"', the motives of the clergy were above suspicion. By rejecting the Bill the House was giving a handle to its enemies. The Bishop of Hereford was equally blunt. The Tory majority were, he said, 'digging the grave' of their own 'inherited privileges'.

But the backwoodsmen were not to be dissuaded. The expression 'drunk as a lord' was no longer accurate, said one. In 'any mess of Yeomanry officers . . . you will see them all drinking barley water'. 'In the north of England', explained another, 'we have very bad weather and like lots to drink.' He quoted a famous aphorism of Lord Salisbury: 'Though he had a great many bedrooms at Hatfield he did not find that that led to his sleeping more.' Lansdowne himself made a powerful, reasoned speech, brushing aside the consequences of rejection. 'The country looks to us', he said, 'to protect it from legislation which we believe to be iniquitous... We shall better deserve both the respect of our fellow countrymen and our own self-respect if straightforwardly and with the courage of our opinions we reject the Bill.'

After three days' debate the House divided and at 7.20 p.m. on Friday, 27th November 1908, the Bill that was to crown eighty years of effort by the temperance movement was thrown out, by 272 votes to 96. It was the House of Lords' last great triumph. On that November evening the dukes and earls and marquesses dispersed to their clubs for dinner, conscious of a good job well done. The Licensing Bill never was passed. But five months later Lloyd George introduced the famous Budget which finally goaded them on to self-destruction.

*Chapter Twenty-three*

# THE GREATEST ENEMY

'We are fighting Germany, Austria and drink and the greatest of these deadly foes is drink.'
— David Lloyd George, M.P., 29th March 1915

THE OUTBREAK of war, on 4th August 1914, presented the temperance movement with both a challenge and an opportunity. In the first flush of patriotism there was a rush to the public house to press drink upon any man in uniform, but simultaneously a mood of positively masochistic self-sacrifice swept the country. As early as the 10th August suggestions were made about 'restricting the facilities for obtaining intoxicating drink during the war', and soon a teetotal magistrate was hopefully telegraphing the Home Office seeking the power to close all the local public houses, although there were no military camps within miles. Some of the first orders under the Defence of the Realm Act empowered the naval and military authorities to enforce restricted opening hours in any military or naval area, but by the 25th August the first anti-drink enthusiasm was already subsiding, and the government's Intoxicating Liquor (Temporary Restrictions) Bill had a distinctly rough passage. The Bill, which gave to licensing justices the power to shorten opening hours during the war to prevent public disorder, provoked many complaints that the government, thwarted in 1908, was 'waving the flag and seeking to advance by a side wind the cause of temperance'. The newly-mustered Territorials needed a place to meet and it would be intolerable 'if a working man hears of a great victory and wants to discuss it with a pal and . . . cannot get a glass of beer'.

Faced by a suspicious House, the Home Secretary promised that prohibition would not be proposed except in a desperate emergency and that magistrates would not be able to impose prohibition, or closing before 9 p.m., without the Home Office's consent. Even in its milder form, however, the Act had a dramatic effect. By the end of the year, restricted hours were in operation in half the 1,000 licensing districts in England and Wales, in addition to areas where military orders were in force. Pre-war hours in towns had usually been from 6 a.m. to 11 p.m. or, in London, 5 a.m. to 12.30 a.m. and from 6 a.m. to 10 p.m. in the country. (Scottish hours were 10 a.m. to 9, 10 or, exceptionally, 11 p.m.) Now in most places the public houses opened at 8 or 9 a.m. and closed again at 9 or 10 p.m., with, in the military areas, an afternoon break as well, its first appearance on weekdays.

Shorter hours rapidly proved remarkably effective in reducing drunkenness, even *The Brewers Gazette* admitting in September that 11 p.m. closing had produced 'A transformation of the night scenes of London' so that many once-rowdy areas 'have suddenly become peaceful and respectable'. Further improvements were claimed when, a month later, hours were still further reduced, a London grand jury being told in April 1915 that 'The closing of the public houses at 10 o'clock has undoubtedly produced a wonderful result.'

The teetotallers had always disliked heavy taxation on drink on the grounds that it discouraged temperance legislation, but it proved the second great remedy for wartime drunkenness. In his war budget of November 1914, Lloyd George increased the 'absurdly low' duty on beer by putting 'a halfpenny on the half pint'. 'Every half pint that a man drinks', he explained, 'he will be contributing to . . . carrying on the war.' Soon a brewers' advertisement was urging the public, 'Drink the national beverage and help your country . . . Order a pint of beer and drive a nail into the Kaiser's coffin. If you can't manage a pint order half a pint and drive a tin-tack.'

Lloyd George was an enthusiastic believer in another wartime expedient which became permanent, weaker beer. 'Light beers', proclaimed the Chancellor, 'contain only from 5 to 7% of proof spirit, just a little above ginger ale'—normal beer contained 9–10%.[1] In December the brewers enterprisingly issued a statement: 'Beer as a temperance drink', which unfavourably compared such outlandish foreign products as vodka and absinthe to 'mild and wholesome beer ... the national beverage of Englishmen ... If we can't go to the front, we can help our country (and our own well being) by changing our cocoa and ginger-beer into ale.' Lloyd George also affronted the temperance movement by increasing the tea duty to catch 'the elusive teetotaller',[2] but when in April 1915 he proposed to quadruple the duty on wine, to double the duty on spirits and to impose a graduated 'surtax' on heavy beer, such as stout, he had to retreat, in the face of violent opposition from the Irish. William O'Brien said that the taxes would ruin the whiskey distillers and Guinness's brewery in Cork and 'the result will be as appalling as if that city was bombarded and sacked by the Germans'. Tim Healy predicted that instead of British troops being greeted with shouts of 'God save the King' as they marched through Dublin, the angry population would once again be singing 'God save Ireland'. The Asquith government, anxious to conciliate Irish opinion, dropped the taxes; twelve months later came the Easter Rising.

'Although I lost this opening round', Lloyd George recorded in his *War Memoirs*, 'I succeeded in subsequent years in carrying through the policy of high taxation of alcoholic beverages, dilution of spirits and encouragement of lighter beers ... The nation sang music-hall ditties bewailing "Lloyd George's Be-e-e-er" but the statistics of insobriety showed a rapid decline.' In 1917 beer prices, rising rapidly, were fixed by law at 4d. or 5d. a pint for a far weaker brew than had formerly cost 3d. or 4d. The price of spirits, also diluted, increased even faster, from between 2d. and 4d. a tot at the outbreak of war to 6d., 9d. or more by its end.

A major problem for both government and teetotallers was

[1] Proof spirit is about 58% alcohol by volume.

[2] Soft drinks were, he explained, mainly drunk with spirits.

the treating of soldiers by civilians, despite an Order making it an offence to ply any man on defence duties with drink. 'Lord Kitchener', ran an appeal issued by the new Secretary of State in October, 'begs everyone to avoid treating the men to drink.' To his troops in the British Expeditionary Force he issued an optimistic order: 'You may find temptation both in wine and women. You must entirely resist both temptations.' Kitchener himself became an abstainer 'for the duration', but few of his men responded to a public appeal from his sister to follow their commander's lead. Other anti-treating appeals, too, achieved little success, one brigadier-general complaining unconvincingly that 'At Perth whisky was literally forced down the throats of my men.' From July 1915 onwards it became illegal, in one area after another, to buy another man a drink, but generous civilians sometimes found ways round the law. A teetotal pamphlet related in 1917 how a young Lincoln V.C. found 120 pints of beer, paid for by his neighbours, waiting for him at his local when he came on leave, so that he 'was very nearly dead with it before he was rescued', while at Sheffield three convalescent soldiers, too lavishly entertained, were found lying incapable on the tramlines.

Even more serious from the teetotallers' point of view were the many young men who, according to temperance publications, broke their pledge on enlisting. 'Our boy', wrote one father piteously, 'never saw drink before ... he joined the Army ... but when he came home to see his mother he was drunk every night.' A 'young officer' wrote in shocked astonishment that on guest night several members of his mess were 'under the table ... One man accounted for ten glasses of champagne.' The hardened regular, explained one pamphlet, knew how to carry his drink, but 'the new Army includes men of a very different type ... They have for the most part been excluded from many unpleasant realities ... Their education and upbringing are not such as to mould firmness of character.'

While these same young men were acquiring the necessary firmness of character on the Somme and at Passchendaele, the teetotallers were busily trying to remove the one comfort left to the fighting man by an hysterical campaign against the rum ration. The campaign was led by the teetotal surgeon, Sir Victor Horsley, who in January 1915 published in *The British Medical Journal* an article later reprinted as a penny pamphlet, *The Rum Ration in the British Army: The Alleged Responsibility of the Medical Profession for its Re-Introduction.* This recalled how British troops had first acquired the spirit-drinking habit during Marlborough's campaigns in the Low Countries. 'Now our army in Flanders is again being taught (by the issue of rum from home) to become victims of the spirit-drinking habit.' Current Regulations, said Horsley, which laid down that 'a free ration of . . . one sixty-fourth of a gallon of rum' could be issued only 'on very exceptional occasions, as when the troops have been drenched or chilled through exposure', and then only 'under the authority of the General Officer Commanding, when certified by the Senior Medical Officer to be absolutely necessary', were being ignored. Rum was in practice being distributed to all troops in France at least once a day and sometimes twice, without prescription, although its only result would be to make an efficient soldier 'heady and excitable, incapable of his normal physical endurance . . . and intolerant of discipline'.

After joining the Royal Army Medical Corps, Horsley was soon sending back scandalised letters from France and the Middle East about commanders who rewarded troops who had fought well with beer and who took up shipping space with 'cases of champagne, port, whisky, etc., for the officers' mess'. 'The King's example', he admitted in a memorable understatement, 'is taking time to work . . . Our Staff is planted thickly . . .with alcoholics.' It was, however, poor Sir Victor who died in Mesopotamia at fifty-nine because, according to an unkind writer in *The Hospital*, 'being a teetotaller, he thought he was proof against heat-stroke'.

Pestered by letters and parliamentary questions about the famous Regulations, Lord Kitchener and the War Office brazenly insisted that rum was 'only issued to the troops on special occasions . . . strictly in accordance with medical advice', and denied that it was ever added to the regimental tea or pressed upon men going into action. The agitation reflected the special place which rum had always occupied in temperance demonology,[1] perhaps because of the damage the almost-universal faith in its special properties had done to the teetotal cause. As one M.P. told the House in 1918, rum had 'this wonderful advantage that it goes to the finger-tips'. That was why it had come into use 'when on our sailing ships ropes had to be handled', and made a soldier 'able to perform the duty of handling his rifle even in the coldest weather'. The rum ration found many other defenders. *The Times* correspondent reported that its arrival 'put new heart into every man' during an epic all-night action on the Ypres–Menin road, and an R.A.M.C. captain acknowledged in *The British Medical Journal* in March 1915 that when 'done to the world on the Mons retreat . . . a tot of rum carried me on to my destination'. A hitherto teetotal doctor said he would like to see his former allies in the trenches, where 'They would find that the rum ration was an absolute necessity'. Experience suggested, too, that rum was a useful prophylactic against shell-shock, the British Medical Association's annual meeting being told in 1922 that a high proportion of shell-shock cases had been teetotallers.

In teetotal eyes the greatest heroes of the war were those who had held firm to their pledge amid shot and shell, like the noble lieutenant who threw his rum on the ground even when threatened with punishment, and the colonel who, when asked by the adjutant if he was to distribute the rum, replied 'in front of the chaplain . . . "No! Damn the rum! To hell with the rum!"' Advertisements in temperance publications showed 'Old Bill' type figures drinking Fry's cocoa in shell holes and in 1918 one M.P. alleged that the whole agitation was 'engineered and financed by the . . . men who make cocoa'.

[1] In America it was often used as a generic term for alcohol, as explained in one temperance poem:

> 'Hail mighty rum! And by this general name  
> I call each species — whisky, gin or brandy;  
> (The kinds are various — but the effect's the same,  
> And so I choose a name that's short and handy).'

The temperance movement did valuable work in providing 'dry' recreation huts and mobile tea-bars for the troops, both in France and at home, one author in 1917 even referring to 'The longest and most momentous battle of the war: the Y.M.C.A. versus the Wet Canteen.' The teetotallers' chief energies, however, were directed to the campaign for wartime prohibition. One argument constantly advanced was 'The example of the Allies', especially Russia, for immediately on mobilisation the Tsar had issued an edict closing all vodka shops in military areas, although first-class hotels and restaurants were exempt. This move, wrongly described as 'national prohibition', turned Nicholas II, most unusually, into a popular hero of the British press. 'The Tsar', declared a writer in *The Daily Chronicle*, 'saved Paris, if not international law and liberty, by the alcohol-free speed of the Russian mobilisation.' 'Without a murmur of protest the most drunken city in Europe was transformed into a temple of sobriety', reported *The Times* Moscow correspondent. 'In sternly prohibiting the sale of spirituous liquor', commented its leader-writer, 'Russia has already vanquished a greater foe than the Germans.' *The Daily Mail* Petrograd correspondent observed naïvely that prohibition must be popular since 'There are no meetings, no letters to the newspapers, no controversy.' 'The Tsar', enthused the author of *Alcohol and the War, the Example of Russia,* 'has done more for the temperance movement than a whole century of preaching . . . The prohibition of strong drink . . . is one of the great factors in the splendid showing . . . being made by the Russian armies today.'

France, too, was favourably compared by the teetotallers to their own country when, on the outbreak of war, the French government banned the sale of absinthe in many areas, including Paris, and in February 1915 made its manufacture illegal everywhere. In 1913 the French had drunk fifty-three million gallons of 'the green devil', a ferocious mixture prepared by soaking wormwood, cinnamon and other herbs in alcohol and containing 72% pure spirit. 'With the enemy hacking its way towards Paris', wrote the author of *Drink and the War from the Patriotic Point of View* in 1915, 'half-measures were futile

. . . France did not hesitate. Absinthe and similar drinks were forbidden throughout the country.'

The French soldier in fact still got his two-thirds of a pint of wine a day, until a breakdown in the supply proved one of the precipitating causes of the 1917 mutinies. By then, with Russia beaten and France on the verge of collapse, the prohibitionists were turning for inspiration to the Italian Army, which had recently banned spirits. This was another unlucky choice, as eight months later it collapsed at Caporetto. By now the prohibitionists were growing desperate for examples. 'China', it was pointed out, 'has thrown out opium . . . and even Mexico has risen to the moral heights of stopping her bullfights in these last few months.'

The entry of the United States into the war in April 1917 provided the teetotallers, too, with a timely ally for prohibition was said to be sweeping America 'like a great prairie fire', and the arrival of troops from dominions with large 'dry' areas also supplied a new argument. It was, said the prohibitionists, the mother country's duty to protect these young men who apparently—such was the moral training provided by prohibition—made for the nearest bar as soon as they came off the boat, and remained till carried out. England, alleged Arthur Mee, in May 1917 in *The Fiddlers*, was 'straining the bonds of Empire'. Because Parliament refused to bring in prohibition, drunken Canadian and British soldiers had committed murder, suicide and even bestiality, while 'the drink trade . . . the great confederate of V.D.' was wholly responsible for the Army's 100,000 cases of venereal disease since 1914. It had been aided, said Mee, by an Austrian prostitute in Lambeth who was doing her bit for her native land by deliberately infecting British soldiers, for which—a fine circumstantial detail illustrating Teutonic meanness—her government paid her fifteen shillings a week.

In *Defeat or Victory?* in the same year, Mee alleged that Canada would have sent half a million men to Britain, instead of 400,000, had not Canadian mothers feared the moral ruin of their sons. 'We handed the Canadian Army over to the drink canteens.' Eventually, although half a million copies of Mee's pamphlets were sold, *The Fiddlers* and *Defeat or Victory?* were banned in Australia and South Africa as a threat to the war effort and in Canada even to possess a copy became an offence punishable by five years in jail. The charges about V.D. were effectively refuted after the war by a British colonel who reported that 300 of the 1,200 soldiers he had treated had been total abstainers, while only 10 had been drunk when infected and 220 'jolly'. A teetotaller was actually more likely to get V.D., since 'The total abstainers may have sought sexual gratification as a relief . . . when a moderate drinker would be content with his customary dose of alcohol.'

Far more serious than drinking at the Front was drinking at home, particularly among the newly-prosperous shipyard and munition workers. 'Saint Tuesday' and even 'Saint Wednesday' were now kept as well as 'Saint Monday', and men regularly turned up for work crippled by hangovers or carrying hidden bottles of spirits. 'Drunk men, nominally at work, have had to be removed', the Captain Superintendent of the Clyde District reported to the Admiralty in March 1915. Recent work on the bottom of one warship 'was so badly carried out . . . that it could not have been done by men who were sober'. 'My destroyer dockings and refits . . . take twice as long as they need to', complained Admiral Jellicoe in the same month. To prepare a transport for sea, reported the Director of Transport, was taking twenty-two days instead of seven. 'The firemen go on board . . . drunk, making it impossible to get up a full head of steam . . . and endangering the lives of thousands of troops by making the vessels a target for submarines.' Almost equally serious was 'slacking' in munitions factories, where, as in the shipyards, a few missing key men could disrupt a whole works; in one shell factory alone in March 1915 a tenth of normal working hours was lost through drink. In the shipyards, although some men were working seventy, eighty or even a hundred hours a week, loss of a third of normal output from drink was not uncommon.

Lloyd George, who in May 1915 became Minister of Munitions and, in December 1916, Prime Minister, had long been concerned with the drink question. In February 1915 he said at Bangor, in a much-quoted speech, that 'Drink is doing more damage in the war than all the German submarines put together', and a month later he told a deputation of shipbuilding employers, who pleaded for wartime prohibition, that 'We are fighting Germany, Austria and drink and the greatest of these deadly foes is drink.' Later, he persuaded the King 'to set an example by giving up all alcoholic liquor' for the duration and banning it throughout his household. 'I hate doing it, but hope it will do good', King George noted sadly in his diary on 6th April 1915. His hopes were misplaced. Despite Lloyd George's glowing predictions that 'all classes would hasten to follow the lead thus given by the Sovereign', few of his subjects adopted 'the King's Pledge'.

A week later a committee of enquiry set up by Lloyd George advised him that for £250 million the nation could buy out every brewery and public house in England and Wales—distilleries and grocers' licences would cost more—to run them as a public service. From sheer patriotism the Conservative leaders and many leading brewers were willing to support the scheme, 'but', wrote Lloyd George, 'a powerful section of temperance advocates ... brought such pressure to bear on the Prime Minister that he feared serious trouble inside the Party and in view of the urgency of the problem ... I decided for the time being to proceed with a more limited reform'. This was all that was ever achieved, for when in January 1917 the Food Controller also urged state purchase, to save food, 'The War Cabinet decided that the question ... should be deferred until other urgent measures had been settled.' Thus a unique opportunity to solve the drink problem and obtain for the taxpayer a valuable asset was lost for ever. Some temperance societies issued leaflets attacking 'Lloyd George, Publican', the National Temperance Federation rejected the suggestion of 'a union between the State and the liquor traffic', the Good Templars repudiated 'the iniquitous principle of state ownership', and the secretary of the United Kingdom Alliance declared that even if state ownership were to cut the consumption of drink by half, they ought still to oppose it. If nationalisation comes, 'It will', he told the Free Church Council, 'be your hands that ... pass the drink into the hands of your brother or sister trembling with eager unholy excitement for the deadly draught ... All these ruined souls will be *your* servants for whom you must answer to Almighty God!' Even worse, a public house might become 'a safe place for the wife and child to go as well as for the man himself', and hopes of prohibition would have to be abandoned, just when 'The promised land lies before us'.

After his recent experiences, Lloyd George told the House of Commons on 29th April 1915, in introducing his Defence of the Realm (Amendment No. 3) Bill, he felt 'prepared to take politically a pledge never to touch it again ... Every government that has ever touched alcohol has burned its fingers in its lurid flames.' The government had, he admitted, 'received ... from the most unlikely quarters proposals for complete prohibition ... Before we do that we are bound to try everything short of it.' Ministers had turned down, too, the 'half-way house' of prohibiting spirits, which would be 'unfair to local tastes', i.e. Scotland. Instead they proposed to hand over authority to a new Central Liquor Control Board, answerable neither to Parliament nor the magistrates, and able, if asked by the military or munitions authorities, to impose any restrictions it liked in any area it chose. The Board could close the public houses completely in a designated area, limit hours, ban spirits, insist on food being served, impose any other conditions it chose, and, if necessary, buy, build and run its own breweries, public houses and canteens; compensation would be paid to those taken over, but against the Board's decisions there was no appeal.

This drastic scheme, intended to remain in force until a year after the end of the war, was received with almost unanimous goodwill. Sir Thomas Whittaker acknowledged that 'this is not the time for controversy', Bonar Law also welcomed the Bill for the Conservatives and Arthur Henderson for the Labour Party loyally supported an immediate second reading. 'I am', he admitted, 'a temperance fanatic', but 'this crisis ... demands ... any sacrifice, even the sacrifice of ... theories ... we have been holding ... a lifetime'. Only the out and out prohibitionists failed to rise to the level of events, their leader, Leif Jones, President of the Alliance, declaring that 'The government have no right to jump the country into experiments upon this matter.' In the Lords the Bill was not even debated, the only Conservative to speak on it being Lord Lansdowne, who said that 'Ministers ... deserve credit for their courage.' Within three weeks, on 19th May 1915, the new Bill was law.

The twelve-member Central Liquor Control Board, under Lord D'Abernon, included representatives of the Home Office, the Admiralty, industry and the Labour Party, a brewer and a teetotaller. Its first Order, in July 1915, applied only to Newhaven, but by December control had been extended to half the population and by the end of 1916 to all but three million of the nation's forty-one million people, the excluded districts being a few rural areas. Most places now endured the shortest licensing hours in British history, usually from 12 noon to 2.30 p.m. and 6 or 6.30 to 9 or 9.30 p.m., but in the naval area of Ross and Cromarty one could buy a drink only between 5 and 7 p.m. Sunday hours were also sharply reduced everywhere and the 'bona fide traveller' abolished. Some public houses were compelled to serve food; spirits for 'off' drinking could only be sold in the afternoon and, to discourage pocket flasks, at least a quart at a time, while their sale in railway refreshment rooms was forbidden altogether. Soon the dilution of spirits below their former strength became compulsory, despite the warning from one whisky-loving M.P. that 'you cannot reduce it to thirty degrees below proof without making it muddy, murky and unattractive'.[1] 'The long pull', by which slightly more beer was served than had been ordered, became illegal and publicans were also forbidden to supply drink on credit or to canvass for orders.

These, and many similar changes, offered limitless oppor-

[1] This is now the standard strength. Rum served in the trenches had been only 4.5 degrees below proof, as the naval rum ration still is today.

tunities for complaints, often about matters, like the shortage of beer, for which the Board was not to blame. Probably nothing caused as much irritation, however, as its 'No treating' Order. There were questions in the House about a Liverpool workman who was given three months' hard labour for treating a friend, while an unfortunate husband at Bristol who was fined for buying his wife a drink was the subject of much heavy Parliamentary humour. Did not 'an endowment of worldly goods include the provision of refreshment?' the minister was asked, but when the government invited suggestions on how a publican could distinguish a man's wife from other lady companions no answers were forthcoming. More serious was the notorious 'Brandy for the rescuer' case in 1916, when a passer-by who had pulled a drowning man out of the Thames was refused brandy at a nearby public house because it was out of hours, thus, according to the coroner, endangering his life—the rescued man had died.

The Board began to use its power to buy out existing interests and open 'state pubs' early in 1916, when it compulsorily acquired four public houses and an off-licence serving an isolated war factory at Enfield Lock, and later in the naval base areas of Invergordon and Cromarty, it took over twenty-two more. These ventures were, however, merely a rehearsal for the great 'Carlisle experiment'. At Gretna, on the Scottish border, an enormous explosives factory had grown up on a site nine miles long. Its construction alone involved 20,000 men and when in full operation it would add 20–30,000 people to a thinly populated rural area, containing no large town, except Carlisle. A local Wesleyan minister described how 'June 1916 witnessed the coming of a new population. Into this quiet city of 50,000 inhabitants . . . there poured 10,000 to 12,000 of the navvy class whose hard-drinking propensity is proverbial . . . Men fought like beasts; fierce fights raged round the doors of public houses . . . Almost every alley was littered with prostrate drunken men. The main thoroughfare of Carlisle was Bedlam and the returning trains to Gretna . . . are memories that cause one to shudder.' In the first half of 1916 there were eight times as many convictions for drunkenness and for assaults on the police as a year before, while in Annan, across the Scottish border, with its 5,000 people, convictions for drunkenness in the same period rose spectacularly from six to 146.

Although often accused of empire-building, 'The Board did not', explained a government spokesman in Parliament in October 1916, 'say "Let us go in for a great social experiment in the nationalisation of the drink traffic." Little by little, step by step, circumstances compelled the Board to take action.' When it was forced to act, however, in July 1916, the Board did so boldly. After discussions with the trade and the local authorities, it found itself responsible for an area of fifty square miles, stretching from Dumfriesshire to Maryport in Cumberland, and containing 140,000 people, although Carlisle, Annan and Maryport, with a population of 10,000, were the only places of any size. Within this area the Board took over all but forty-seven of the 368 licensed premises, of which 123 ceased to sell drink. In Carlisle itself the number of public houses was cut from 119 to 69 and seven 'grocers' licences' withdrawn, the remaining three shops being allowed to sell drink alone. Three of the five local breweries were closed; the bottling of beer was confined to one plant instead of twelve and spirit blending to one instead of seventeen. This policy of rationalisation, directed by a resident manager with the help of a local advisory committee, was accompanied by many purely restrictive measures. The sale of spirits to anyone under eighteen was forbidden, nor could anyone buy them on Saturday or public holidays, or, for most of 1917, anywhere near the Gretna factory. Even beer could only be served to under eighteens with a meal. Former publicans, converted into salaried managers, loyally carried out the Board's orders to prevent treating, to serve food and to raise the whole status of the public house as a social centre.

Like Gothenburg, Carlisle became a place of pilgrimage for temperance enthusiasts. There was much to see. Most villages now had only one public house, since those in 'passages or narrow lanes' had disappeared. To provide a 'dry' meeting-place one former inn had been converted into a Trades Hall, while many public houses had been rebuilt, with tea-rooms or restaurants included, which served soup, sandwiches, pies and hot non-alcoholic drinks all day. 'Those remarkable advertisements which render so many public houses an eyesore from the street', noted one observer, 'were taken down; bottles and mirrors were removed from the windows and replaced by neat green curtains. The name of the house was inconspicuously painted over the door ... Inside rooms were rendered more comfortable by ... the provision of seats and more cheerful by better decoration.' The Board had some success in discouraging 'vertical drinking', but its efforts to get rid of small 'snugs' and 'smoke rooms' were abandoned, for by 1918 the General Manager had discovered that 'The British drinker does not appear to like too large an open space.'

The opening of *The Gretna Tavern* in a disused post office in July 1916, the first public house ever designed to discourage drinking, was a national event. *The Times* described the building as 'neither dingy like the old style of pothouses, nor garish like the new', and after a glowing account of the interior, 'spacious, lofty and well lighted', with its 'stand for newspapers ... piano, gramophone', and its 'long open bar' serving only beer or soft drinks, summed up: 'The idea is to encourage people to stop for rational recreation by making them comfortable, but not for mere drinking.' Even Leif Jones, M.P., conceded that the Board had made the actual bar 'as uncomfortable and unattractive as they can', though it would have done even 'better to have that tavern without drink'.

During the next few months the Board opened several more establishments, including at Annan a recreation centre for workmen, containing a cinema, billiard tables, and a bowling green, but lacking a bar—beer was served only at tables—and a 'model tavern' built in red stone. 'If architecture can lift the public house out of debasing associations', remarked *The Times* correspondent, 'it is done here', and before long private brewers were sending their architects to Carlisle to study the latest trends in public house design.

By March 1918 the Carlisle state management scheme was

earning a profit of 15%, more than most private companies, though drunkenness had been drastically reduced. After the war everyone from the Chief Constable to the Bishop of Carlisle favoured its continuance and even the local nonconformist ministers grudgingly admitted that 'if the trade is still to be with us, the experiment is a step in the right direction'. Although the Enfield properties were sold off in 1922, the nation still owns fifteen public houses and hotels in Cromarty, fourteen in Gretna, and 150 in Carlisle itself, plus a few off-licences. The two Scottish schemes together made a profit of £41,000 in 1966/67 and the Carlisle State Management District yielded £220,000, while Britain's only nationalised beer was commended in a Consumers' Association survey in 1960.

By 1917, with sugar, butter and meat desperately scarce and queues a mile long for potatoes, the prohibitionists had a new slogan, 'Bread before beer'. This was the argument constantly pressed by Leif Jones, a Nottingham M.P., and since 1906 President of the Alliance. The son of a Welsh Congregational minister, Jones had, on coming down from Oxford, found himself a wealthy patroness and, though only fifty-two in 1914, he chose as his war work adding to the government's difficulties on licensing. It was said that 'He piloted the Alliance along the "straight road" past that "stile" which led to the seductive "by path meadow" of nationalisation.' Not surprisingly, he lost his seat at the end of the war. He later sat briefly for Camborne, once Sir Wilfrid Lawson's refuge, but was finally rejected even here and consoled with a barony in 1932 as Lord Rhayader, the Welsh for 'waterfall'. He died in 1939.

As early as November 1915, Leif Jones had complained of 'the waste of food in making the drink', and by May 1917, when a Royal Proclamation was issued calling on everyone to save food, not only teetotallers were supporting him. 'The submarine has settled this question, not the temperance party', said one speaker. Another described the use of cereals in manufacturing beer and whisky as 'little short of treason to the state'. The National Prohibition Party, barely heard of since its birth in the eighteen-eighties, had already emerged from obscurity to make the most of its brief opportunity. In July 1916 its monthly magazine, *The Prohibitionist*, pictured Lloyd George accepting money from a villainous Carlisle brewer, with the caption 'Partners'. In February 1917 a solid citizen was seen surrendering his sons and money to the war but still clutching his beer barrel. January 1918 produced the largest headline of the war, 'BEER BEFORE BREAD! Grave government decision'. But December 1918 brought even worse news. Despite a nation allegedly inflamed against drink, the unexpectedness of the general election meant that 'our Prohibition candidate' could not after all take the field.

Far more dangerous than such open advocates of prohibition were the movements which masqueraded under innocuous-sounding names, and claimed—always a suspicious sign—to be non-party and to contain many practical businessmen. The National Efficiency Committee in 1915 gave way to the Strength of Britain movement, founded in October 1916, which favoured state purchase of the trade, but only to enforce wartime prohibition. Its list of supporters included 100 admirals and generals, 200 baronets and knights, 500 magistrates and, of course, numerous 'men and women of goodwill'. Significantly, the Labour Party would have nothing to do with it. *The Strength of Britain Book*, issued in February 1917, contained a calendar on which every twelfth day was marked 'On this day brewers may destroy all the nation's food'. The movement's chief propagandist was Arthur Mee, who published some twenty anti-drink tracts. His masterpiece, *The Fiddlers*, was published in May 1917. 'How long will you go on fiddling? Till we starve?' asked a hungry-looking woman and child on the cover, and inside 'the bread famine' was blamed on 'the wilful destruction of 4.8 million tons of food' by 'the drink trade'. In *The Parasite*, issued in December, he returned to this theme. 'Give ... crumbs to the birds and you are fined £5; give a loaf to the brewer and you are patriotic ... The beer drinkers in the United Kingdom are eating their own rations and drinking somebody else's.'

Although, to save raw materials and labour, beer production

had been cut from the pre-war thirty-six million barrels to twenty-six million by 1916, when, early in 1917, the government decided on a further reduction to ten million, they soon had second thoughts. Eight Commissioners who went on tour that summer found that lack of beer was a universal cause of industrial unrest. To meet in 'The public house . . .', one later wrote, 'and discuss the eccentricities of centralised government was to the tired worker a pleasant relaxation leading to forgiveness . . . of the powers that be . . . To listen in a dry state at a street corner . . . was bound to stir up . . . social unrest . . . Bureaucracy in the absence of . . . vodka seems to have been the moving cause of Bolshevism in Russia.'

The government wisely decided to brew another six million gallons of light beer, the Parliamentary Secretary to the Minister of Food explaining that many employers had asked for more beer 'in the interests of efficiency and . . . contentment', while huge heaps of bread were being wasted in canteens for lack of beer to wash it down. Instead of threatening the working man's hard-earned pint, why did not the teetotallers campaign against West End shops which offered chocolates at 52s. 6d. a box when 'many people are finding it difficult to get . . . a pound of sugar'? The real victim of further restrictions, explained the Minister of Munitions, would be the north country housewife who used brewers' yeast to make bread. As for spirits, most distilleries were turning out industrial alcohol and others yielding valuable by-products for feeding pigs and cattle. It was, said one ingenious back-bencher, the teetotallers who were really to blame for one vital shortage, since 'the fanatical campaign' against brewing had meant a sharp drop in 'the cheapest and best food' for cows, 'brewers' grains'. Thus 'In striking in this unreasonable manner at the brewing trade these fanatics are depriving the children of the country of the milk of which they stand so much in need.'

'OUR COFFEE ROOM', AT DORKING, C. 1876

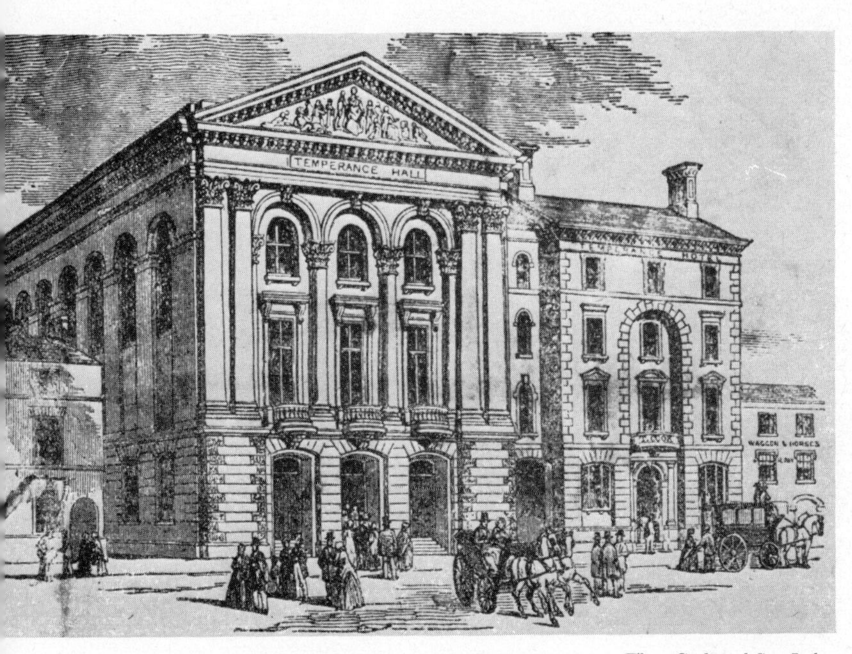


*Thos. Cook and Son Ltd.*

THE TEMPERANCE HALL, LEICESTER, WITH THOMAS COOK'S TEMPERANCE HOTEL

LICENSING
BILL
Bernard Partridge
A HANDY CUSTODIAN.
"YES, WE OUGHT TO GET PAST THE OTHERS PRETTY EASILY. BUT *THAT'S* THE FELLOW I'M AFRAID OF."


*'Punch'*

LLOYD GEORGE (*LEFT*) AND ASQUITH DISCUSS HOW THEY CAN GET THE LICENSING BILL PAST 'GOALKEEPER' LORD LANSDOWNE, 1908

*Chapter Twenty-four*

## TEN MINUTES MORE

'The amendment I have moved reduces from fifteen minutes to ten minutes the period of drinking-up time.'

— DENNIS VOSPER, M.P., House of Commons, 5th June 1961

THE FIRST WORLD WAR not merely demonstrated that Great Britain would never accept prohibition; it also destroyed the temperance movement's *raison d'être*. By 1919 shorter hours, higher prices, more civilised public houses and all the other 'true temperance' measures which had been tried had achieved a near-miracle. The consumption of all forms of drink, in terms of absolute alcohol, had dropped from 89 million gallons in 1914 to 37 million in 1918, and the number of cases of drunkenness in England and Wales from 184,000 to 29,000, while deaths from alcoholism had been cut by five-sixths. The manager of the largest bachelor lodging-house in Newcastle applied another test, unknown to statisticians. He now 'led, comparatively speaking, a gentleman's life', his daily rounds yielding only four dozen empty bottles instead of three gross.

No longer, except in a few black spots, did children gather outside the public houses on Saturday night to see the drunks thrown out. No longer did anxious wives search the gutters for stupefied husbands. Justly did Lloyd George, the chief architect of this social revolution, tell a prohibition deputation in 1917 that 'by confining our objectives to practical and attainable limits we had been able in the last year or two to achieve a far bigger advance towards national sobriety than had hitherto been effected . . . by all persuasive and legislative efforts in combination'. The M.P. was right, too, who said in February 1917 that 'great masses of people . . . do not wish to go back to the old state of things. Men who were not teetotallers . . . do not wish to have in their own streets . . . the sort of squalor which used to be found there three or four years ago.'

Wartime restrictions began gradually to be withdrawn in Great Britain from February 1919, just when in the United States the 36th state was ratifying the eighteenth amendment which enforced prohibition on the whole country from midnight on Friday, 16th January 1920. This gave the teetotallers new heart and soon there were rumours of a 'Prohibition Plot', one newspaper warning of 'conspirators . . . coming from America to try and turn Britain dry'. The chief conspirator, W. E. 'Pussyfoot' Johnson, was invited to England by the United Kingdom Alliance—his nickname, based on his stealthy work in hunting down illicit drink, became a synonym for 'teetotaller'. In November 1919 he took part in a debate with the Anti-Prohibition League in Essex Hall off the Strand, which was broken up by medical students armed with bags of flour and stink bombs. Johnson was dragged from the platform and carried off to King's College where he was publicly 'christened' on the balcony with a bottle of beer tipped over his head. The students then paraded him round the West End on a delivery van drawn by themselves, in a procession led by a tin-trumpet band and a banner showing drawings of a cat and a flagon of beer. 'Behind the banner, smiling and bowing to the left and right, came "Pussyfoot" himself', reported *The Times*. 'Then came a battalion of students, marching in fours . . . The marching song was . . . "Who've we got? Pussyfoot!"' One banner succinctly explained the demonstrators' attitude:

Mr. Pussyfoot, Miaow-wow!
Mr. Pussyfoot, Miaow-wow!
Fancy coming from America to try
To make Old England dry!

Uncle Sam stood it like a lamb,
But if you think we are going to allow
Any crank of a Yank to put us on the water tank—
Mr. Pussyfoot, Miaow-wow!

Mr. Pussyfoot was eventually rescued by the police after two hours, declaring that he had 'had a good time', though the rag had a tragic sequel, for a stone thrown during it cost Pussyfoot the sight of one eye. The press publicly apologised and Pussyfoot bravely continued his tour, and even made a gramophone record, *What I see with my blind eye*, which described the 'dry' world ahead.

Pussyfoot's blind eye had, however, let him down so far as Great Britain was concerned, although the Licensing Act of 1921 made permanent many wartime restrictions. The justices regained their former powers; the Control Board vanished and the Carlisle State District and its Scottish counterparts passed into the care of the Home Office and the Scottish Office. The afternoon break, however, had come to stay and opening hours, sixteen to nineteen-and-a-half pre-war, were now fixed at eight or nine, usually between 11 a.m. and 10 p.m., though closing time could be extended till 10.30, or in London till 11 p.m. On Sundays, no public house could now open for more than five hours altogether, ending at 10 p.m. Beer and spirits, though stronger than during the war, never regained their pre-war potency. 'The long pull', the 'on' sale of drink on credit and the bona-fide traveller had also vanished for good, while, most important of all, high prices had come to stay.

A curious feature of this period was the emergence of 'pseudo-temperance societies' financed by the trade to disrupt the prohibition movement. In 1920 the normally decorous annual conference of the Western Temperance League was almost wrecked by a delegation from the Fellowship of Freedom and Reform, which howled down 'Pussyfoot' Johnson until opening time. The League counter-attacked with a pamphlet exposing 'camouflaged brewers' fellowships' as the 'submarine flotilla of the liquor trade', but according to the League's historian, 'if a Fellowship official had not been convicted and fined in 1924 ... for disturbing a League meeting at Yeovil, the holding of temperance meetings in the West ... would have become well-nigh impossible owing to ... organised rowdyism'. 'Front' organisations of this kind were expressly condemned by the Royal Commission on Licensing a few years later.

The threat of prohibition also stimulated the trade into more open efforts to defend itself. Soldiers, surgeons and clergy, sportsmen and centenarians, all now testified to the blessings drink had brought them, and the nation's heavy expenditure on alcohol[1] was claimed as proof of public-spiritedness; the drinkers were generously keeping the country solvent, while the teetotallers were meanly evading their fair share of taxation, estimated at an extra £20 a year. *True Temperance Monographs*, published in 1921, exploded several teetotal myths. One parish clergyman had observed that 'the favourite drink ... amongst criminals in the slums of a large city ... was invariably cocoa', while there had been before prohibition more divorces in 'dry' states in the United States than in 'wet' ones. The book's sponsors, the True Temperance Association, no longer defended alcohol primarily for its food value. 'What the great majority of people drink alcohol for is not because they like the taste of it, nor because they are thirsty, but ... because it makes them feel jolly', acknowledged a leading mental specialist. 'What objection can there possibly be to anything which increases the sum of human happiness to the same extent as wine?' asked an eminent physician. Its only rival was beer, for 'It is almost impossible to conceive anything more delicious than a draught of cold beer when one is thirsty. One wishes one had a neck like a giraffe so as to feel the cold liquid trickling down two yards of gullet.' In 1922 one famous writer, Sir Arthur Quiller-Couch, issued a much-publicised statement that 'A total abstainer ... is in the nature of things imperfectly equipped for high literature, because ... its creation and ... full enjoyment demands total manhood, of which teetotal manhood is obviously a modification.' Leif Jones, a well-read bachelor, went down to

[1] Due to increased prices this was, of course, higher than ever, though drink consumption was lower.

Cornwall to denounce the traitor 'Q' on his native soil, and to attack drinking authors, whose works contained 'rollicking descriptions of drinking bouts' and were 'at times grossly coarse ... in regard to sexual matters'. A London newspaper commented lightheartedly, 'A couple of stouts, a couple of ports, a good stiff Scotch splash, and you cannot think what a merry and bright little trifle *Paradise Lost* seems.'

The *Handbook for Speakers and Writers on the So-called Temperance Question*, a 500-page compendium published by the Freedom Association in 1932, made the Rev. J. M. Morrell's rival work fifty years before seem slight and amateurish. *Was* drink chiefly responsible for poverty? The *Handbook* proved by quotations from Philip Snowden that it was not. *Did* drink cause almost all crime? The Home Office's most recent memorandum stressed that on the contrary crime demanded a clear head. *Did* drink lead to ill-treatment of children? The National Society for the Prevention of Cruelty to Children considered it important in 1931 in only one case in ten. *Did* drink produce insanity? As consumption of alcohol had slumped madness had increased, while the medical superintendent of one Dorset asylum had pronounced 'the black teapot ... a tragic factor in the creation of lunatics'. Teetotalism was a menace to general health, too: the War Office had warned its typists against excessive tea-drinking and a French doctor had found a link between appendicitis and abstinence. As for prohibition, 'Young men accustomed to get liquor', the Washington correspondent of *The Morning Post* had reported in 1921, 'have turned to drugs.'

Such arguments were by now almost redundant for the temperance movement was clearly in decline. The once-mighty Church of England Temperance Society had already lost two-thirds of its subscribers and the Good Templars had shrunk by 1931 to 27,000 adult members. The Band of Hope's strength had declined by half in twenty years and the young Rechabites had lost 17,000 members in twelve months. Its concert party, maliciously noted the *Handbook*, was known as 'The Remnants'. Even more significantly, the British Women's Total

Abstinence Union was now campaigning against the corrupting effect of some cinema-going, 'the drink question alone being apparently no longer a sufficient draw'.[1]

By now the British temperance movement had also been discredited by the total and disastrous failure of American prohibition. Far from preventing crime, prohibition had created an army of vicious gangsters and had driven formerly virtuous citizens into law-breaking, while the hospitals, instead of being emptied, were crammed with thousands of crippled and blinded victims of near-lethal 'hooch'. Prohibition was finally abandoned in 1933, but before this it had been resoundingly trounced in Great Britain. The first local option polls in Scotland under the 1913 Temperance (Scotland) Act, held in 1920, resulted in an overwhelming defeat for the prohibitionists, despite the importation of 'Pussyfoot' Johnson and a team of lavishly-paid agitators. Of 900 areas in Scotland containing public houses only 500 called for a poll and only 40 of these voted for 'no licence', while subsequent polls showed a steady erosion of temperance strength. The prohibitionists scored, however, a sensational victory in 1922 when 'Britain's first prohibition candidate', Edwin Scrymgeour, defeated Winston Churchill at Dundee. Scrymgeour introduced a Prohibition Bill in the following year, when it was thrown out by 236 votes to 14, and in 1931 he tried again, with slightly better results, 137 to 18. He left the House in 1931 and died in 1947.

The economic depression struck a further blow at the temperance movement, for it was self-evidently ridiculous to tell the millions of sober and hungry unemployed that their troubles were due to drink. The National Commercial Temperance League, founded in 1891 to promote 'total abstinence as a business asset', did, however, circularise businessmen with a novel pledge: 'To assist employment I agree to abstain from the use of intoxicating liquors . . . throughout 1925', and in 1932 the nonconformist-dominated Temperance Council of the Christian Churches called on the whole nation to abstain as an aid to

[1] The two were sometimes linked. An American investigator who watched 115 films discovered 'liquor situations' in 78%.

economic recovery. The teetotal Rouse the Nation Council, consisting largely of 'unemployed legislators', defeated in 1931, failed signally to live up to its name. Had Joseph Livesey still been alive no doubt he would have been turning Preston upside down organising public works for the unemployed, but the Livesey era was past. The response of the Good Templars to the challenge of the times was to pass a resolution in 1931 deploring 'the installation of wireless equipment in the state liquor shops of Carlisle'.

The success of the Carlisle experiment confirmed the belief of the Labour Party, which in 1919 had become the official Opposition, in nationalisation of the trade. In November 1919 Arthur Greenwood, a future deputy leader of the Party, told a conference that 'organised Labour is solidly and overwhelmingly in favour of public ownership . . . Prohibition . . . does not stand a chance . . . The country . . . was not going to be deprived of its beer.' A nationalisation Bill, though drafted, was never introduced, but in 1929 the second Labour government did appoint a Royal Commission on Licensing, with Lord Amulree as chairman, and a similar, separate, Commission for Scotland. The *Report* of the English Commission, published in 1932, was in every sense a 'thin' document, and did little more than repudiate local option and recommend further experiments on Carlisle lines. (The Scottish Commission, on the other hand, wanted to see the Gretna and Cromarty schemes wound up.) The Commission's 'ideal' was, it said, 'to make the public house . . . a place where the public can obtain general refreshment . . . in decent, pleasant and comfortable surroundings' which were 'a direct discouragement to insobriety'.

This was, of course, a familiar aim. The True Temperance Association had during the war made the sensible suggestion that 'improved' houses should pay a lower licence duty and be exempt from the compensation levy, predicting that 'with imagination and commonsense, the pub has a magnificent future'. Several Bills to encourage 'improved' houses were introduced into Parliament from 1918 onwards, often supported by the argument that no Chancellor would ever find the £300 to £600 million needed to nationalise the trade. The temperance movement insisted that the whole agitation was a brewers' plot. 'Until prohibition comes, our hope lies in preventing ... the rising generation from becoming habituated to ... intoxicants', argued *The Alliance Almanack* for 1920. The trade's provision of 'improved' houses was merely 'its advertisement ... "Wanted! Boys and girls"'.

The 1920s and 1930s were a great period of public house building, particularly on by-passes and new housing estates, and these spacious, custom-designed premises infuriated twentieth-century reformers as the gin palace had enraged their forebears. '"The Improved Public House"', wrote a future President of the Alliance, was 'an insidious danger to the future sobriety of the nation ...' While 'a few far-seeing municipal authorities' banned all licences on their estates, 'in other places ... like Birmingham, Manchester and London, the erection of very large and attractive-looking public houses is deliberately encouraged'.

The author recorded with disgust a visit around 1938 to one such establishment opened by the Chairman of the London County Council and blessed by the local vicar. 'In the whole of the premises there were 678 adult persons ... This so-called "Improved public house" was doing more harm ... than would half-a-dozen licensed houses of the ordinary type.' Not surprisingly, the trade's defenders took a different view. One True Temperance Association author commented admiringly on a large new public house near Birmingham: 'The lofty ceilings, the beautiful oak panelling, the Turkey carpets, the mosaic pavements and polished copper tables produce an impression of dignity which is almost incongruous. As a visitor said, "One has the feeling of entering into a cathedral rather than a public house."'

A remark by the Director of the Brewers' Society in 1933 that 'We want to get the beer-drinking habit instilled into thousands, almost millions of young men who do not at present know the taste of beer', led to a tremendous outcry by the teetotallers and they were also indignant about a mock-Rechabite society, the

Ancient Order of Frothblowers, whose declaration of principles asked, 'Do you gollop your beer with zest?' Most temperance propaganda had, however, a more familiar ring. What the Lord Chief Justice had said in 1878 was still being quoted in a pamphlet published in the 1930s, which even revived the 'two wines' theory and warned of the danger—a real one a century earlier—of the suffocation or 'overlying' of infants by drunken nurses. The court reports, too, remained a rich mine of material. *The Alliance Yearbook* for 1928 contained a vintage collection from *The News of the World*, from 'Schoolmaster arrested for grave charges; "Had had two or three sherries"' to 'Baronet—heavy drinker—strips and blacks girl'. But the trade, too, had perhaps changed less than its admirers claimed. The author of *The English Public House As It Is* in 1927 found many profitable taverns still cramped and squalid and though in one bar the customers had listened to the Sunday evening service on the newly-installed radio, in another, in the Midlands, 'Maud' had sat on the drinkers' laps and urged them to 'Tell us that one about the parson'.

The most detailed study of the British drinking scene ever made was undertaken between 1936 and 1939 by the social survey organisation Mass Observation. Its report, *The Pub and the People*, published in 1943, on life in the Lancashire textile town of Bolton—thinly disguised as 'Worktown'—revealed such little known facts as that drink was a theme in 13% of 224 Blackpool picture postcards—sex occurred in 31%; that a Weymouth Methodist minister was concerned about tortoise racing in public houses; that distillers and brewers bribed comedians to mention their products by name; and that about 15% of the adult population visited a public house at least once a week. As for the corruption of the young, more under-21s in Worktown patronised the milk-bars—the first had opened in 1937—than the public house and some brewers were even contemplating serving milk shakes.

Worktown also provided a history in microcosm of the temperance movement. Its first temperance society had been founded in 1831, it had been a centre of temperance literature from 1850 to 1880, and the clearing off of the debt on the Temperance Hall in 1859 had involved a three-day celebration and a bazaar that raised £900. Now the Temperance Hall was a cinema—the income financed the one remaining professional temperance worker—smoking and football pools were attacked more vigorously than drink, and only the members of the Holiness Tabernacle, who considered the cinema sinful and communicated in raspberry juice, remained solid for the old cause. The town's Temperance Union still existed on paper and in 1937 even, though unsuccessfully, opposed an extension of licensed hours for the Coronation. Its claim in 1936 to have held twenty-one meetings on the steps of the Town Hall, attended by 7,100, did not stand up to the shrewd eyes of Mass Observation: the actual attendance at two meetings it inspected had been respectively nine and thirty-five. Even the Union's annual meeting had attracted only twenty people, mainly elderly, the most vocal being a man of ninety-four who accused the Roman Catholics of holding drinking orgies in their churches. The Union President, a Baptist clergyman, had frankly admitted that temperance work now mainly attracted fanatics, while the Secretary had complained that 'The Sunday schools and churches are . . . full of complacency. They say there's no drunkenness . . . All the Bands of Hope seem to have gone.'

During the Second World War from 1939 to 1945 there was no Central Control Board and no active prohibition movement and only the shortage and high prices of wine and spirits, and the doleful notice 'Sorry no beer' on many a bar recalled the excitements of twenty years before. When, in 1945, the Labour Party came to real power for the first time, it was preoccupied with other matters than the trade and though in 1949 and 1951 back-benchers put down Bills to abolish the tied house these were never debated. In 1948 the government introduced a modest measure to extend state management to the New Towns, which then housed some 64,000 people but were destined to accommodate a million, and old battles were briefly refought. The teetotal Home Secretary, James Chuter Ede, disclaimed any desire 'to enter into the troubled controversies of amendments of the licensing law'; the Labour M.P. for Carlisle claimed it as 'a symbol of social progress and enlightened reform'; a Tory back-bencher thought the Bill 'the thin end of the pledge' and a Welsh Liberal denounced any state contact with 'an evil trade'. Outside the House, *The Morning Advertiser* threatened that brewers and publicans would 'act on political lines if necessary', the less responsible papers published cartoons showing the poor citizen being forced to ask a black-coated bureaucrat for a permit to buy a glass of beer, and 200 misguided citizens, believing that 'all pubs, hotels and inns are to be nationalised and that dominoes and darts will be prohibited', were persuaded to write to one M.P. alone. The Bill duly went through, by 305 votes to 187, but it was repealed four years later by the victorious Conservatives, the New Towns being, according to Labour members, shared out among the brewers as the spoils of victory.

Throughout the 1950s the ghost of the once-powerful temperance movement continued to haunt M.P.s. When, in 1952, a back-bencher proposed 'that certain of the more irksome restrictions on the sale of intoxicating liquor could be relaxed', it was 'the discouragement often caused to foreign visitors', not the interference with the British citizen's liberty, which was mentioned first. The imminence of Coronation Year did not deter the Baptist, Sir Cyril Black, from arguing that 'We should be earning foreign currency . . . at the price of the degradation of the manhood and womanhood of our people', or a Midlands member from warning that 'the booze trade . . . is even more dangerous today with its . . . chromium-plated "pubs" and "pubs" built in the Old Gothic style'.

With such antiquated bigotry still rampant, a later Conservative government and its Home Secretary, R. A. Butler, deserved full credit for bravely introducing a Licensing Bill designed 'to suit the general interest' by providing 'a modest increase in the total number of hours and a slightly later closing hour, together with greater uniformity'. The second reading, on 28th November 1960, marked the final, long overdue, turn of the temperance tide. Opening hours were, if the House agreed, to be raised to nine-and-a-half a day—11 a.m. to 3 p.m. and 5.30 to 11 p.m., or, at the justices' discretion, to 10.30 p.m. outside London; Sunday midday opening hours were to be extended from 2 p.m. to 3 p.m.; the frantic rush to finish drinks at closing time was to be prevented by allowing 'a quarter of an hour grace for drinking up after the end of permitted hours'; off-sales were to be allowed during normal shopping hours, licences were to be reclassified, being available to restaurants and hotels almost on demand; hotels were to have more freedom to serve drinks out of hours; legislation affecting clubs was to be tightened up; and liqueur chocolates could be sold in unlicensed shops.

As usual, both publicans and teetotallers raised a wail of indignation against the Bill and joined forces against the drinker. *The Alliance News* approvingly reprinted, along with letters from such representative organs of opinion as *The Sunday School Chronicle* and *The Baptist Times*, correspondence sent to *The Morning Advertiser*, where a Berkshire hotelier had criticised 'the extra fifteen minutes drinking-up time and . . . later opening', and a north London publican wanted to know 'What lunatic has connived at this . . . villainous . . . twelve to three scheme for Sunday?' Although from 75% to 98% of the trade were said to oppose all the Bill's provisions, except those making life harder for the clubs, one Welshman denounced it as 'a brewer's ramp', while Sir Cyril Black was, as usual, 'gravely concerned at the lowering of the moral standards in so many directions', and another high Tory, Sir Cyril Osborne, anxious 'to protect the weaker brethren'. It was soon clear that no party had a monopoly of intolerance. George Thomas, a Socialist from Cardiff, was, needlessly it has since proved, anxious about the sale of liqueur chocolates to children, while Sir Frank Soskice, later a short-lived and undistinguished Labour Home Secretary, thought a proposed extra half-hour on Sunday evening 'a revolutionary change', a remark greeted by incredulous guffaws. The best sense was spoken from the back benches. Instead of concessions to 'the trade lobby' and 'the teetotal lobby', asked the Labour M.P. Tom Driberg, what about some to the 'millions of ordinary moderate drinkers'?

But this was altogether too novel a notion for any government to accept and soon ministers, if not in full retreat, were making a series of tactical withdrawals. To please the publicans the government meekly dropped the extra hour on Sunday afternoon, though adding an extra thirty minutes at the end of the evening.[1] To please the teetotallers, who feared that with caterers' licences easier to get every back-street café would ply its patrons with liquor over their egg and chips, the government agreed to define a legally acceptable meal. To please both, the government spokesman, professing himself 'quite unrepentant' about drinking-up time, cravenly cut it to ten minutes. Worst of all, the vital principle of uniformity of hours was sacrificed to temperance fanaticism, so that evening opening time, 5.30 p.m. in London, remained in most other places at 6 p.m., and closing time oscillated between 10.30 and 11 p.m. according to area, season and day of the week. Only the liqueur chocolate was, as promised, duly set free.

Against the most vocal and least representative pressure group of all, the Welsh nonconformists, the government did, however, stand firm. Welsh Sunday closing, forced through the House by a militant minority when only one Welsh citizen in ten had the vote, had long since become a national scandal, for 60% of the adult male population belonged to drinking clubs and 10% of all alcohol drunk in Wales was consumed on a Sunday. The government cunningly hoisted the teetotallers with their own petard by proposing local option, through a plebiscite in each county. This plan to 'let the voice of the people decide' threw the teetotallers into a fury. The Liberal leader, Clement Davies, opposed the Bill on the curious ground that it would give power to 'a majority . . . who rarely enter fully into the life of the nation'. A former Labour minister thought the Bill would 'outrage nonconformist sentiment in Wales'—other Welshmen apparently did not count. A Vice-President of the Band of Hope incautiously admitted that 'Many people think that to be a temperance worker means that

[1] The most irritating restriction of all, Sunday closing until 7 p.m., remained unchanged.

there is something wrong with us.' Supporters of 'freedom for Wales' suggested a national ballot instead, but the teetotallers liked this even less, well knowing that this meant the whole of Wales being liberated. Their suggestion was that the Bill should be referred to an all-Welsh Committee so that, as one dissident Welsh M.P. said, it could 'be taken down to the cellar and strangled . . . What argument', asked the same brave member, Iowerth Thomas from the Rhondda, 'can be put forward, especially by radical democrats, to deny two-and-a-half million people in Wales the same rights, liberties and freedom enjoyed by those forty-five million people over the border?' He urged the House 'to liberate the people of Wales from the tyranny and the bigotry that has dominated their lives for over eighty years'. On a free vote, and despite a national day of prayer on their behalf in the chapels of North Wales, tyranny and bigotry were duly defeated by 177 to 56, and three months after, on 3rd August 1961, the Licensing Act had become law, the Sunday-opening poll in Wales completed their rout. About half the electorate voted and a clear majority, 454,000 to 391,000, favoured Sunday opening. All four county boroughs, including Cardiff, and five of the thirteen counties, decided to unlock the public house doors. The eight other counties, largely in the rural north, opted to stay dry.

Outside Wales, temperance has lost its hold even on the nonconformists. The stories of Free Churchmen with beer hidden in the coal cellar which got a laugh in Worktown in the 1930s would today seem hopelessly dated, and a survey of Methodist ministers in 1962 showed that a quarter did not practise total abstinence and half those who did did not believe in it. 'Temperance Sunday', once an important event, has been renamed 'Citizenship Sunday', while the Church of England Temperance Society has disappeared, although the Church's Social Problems Division still works among alcoholics.

To assess the strength of the temperance movement today is difficult, for many of the old societies have vanished, the survivors are unable, or unwilling, even to estimate their own membership, and no one organisation represents them all. The most active bodies today are those which aim to influence legislation, the United Kingdom Alliance and the National Temperance Federation. The former, which still includes non-abstainers, has a mailing list of about 11,000 and though still working for the ultimate suppression of the 'liquor traffic' no longer quotes prohibition as an immediate aim. The Federation has 23 societies affiliated to it, some purely administrative, and estimates their total membership at about 520,000. This figure is far from authoritative, however, since eleven societies provided no information and there is clearly much overlapping membership. The Rechabites are probably the largest non-religious organisation, with about 120,000 adult members in Great Britain, followed by another friendly society, the Sons of Temperance, with 75,000. Among religious societies the strongest are the Church of Scotland's Women Section with 124,000 members and the United Free Church of Scotland, with 23,000. The most powerful not specifically religious women's organisation is the 15,000-strong National British Women's Total Abstinence Union. In 1967 there were also some 15,000 Good Templars in the United Kingdom and the movement still maintained its own children's home. The British National Temperance League, with headquarters in Sheffield, has about a hundred affiliated societies, but no figures for their membership; the British Temperance Society, misleadingly, is not a general organisation but part of the Seventh Day Adventist religious sect.

Many local temperance societies have handed over their affairs and assets to a regional association, like the Western Temperance League, based on Bristol, which now has 120 societies affiliated to it, compared to about 350 ninety years ago. The League, which covers an area with a population of nearly six million, has about 2,000 individual members, or one person in every 3,000. The North of England Temperance League, covering the five northernmost counties, which contain 3,300,000 people, draws support from forty local societies, with 5,000 members, so that in this area approximately one person in 660 is a paid-up, active teetotaller, plus others who belong to societies outside the League. In 1892 the comparable figure, allowing for the smaller population, was about one in forty-four. Even the surviving few have some nuisance value, however. In 1961 local temperance organisations successfully interfered with nearly half of the eighty licensing applications they opposed, while the Temperance Council of the Christian Churches by frustrating—with trade support—the efforts of some self-service stores to sell drink, has managed to inconvenience many shoppers or to drive them instead into the wine-merchants and the public houses to buy their wine or beer.

The drop in support for children's temperance organisations has been even more marked. The Band of Hope has no statistics about local societies but one press article in 1962 estimated their total support at only 'a few thousands'. Even more revealingly, many societies have dropped the traditional name, preferring non-committal titles like 'The Amethyst Club'.

The number of people in Great Britain who abstain from drink on grounds of principle rather than preference is also hard to determine. One expert calculates that, assuming all Salvation Army members are teetotallers and about half those in other nonconformist churches, the total is around three million; this is perhaps on the high side.

The deterioration in the quality, as well as the numerical strength, of the temperance movement is well illustrated by the extent to which, as was already happening in the 1930s, it is now seeking fresh targets for attack. Now that it is television, not the 'talkies', which is new, the National British Women's Total Abstinence Union is alarmed about violence and immorality on the small screen, while other temperance organisations oppose gambling and smoking. One, even more optimistic, recently achieved a brief notoriety by proposing a 'Chastity Pledge', under which girls would promise to abstain from premarital intercourse, as well, presumably, as alcohol.[1] Today a popular target is drugs. Ironically the same organisations which

[1] Thus recalling the classic story of Lady Astor declaring 'I would rather commit adultery than have a drink' and the heckler shouting 'Who wouldn't?'

successfully campaigned to prevent young people enjoying a harmless shandy or soft drink in a well-run public house, now complain that they are acquiring far more dangerous drugs in unlicensed coffee bars. Indeed, although a new golden age was promised once drunkenness was banished, the millennium seems strangely slow in arriving. Crime, divorce and immorality, far from disappearing, have actually increased since the demon drink has been tamed, the General Secretary of the Band of Hope warning as recently as 1964 that with 'juvenile delinquency ... promiscuity and drug taking ... rapidly undermining the nation ... the collapse of our civilisation' was an imminent possibility.

In Parliament, where temperance opinion was once under-represented, it is today grossly, even dangerously, over-represented. The temperance group of M.P.s numbers about 130 out of 630 members, though few attend its meetings and not all are abstainers. The group's chairman, Sir Cyril Black, an ultra-Conservative Wimbledon property millionaire, has little obvious resemblance to that poor and Radical Preston cheese-maker, Joseph Livesey, or to the first parliamentary water-drinker, James Silk Buckingham, who was derided as a visionary in the 1830s for wishing to humanise the penal system and to abolish the death penalty. His successor in the 1960s favours the return of the birch and the restoration of capital punishment.

The temperance movement today has, in fact, little in common with its past. Its progressive love of humanity has degenerated into reactionary opposition to 'softness', its old comradeship has withered into fraternal distrust, its desire to improve the quality of life has congealed into a joyless puritanism. The history of this once great movement has, however, much to teach us today: the astonishing change in public opinion and legislation which can be accomplished by a small band of dedicated and courageous men and women; the readiness to submit to restrictions and compromises which a majority will show for the sake of peace from a noisy and persistent minority; above all, perhaps, the menace to society represented by reformers who have outlived their usefulness.

# A NOTE ON SOURCES

*The place of publication is London, unless otherwise stated. Publishers are omitted, except in the case of relatively recent books, and authors' qualifications are not given except where directly relevant. A few publications which I have been unable to consult, but which seem from contemporary references to have been important, are included. Complete particulars are given only the first time a book is mentioned.*

## GENERAL ACCOUNTS

The indispensable source is James Dawson Burns, D.D., *A Consecutive Narrative of the Rise, Development and Extension of the Temperance Reform*, commonly known as Dawson Burns's *Temperance History* (Volume I, no date but circa 1881, Volume II n.d. but c.1890), a year by year diary of the movement with an excellent classified index. Where a temperance or teetotal historian is referred to in the text Burns is meant, unless otherwise indicated here. The other standard works are Peter T. Winskill, *The Temperance Movement and its Workers* (4 volumes, Blackie, 1892) and *The Comprehensive History of the Rise and Progress of the Temperance Reformation from the Earliest Period to September 1881* (Warrington, 1881) and the Rev. Henry Carter, *The English Temperance Movement, Volume I, 1830–1899* (Epworth Press, 1933, no more published). On the first years of the movement, Samuel Cowling, *History of the Temperance Movement in Great Britain and Ireland from the Earliest Date to the Present Time (1862)* is also very useful. A very slight, but more recent, survey is Sir

R. Murray Hyslop, *The Centenary of the Temperance Movement, 1832–1932* (1931). References to events in the United States throughout the book are mainly based on J. C. Furnas, *The Life and Times of the Late Demon Rum* (W. H. Allen, 1965)—the nearest American equivalent to the present book—and Andrew Sinclair, *Prohibition* (Faber, 1962).

Periodical publications drawn on throughout the book were *Hansard's Parliamentary Debates*; *The Annual Register*; and *The Times*. Temperance magazines consulted are indicated under the various chapter headings.

## CHAPTER ONE

The main source was Richard V. French, *Nineteen Centuries of Drink in England* (2nd edition, n.d., but c.1884). I also used Samuel Morewood, *An Essay on the Inventions and Customs of Both Ancients and Moderns in the Use of Intoxicating Liquors* (1824), Sidney and Beatrice Webb, *The History of Liquor Licensing in England, principally from 1700 to 1830* (Longmans, 1903), M. Dorothy George, *London Life in the Eighteenth Century* (Penguin, 1966), Arthur Shadwell, M.D., *Drink, Temperance and Legislation* (Longmans, 1903) and John H. Hutchins, *Jonas Hanway 1712–1786* (S.P.C.K., 1940). The Dublin clergyman is quoted by Dr. Ralph Charles Grindrod, *Bacchus, An Essay on the Nature, Causes, Effects and Cure of Drunkenness* (1839). Hanway's indictment of tea is quoted in *True Temperance Monographs* (True Temperance Association, 1921) and by J. M. Scott, *The Tea Story* (Heinemann, 1964). On beer, in this and other chapters, I used H. A. Monckton, *A History of English Ale and Beer* (The Bodley Head, 1966).

## CHAPTER TWO

The Webbs are a main source. The beer-drinker quoted is Morewood, the doctor who defended vitriol Shadwell. The description of May morning in Edinburgh is quoted by John Dunlop, *The Philosophy of Artificial and Compulsory Drinking Usages in Great Britain and Ireland* (1839), a major source for much of the chapter. The description of the coming-of-age feast and of funerals in Skye are quoted by Grindrod, of William IV's coronation by Ralph E. Turner, *James Silk Buckingham 1786–1855* (Williams and Norgate, 1934), and of the Horsham election by George B. Wilson, *Alcohol and the Nation* (Nicholson and Watson, 1940).

## CHAPTER THREE

The principal sources are the *Evidence* heard by *The Select Committee Appointed to Enquire into the State and Management of Houses in which Beer is Sold by Retail* and the *Report of the Select Committee Appointed to Enquire into the State and Management of Houses ... Commonly Called Beershops*, the official Report referred to. Other sources are the Rev. Thomas Page, *An Earnest Appeal to the Nation at large on the Mischievous Effects of Beerhouses* (1846) and J. Russom, *The Evil Effects of Beershops* (1849). The exterior of a gin-palace was described by a witness in *Evidence* heard by the *Select Committee on Drunkenness* (1834), and the interior by Mrs. Henry Wood, *Danesbury House* (1860).

## CHAPTER FOUR

On Joseph Livesey, the Preston resident referred to, my chief source was John Pearce (editor), *The Life and Teachings of Joseph Livesey* (1887), supplemented by Ernest H. Hayes, *The Cheese-factor's Vow* (Wallington, n.d. but c.1950) and *The Preston Temperance Advocate*. On the much-debated question of the order in which the first societies were founded I have generally followed Winskill, who made a special study of this subject.

## CHAPTER FIVE

The Malt Liquor Lecture was reproduced by Pearce. Other sources on the origins of the movement are William Logan, *Early Heroes of the Temperance Reformation* (1873) and Jabez Inwards, *Memorials of Temperance Workers* (1879), particularly useful on how the pioneers died. The beer-barrel incident and the first teetotal procession are described by W. Pilkington, *The Struggles and Triumphs of Teetotalism, a Lecture* (Preston, n.d. but c.1895).

## CHAPTER SIX

On the origins of individual societies I used the following: William E. A. Axon, *The Social Results of Temperance in Blackburn* (1886); John Farley Rutter, *Short History of the Mere Temperance Society* (1890); Frank Bates, *Lights and Landmarks of the Teetotal Movement in Northamptonshire* (Northampton, 1898); William Pickwell, *The Temperance Movement in the City of York* (York, 1886), a most useful account of the growth of teetotalism in one town, with a list of twelve 'early objections and prejudices' against teetotalism with the answers to them; J. P. Draper, *Jubilee Sketch of the Fitzroy Teetotal Association* (1889) and *Memorial Days* (also about the Fitzroy Association) (1898); Jack Young, *How the Movement Came to Tynemouth* (1932); and *Middlesbrough Temperance Society, Souvenir of the Centenary Celebrations* (1936). Dr. Henry Mudge's sermon was reprinted as *The Fruits of Teetotalism* (Falmouth, 1839). Winskill described Captain Bailey's scruples.

## CHAPTER SEVEN

The chief authority is Thomas Hudson, *Temperance Pioneers of the West* (1887). I also used two privately-printed pamphlets,

Arthur G. Barker, *The Temperance Century in the West* (Western Temperance League, 1937) and Roger Clarke, *The Street Teetotal Society, 1835–1935* (1935). Teare's rough reception at Street is described by Pilkington. On Teare's life I used the memoir which appears as an introduction to Frederick Powell, *Bacchus Dethroned* (1871), the first James Teare Prize Essay, and James Stephenson, Joseph Dearden and George Toulmin, '*The Origin and Success of Teetotalism*', *Refutation* (Preston, 1864), though Teare's book, which prompted the *Refutation*, I was unable to consult. The information about the Joseph Eaton legacies came from Dawson Burns and from the *Annual Report* of the United Kingdom Alliance for the year ending 30th September 1966. The American visitor was John B. Gough and the suggestion about classifying temperance hotels was reported in *The Western Temperance Herald* for January 1899.

## CHAPTER EIGHT

Thomas Whittaker, *Life's Battles in Temperance Armour* (1892), was supplemented by his pamphlet *Facts and Feelings or Storms by Sea and Land as Illustrated by the Loss of the Lifeboat Crew at Whitby on February 9th and the Narrow Escape of Thos. Whittaker, Temperance Advocate, at Scarborough, March 5th 1861* (Scarborough, 1861), by a brief note in J. M. Blakey, *Some Scarborough Faces* (*Past and Present*) (Scarborough, 1901)—the source of the Hyde Park challenge story—and by information supplied privately by Mr. Meredith Whittaker.

## CHAPTER NINE

Sources not already listed were Joseph Brotherton, *The First Teetotal Tract on Abstinence from Intoxicating Liquor* (1821, reprinted 1890), and James Silk Buckingham, *Autobiography* (2 volumes, Longmans, 1855).

## CHAPTER TEN

The principal source is the Rev. Jonathan Turner, *Teetotalism Illustrated by Facts, including a Brief View of Teetotal Sayings and Doings in St. Ives and the West of Cornwall* (London and Exeter, 1842): I also used Anon. (in fact F. J. Vibert), *A Vindication of the Case of the Teetotal Wesleyan Methodists of St. Ives, Cornwall, with an Incidental Exposure of the Domination of the Wesleyan Priesthood* (Penzance, 1842); *A Lancet for a Knife, or Jonathan Turner Bled to Death, by the Author of the St. Ives Case* (Penzance, 1843) and *A Forerunner, by the Writer of the St. Ives Case* (Hayle, n.d. but c.1843); John Ellis, *A Letter to the Rev. Jonathan Turner, Wesleyan Minister, Exeter, Occasioned by Reading his Pamphlet Entitled 'Teetotalism, Illustrated by Facts'* (Exeter, 1843) and *Thomas S. Burgon, The Practicability of Teetotalism, Shewn by the Sayings and Doings of the Teetotallers in St. Ives and the West of Cornwall, Intended as a Defence against the Attacks of the Rev. J. Turner's Tract entitled 'Teetotalism Illustrated by Facts'* (Penzance, 1843). On general criticism of the movement, I used Democritus, *A Medical Moral and Christian Dissection of Teetotalism* (1846), Thomas Smeeton, *Confessions of a Convert from Teetotalism to Temperance* (1849) and *Household Words* for 23rd August 1851. The great pitmen's strike is described by Winskill.

## CHAPTER ELEVEN

The outstanding source is John Francis Maguire, *Father Mathew, a Biography* (1863). Two recent biographies which claim to add new material and correct inaccuracies in Maguire are the Rev. Patrick Rogers, *Father Theobald Mathew* (Browne and Nolan, Dublin, 1943) and the Rev. Father Augustine, *Footprints of Father Theobald Mathew, Apostle of Temperance* (Dublin, 1947), the 'modern research' referred to. I also consulted S. H. Burke, *The Rise and Progress of Father Mathew's*

*Temperance Mission* (1885); the Rev. W. H. Cologan, *Father Mathew, The Apostle of Temperance* (n.d. but c.1890); and S. R. Wells, *Father Mathew, The Temperance Apostle* (New York, n.d. but c.1867). The story of the heresy porter occurs in Patrick Lynch and John Vaizey, *Guinness's Brewery in the Irish Economy, 1758–1876* (Cambridge University Press, 1960).

## CHAPTER TWELVE

The title quotation and several of the songs referred to come from the Rev. J. A. Sharp (editor), *The New Temperance Hymnal* (1909); my chief source was Frederick Smith (editor), *The Jubilee of the Band of Hope Movement* (U.K. Band of Hope Union, 1897). The pamphlet by George Cruikshank referred to is *The Glass and the New Crystal Palace* (1853). The specimen programme for Bands of Hope is given by J. Milton Smith, *The Band of Hope in the Sunday School* (n.d. but c.1881). Temperance textbooks for children which I consulted included: Mrs. Clara Balfour, *Morning Dewdrops, or the Juvenile Abstainer* (many editions, from 1843 onwards); J. James Ridge, *The Band of Hope Catechism* (n.d. but c.1894); J. Glyn Davies, *A Temperance Catechism* (R. E. Jones, Conway, n.d.); Charles Wakeley, *The Temperance Manual for the Young* (n.d. but c.1891); Frederick Smith, *Simple Lessons for Young Abstainers* (1894); Ebenezer Clarke, *The Worship of Bacchus, a Great Delusion* (abridged edition, n.d. but c.1894); Anon., *The Land where Jack Dwelt* (Church of England Temperance Society, n.d. but c.1890) and *The Temperance Alphabet for Bands of Hope* (1871); *Temperance Picture Books No. 1 and No. 2* (C.E.T.S., n.d. but c.1891); *The Musical Temperance Alphabet* (n.d. but c.1894); Dr. Benjamin W. Richardson, *The Temperance Lesson Book* (1878) and *Drink and Strong Drink, a Series of Readings for Schools and Families* (1882); A. Jolliffe, *Simple Temperance Teaching for Children* (1891) and *The Child's Textbook of Easy Temperance Lessons* (1916); the Rev. William Spiers, *Giant Alcohol, or Talks with the Young on the Science of Temperance* (1907); Miss E. Holmes Harvey, *A New Temperance Catechism for Juniors* (n.d. but c.1911); Helen Coomber, *Lessons and Experiments on Scientific Hygiene and Temperance for Elementary School Children* (Macmillan, 1914); Dr. John A. Hunter, *Alcohol and Life, A Manual of Scientific Temperance Teaching for Schools* (Macmillan, 1918). Temperance fiction for children which I read included Mary E. Murray, *A Bit of Blue Ribbon* (n.d.); Miss M. A. Paull, *Sought and Saved* (1880); and the Rev. T. P. Wilson, *Frank Oldfield* (1869). I also consulted *The Souvenir of the Essay Competition in the Hull Elementary Schools on 'Physical Deterioration and Alcoholism'* (1906), and R. H. Crofton, *Anne Jane Carlile and her Descendants* (St. Leonards on Sea, 1950). The appeal to gilded youth is contained in Canon E. G. Sandford, *Temperance at School and the University* (1890) and Dr. Dukes's anxieties about bedtime beer in *Alcohol and Childhood* (1891).

## CHAPTER THIRTEEN

The history of the Alliance is told in Mark H. C. Hayler, *The Vision of a Century, 1853–1953* (U.K. Alliance, 1953) and its foundation is recorded in *The Report of the Provisional Committee* (U.K. Alliance, Manchester, 1853). Details about Thomas Cook come from Burns and Winskill and from private information from Thomas Cook and Son Ltd. The verse on Exeter Hall occurs in Turner. The effects of the Maine Law are described by Furnas. The reference to 'little differences between teetotallers' is found in Winskill, *Comprehensive History*. Livesey's criticism of the Alliance is quoted by Carter. The disguised and martyred teetotallers are mentioned by Burns, the 'empty' glass incident by Jack Young, and events in Shrewsbury by Mrs. J. B. (Charles) Wightman, *Haste to the Rescue* (1862). Other important sources are Frederick R. Lees, *An Argument, Legal and Historical for the Prohibition of the Liquor Traffic* (1855), and Frederick Powell, *Bacchus Dethroned* (1871). I also used Jabez Inwards, *Pictures on the Traffic, Consisting of Remarks on Public House Signs* (1881); Joseph McCorry, *Alcohol As It Was, As It Is And As It Ever Shall Be, the Enemy of the Human Race* (1886); James C. Parker, *Mission Work among Licensed Victuallers* (1892); Edwin Evans, *Are you a Teetotaller?* (1892); W. C. Galton, *The Licensed Victualler's Dialogue and Publican's Prayer* (1896); Tom Glover, *Tom Glover's Reform Bill and Challenge of 100 Guineas and a Few Chips from a Workshop* (1887); and Robert Scott Moffat (editor), *The Times's Drinking Bout* (n.d. but c.1891). Working conditions in public houses are described by the Rev. J. M. Morrell, *Hints and Topics for Temperance Speakers* (1883), a most useful book on many aspects of the subject, and Anon., *The Barmaid Problem* (published by the Joint Committee on the Employment of Barmaids, n.d. but c.1904). Criticism of short measure and poor quality beer is made by Henry Ladd, *The Vital Question of the Day: or How to Suppress Drunkenness from a Publican's Point of View* (Carmarthen, 1877) and the story, *A Good Young Man*, and the series on famous fights are quoted by Anon. (Pseudonym 'The Aldgate Pump'), *Studies of the Bar, or Beer, Bungs and Bruisers* (1874).

## CHAPTER FOURTEEN

My chief sources on Gough were John B. Gough, *Autobiography, Revised and Brought Down to the Present* (1879); *Orations* (1878); *Sunlight and Shadow: or Gleanings from my Life Work* (1891) and Furnas. On Lees I used Frederick Lees, *Dr. F. R. Lees: A Biography* (H. J. Osborn, London, 1904); Frederick R. Lees, *What Was It? The Inner-history of the Temperance Libel Case from the Moral Standpoint, Final Words for History* (1860) and Edward Grubb, *Old and New Temperance Advocacy* (n.d. but c.1858). The building of the hall at Dunse is reported in *The Illustrated London News* for 13th January 1855, and the Gough v. Lees court hearing in *The Times* for 22nd June 1858. The description of Gough's first meeting and the panegyric on cold water are quoted by Winskill, and the Anglican clergyman present was Morrell.

## CHAPTER FIFTEEN

The main sources for the events of 1854 and 1855 are *The Report from the Select Committee on Public Houses, with Evidence*, July 1854, and *The Select Committee on the Sale of Beer Act, First Report*, July 1855. The enthusiasm of Scots for Sunday closing is referred to by R. P. Durnford, *The Englishman's Brief for Sunday Closing* (1898), a valuable summary of previous legislation and of events throughout the British Isles. The information about Francis Berkeley is mainly taken from the *Dictionary of National Biography* and the report of his law-suit from *The Times*. The remarks of Dr. Christopher Wordsworth, Bishop of Lincoln, occur in a speech made in the Corn Exchange, Lincoln, on 28th February 1870 (reprinted, n.d.). J. Beavan, *The History of the Welsh Sunday Closing Act* (Cardiff, 1885) was my main source on Wales. The Carmarthenshire licensee was Henry Ladd. Other sources were the Rev. J. M. Morrell, *Reasons for a Sunday Closing Bill for Cornwall* (1882); Joseph Malins, *Legislation on the Sunday Closing of Public Houses* (1889); A. F. Harvey, *The Royal Commission and Sunday Closing* (1899), which describes the drunkards on the road to Rumney and the 'flying squadron' of police; Anon., *The Drunkard's Plea for Sunday Closing* (1884); *The Western Temperance Herald*, February 1899; and 'A Radical' (in fact A. J. Marriott), *The Public v. the Publican and Teetotal Fanatic* (1892).

## CHAPTER SIXTEEN

Dr. Todd's prescriptions are referred to by Sir Victor Horsley, *What Women can do to Promote Temperance* (n.d. but c.1906), which also includes figures of hospital expenditure on alcohol and milk, and Courtenay C. Weeks, M.R.C.S., *Alcohol in*

*Medical Practice* (H. K. Lewis & Co., 1925). Other sources on the early period are Henry Mudge, surgeon, *Teetotalism, a Manifestation of Love* (n.d. but c.1840); John Higginbotham, surgeon, *Alcohol as a Medicine* (1840); A. Courtney, surgeon, *Alcohol as a Beverage and as a Medicine* (1842); R. Hicks, *The Injurious Effect of Alcohol upon the Human Frame* (1841); and Robert Macnish, *The Anatomy of Drunkenness* (1834), which quotes early examples of spontaneous combustion. Later cases are quoted by Charles Keene, *Albert Lacroix or a Loathsome Living Devil* (n.d. but c.1890), Frederick Powell and Furnas. Other sources are Grindrod, Baker, Democritus, Pearce, for the Livesey quotations; Thomas Hudson, for the story of the ten-year-old boy; and Burns, on the origins of the London Temperance Hospital. Liebig's work is discussed by Burns and Weeks and Burns also refers to William Batchelor, M.R.C.S., *The Trial and Persecution of a Teetotal Surgeon* (1842), which I have been unable to consult. Later sources included: Mrs. R. D. Bolton, *What we Expect of our Doctors* (1886); M.S.B., *Something I Want you Mothers to Know* (1889); J. F. B. Tinling, *For the Sake of the Children* (1890); and William Sharpe, M.D., *Alcohol a Factor in Human Progress* (1882), which praises its beneficial effects. On temperance recipes I used Anon., *Temperance Substitutes for Brandy* (n.d. but c.1890) and *Temperance Drinks for the Harvest and Home* (in English and Welsh, Denbigh, n.d.); Henry Mudge, surgeon, *Advice to Farmers and other Employers with Testimonials in Favour of Teetotalism* (n.d. but c.1840); Mrs. Wightman and Morrell, *Hints and Topics*. Catherine B. Drummond, *An Outline of the Temperance Question* (n.d. but c.1905) gives details of hospital expenditure on alcohol and W. C. Amery, *The Non-Alcoholic System of Workhouse Management* (Birmingham, 1888), describes the campaign against drink in workhouses. References to alcohol in hospital are also found in A. E. Clark-Kennedy, *The London*, Volume II, 1840–1948 (Pitman Medical Publishing Co., 1963). The connection between alcohol and cholera is asserted by the Rev. W. R. Baker, *The Curse of Britain. An Essay on the Evils, Causes and Cure of Intemperance*

(1838), the first full-scale teetotal textbook, and is discussed in detail in my *King Cholera* (Hamish Hamilton, 1966). The key sources on Sir Victor Horsley's work are Sir Victor Horsley, F.R.S., F.R.C.S., and Mary D. Sturge, M.D., *Alcohol and the Human Body* (Macmillan, 1908), and Stephen Paget, *Sir Victor Horsley* (Constable, 1919). The views of Dr. C. A. Mercier and Sir James Crichton Browne, M.D., appear in *True Temperance Monographs* (True Temperance Association, 1921). The examples of teetotal sportsmen are mainly given by Burns and refuted by Ernest E. Williams, *Handbook for Speakers and Writers on the So-Called Temperance Question* (9th edition, revised to September 1932, Freedom Association, n.d.).

## CHAPTER SEVENTEEN

On Dr. F. R. Lees, I used Winskill and Frederick Lees. The literature by Lees himself is vast, but I principally used the following: *Prize Essay on Deuteronomy XIV, 25, 26* (Aberdeen, 1842); *Report on the Public Discussion held at Market Drayton on Tuesday 9th September 1845 between Mr. John H. Barrow, Independent Minister of Market Drayton and Dr. Frederick R. Lees, of Leeds, on the Question 'Is Teetotalism in Harmony with the Divine Word?'* (c.1845); *Prize Essay on the Nature, Elements and Rites of the Christian Eucharist* (1844); *The Bible Wine Question. The Answer to the 'Unanswerable', or an Exposure of the Fallacies of Three Irish Advocates and Eleven Syrian Witnesses* (1876); *Teetotalism in its Relations to the New Testament* (n.d. but in Vol. II of *Collected Works*, 1853); *A Refutation of the Bishop of Lincoln's Extraordinary Attack upon Teetotalism* (n.d. but c.1873); *Teetotalism, the Teaching of the Bible* (1883); and, with the Rev. James Dawson Burns, *The Temperance Bible Commentary* (1868). I also used David Williams, *The Bible, Teetotalism and Dr. Lees* (1859); the Rev. James Dawson Burns, *The Rev. Charles Lee's Objections to Total Abstinence Answered by the Rev. Dawson Burns in a Lecture delivered in Camden Hall, Camden Town, Mon-*

*day 18th December 1865* (1866); the Rev. Benjamin Cervoso, Wesleyan Minister, *Drunkenness, the Enemy of Britain, Arrested by the Hand of God in Teetotalism* (n.d. but c.1840); John L. Penny, *The Test of Christian Conduct Applied to the Use of Intoxicating Liquors in a Letter to Christians* (1840); R. Rackes Bromage, *What the Bible says on Gospel Temperance* (n.d. c.1882); Anon., *The Two Lost Sons. A Warning to the Intemperate* (n.d. but c.1840); George Powell, *The 'Calm Consideration' of the Rev. Jacob Stanley Calmly Considered by an Old Methodist Local Preacher in a Familiar Letter to a Friend in Bristol* (1841); the Bishop of Lincoln (Dr. Christopher Wordsworth), *On Temperance Societies* (1873); John Fordyce, *A Reply to the Bishop of Lincoln on Temperance Societies* (1873); Anon. (in fact A. S. W. Young), *The Blue Ribbon versus the Cross. A Short Letter Addressed to the Vicar of Kingston upon Thames* (1883); W.H.F., *Temperance not Abstinence the Teaching and Example Laid Down in Holy Scripture* (Taunton, 1883); the Rev. George Pope, *The Mind of God on Total Abstinence* (1884); 'A Churchman', *Temperance Fanaticism in Regard to Sacramental Wine, a Letter to the Lord Bishop of Manchester, containing an Exhaustive Enquiry into the Traditions and Practice of the Early Fathers* (1885); the Rev. R. M. Grier, *A Letter of Remonstrance to the Very Rev. Dean of Rochester* (1889); John Kempster, *The Dean and the Drink* (1892), which quotes the Dean's speech; W. W. Edwards, *The Bible on the Side of Total Abstinence* (1895); M. A. Austen Leigh, *True Temperance as Taught by the Bible* (1884), which refers to the 'emblematic' significance of wine; J. W. Kirton, *The Waterdrinkers of the Bible* (1885); the Rev. S. D. Scammell, *Did the Son of God, When upon Earth, Use, Provide or Commend the Use of Intoxicating Drink?* (1890); the Rev. D. V. Lucas, *Wine Bad and Good* (1894); Anon., *Did Our Lord Indeed Speak Sense?* (1895); the Bishop of Lincoln (Dr. Edward Hicks), *The Church and the Liquor Traffic* (n.d. but c.1912); and George Campion, *A Prick to the Teetotal Bubble* (n.d. but c.1896). The conflicting opinions of Irish priests on the pledge are quoted by Augustine. The Roman

Catholic attitude to teetotalism is discussed by the Rev. Joseph Keating, S.J., *The Drink Question* (1914), and Cardinal Manning's views by Sidney Dark, *Manning* (Duckworth, 1936), while the Rev. James Dawson Burns, *Pen Pictures of Temperance Notables* (1895) explains Manning's conversion to total abstinence. Manning and other clerical teetotallers are also described in Frederick Sherlock, *Heroes in the Strife, or The Temperance Testimonies of some Eminent Men* (1881). The rationalist viewpoint is given by G. W. Foote, *The Bible and Beer* (1895). Frank Bates describes the Baptist who administered communion to himself, Keating the man who communicated in tea, and William Pickwell the belief that the temperance movement was a Roman Catholic plot and the need for alcohol to be 'driven out from the shelter of the church'. The sense of disappointment was felt by Scammell. Lees's discovery of non-alcoholic wine is described by Frederick Lees; Frank Wright's wine was advertised in Morrell, *Hints and Topics*. The Welsh clergyman who distributed tickets for drink is described by Henry Ladd and the trials of the teetotallers in South Shields by Jack Young.

## CHAPTER EIGHTEEN

Publications consulted were: Anon., *An Earnest Appeal from the Furnace by a Bottle Hand to His Fellow Workmen* (n.d. but c.1856); the Rev. J. M. Morrell, *A Dog's Protest Against Intemperance* (1885); Mrs. R. D. Bolton, *And So We Bury Our Dead* (1886); the Rev. George Pope, *Thought-Food for Farmers, Labourers and Artisans, Being Reasons for Becoming a Total Abstainer* (1883); John Abbey, *Temperance in the Hay and Harvest Field* (n.d. but c.1892); J. Johnson, *The Economic Aspect of the Temperance Question* (n.d.); J. Milton Smith, *Nuts to Crack for Moderate Drinkers* (n.d. but c.1890); the Rev. J. Dawson Burns, *Country Walks and Temperance Talks* (1901); O. S. Fowler, *Intemperance and Tight Lacing* (Manchester, n.d. but c.1899); Chas. W. Bateman, *Tippling and*

*Temperance* (1890); and Mrs. Henry Wood. The plays and similar works mentioned were: W. H. Smith and A. Gentleman, *The Drunkard* (1844, John Lane, 1943); Anon., *Seven Nights in a Bar-room* (1855, Middlesbrough on Tees, c.1863) based on the novel by R. S. Arthur, *Ten Nights in a Bar-room* (1855); A. H. Foxwell, *An Awkward Half Hour* (n.d. but c.1889); the Rev. Francis Beardsall, *The Trial of John Barleycorn alias Strong Drink* (Manchester, c.1879); C. D. Hickman and W. Darbyshire, *The Trial of John and Jane Temperance* (Manchester, c.1882) and Samuel C. Hall, *The Trial of Sir Jasper. A Temperance Tale in Verse* (c.1873). The list of amateur entertainers and the advertisement for the inebriates' home appear in the Rev. J. Dennis Hird, *The Guide to C.E.T.S. Work in the London Diocese* (1890); the list of temperance songs in an advertisement for *The Temperance Vocalist* at the end of Foxwell, and the song *Oh I am safe* in Philip Phillips, *Self Deceived* (n.d.). I also used *Temperance Placards* (n.d. but c.1854); *Temperance Mottoes* (n.d.); J.A., *The Turkish Bath: An Antidote for the Cravings of the Drunkard* (Dublin, 1859); Anon., *Temperance Pills* (n.d.); J. Harding, *Facts Relating to Intoxicating Drinks* (1840); and *Pearson's Temperance Reciter* (C. A. Pearson Ltd., 1906). The advertisements for pledge cards, printed tickets, etc., appear in Jollife.

## CHAPTER NINETEEN

My chief sources were Mrs. Mary Bayly, *Ragged Homes and How to Mend Them* (1860); Elizabeth Cotton, *Our Coffee Room* (1876) and *More about Our Coffee Room* (1878); and Mrs. Wightman. The description of country coffee rooms comes in the Duchess of Rutland, *How Intemperance Has Been Successfully Combated* (1893); of Yates's Wine Lodges in *The Spectator* for 9th September 1966; and the novel *Rosa Fielding* in Steven Marcus, *The Other Victorians* (Weidenfeld and Nicolson, 1966). On coffee stalls I used Anon., *The Coffee Public House, How to Establish and Manage It* (1878); and

*Practical Hints on Coffee Stall Management* (1886). The figures on tea and coffee consumption occur in Winskill and the information about temperance in the Forces comes from Miss Sarah Robinson, *Christianity and Teetotalism. A Voice from the Army* (n.d. but c.1876). The indulgent reference to 'Bosun' Smith is made by Burns, his anti-Popery activities are mentioned by Michael Reynolds, *Martyr of Ritualism: Father Mackonochie of St. Alban's, Holborn* (Faber, 1965) and his death by Winskill.

## CHAPTER TWENTY

The origin of the Good Templars is described by Joseph Malins, *Life of Joseph Malins* (Templar Press, Birmingham, 1932) and by Mark Hayler, *The Man from Battle: The Joseph Malins Memorial Lecture* (1950). The Temperance Lifeboat Crews are described by Winskill, *Comprehensive History.* Mother Stewart's tour is recorded in Mrs. Eliza Stewart, *The Crusader in Great Britain* (Springfield, Ohio, 1891). The postmen's blue ribbons are mentioned by Winskill. On Sir Wilfrid Lawson the sources are: R. Coad (editor), *Wisdom Grave and Gay. Select Speeches of Sir Wilfrid Lawson* (1889); W. B. Luke, *Sir Wilfrid Lawson* (1900); and George W. E. Russell (editor), *Sir Wilfrid Lawson, a Memoir* (1909). Dilke's view of Lawson is quoted by Roy Jenkins, *Sir Charles Dilke* (Collins, 1958). I also used the Rev. R. M. Grier, *A Reply to the Bishop of Peterborough* (1876). The Convocation Report is quoted by W. S. Caine, William Hoyle and the Rev. Dawson Burns, *Local Option* (1885); the Shaftesbury Estate is described by Burns; the Bessbrook experiment by Winskill. Joseph Livesey's opposition to the Alliance is described by Carter. The disillusioned teetotaller was Winskill, who also described the founding of the National Prohibition Party. The Cornish local optionist was Morrell and the brave nonconformist minister the Rev. Henry Bell, *Christian Temperance Moral Suasion v. Coercive Legislation* (1885). Other sources used were Joseph A. Scofield, *The Dangers and Fallacies of Local Option* (1885); Fred C. Coley,

*Early Closing of Licensed Premises. A Word to the Wise* (n.d. but c.1887); Malthus Questell Holyoake, *Equitable Licensing Reform* (1883); a report of the *Debate between W. Brigham (United Kingdom Alliance) and J. Danvers Power (National Trade Defence Fund)* (Gloucester, 1889); and, on the Osgoldcross by-election, *The Western Temperance Herald* for August 1899. The Scottish trade paper referred to was *The Scottish Guardian* for 29th April 1967.

## CHAPTER TWENTY-ONE

The modern research on the attitude of the trade to the Liberals is by H. J. Hanham, *Elections and Party Management, Politics in the Time of Disraeli and Gladstone* (Longmans, 1959). On Gothenburg I used Bailie Lewis, *The Gothenburg Licensing System. A Lecture* (Edinburgh, 1873) and Joseph Rowntree and Arthur Sherwell, *British 'Gothenburg' Experiments and Public House Trusts* (Hodder and Stoughton, 1901); on municipalisation Joseph Chamberlain, *Public House Reform* (n.d. but c.1877); on *The Boar's Head* and similar experiments Shadwell (an excellent guide to the whole subject); Joseph Malins, *Public House Trusts and Liquor Municipalisation* (n.d. but c.1902), and private information from Canon Walters. On Trust Houses I used Edmund Vale, *Trust House Story* (privately printed, 1949); Jean Wakeman, *Trust House Britain* (Hodder and Stoughton, 1963); and information from the company. On children I used Joseph Malins, *Serving Children with Intoxicants* (Birmingham, 1902); E. S. Turner, *Roads to Ruin* (Michael Joseph, 1950); Anon., *Child Drunkenness* (n.d. but c.1892); and the Rev. L. B. Currie, *Mothers Awake! A Warning* (C.E.T.S., 1911). On temperance sentiment in the 1880s I also consulted George M'Cree, *The 'Queen's Health'. A Word for the Jubilee Year* (1887). The 'moderation' expert was Shadwell. *The Western Temperance Herald* summing up appeared in October 1898 and the complaints about the Guinness shareholders in Winskill.

## CHAPTER TWENTY-TWO

The mock trial is by E. V. Jones, *The Drink Question. Claim for Fair Consideration and Compensation Brought by the Licensed Victuallers against John Bull Esq.* (1892). Scepticism about the effect of reducing the number of public houses is expressed by W. G. Benham, *New Light on the Temperance Question* (1892). *The United Temperance Gazette* for December 1898 recorded the triumphs in the licensing courts. Burns has a useful appendix on the case against compensation and Carter gives details of the Sharp v. Wakefield case. I also used the Rt. Hon. G. Shaw-Lefevre, *The Licensing Question in Hampshire* (Winchester, 1902), and Edwin A. Pratt, *The Licensed Trade* (John Murray, 1907). On Asquith I used Roy Jenkins, *Asquith* (Collins, 1964) and on the struggle for the Licensing Bill, *The Liberal Magazine* for 1908 and 1909 and the following Liberal Publication Department leaflets and pamphlets: *'The Trade' or the People*; *The Licensing Bill of 1908: Speech by H. H. Asquith*; *The Licensing Bill of 1908: Speech by Sir Thomas Whittaker*; *The Licensing Bill: Its two Main Objects*; *The Brewers' Game or 'Heads I Win, Tails you Lose'*; *The Price of Beer*; *The Fall in Brewery Stocks: Who is Responsible?*; *The Licensing Bill: The Compensation Time Limit*; *The Man in the Street and 'the Robbery Bill'*; *The Licensing Bill and Local Rates*; *The Licensing Bill and the Publican*; and *The Licensing Bill: Fewer Public Houses*. The Bishop of London's 'Midnight March' is described in the *Annual Register* for 1908 and his life, including the playing at 'home' incident, in S. C. Carpenter, *Winnington-Ingram. The Biography of Arthur Foley Winnington-Ingram, Bishop of London, 1901–1939* (Hodder and Stoughton, 1949). The Horatio Bottomley incident and the Peckham by-election are described by Colin Cross, *The Liberals in Power, 1905–1914* (Barrie and Rockliff, 1963) and the Labour Party attitude to licensing is explained by Philip Snowden, *Socialism and the Drink Question* (1908).

## CHAPTER TWENTY-THREE

The outstanding source was Arthur Shadwell, *Drink in 1914–1922: A Lesson in Control* (Longmans, 1923). I also used David Lloyd George, *War Memoirs* (Odhams Press edition, 2 volumes, 1934–6); Harold Nicolson, *King George the Fifth* (Constable, 1952); and George B. Wilson, *Leif Jones, Lord Rhyader, Temperance Reformer and Statesman* (U.K. Alliance, n.d. but post-1939) and *Who Was Who*. Temperance publications issued during the war which I consulted were: Lt.-Col. A. H. Williams, *Drink, the Greatest Foe* (n.d.); the Rev. Mathias Lansdown, *Our Allies, Ourselves and the Drink Problem* (n.d.); John Newton, *Alcohol and the War, the Example of Russia* (n.d.); Marr Murray, *Drink and the War from the Patriotic Point of View* (1915); Sir Victor Horsley, *The Rum Ration in the British Army* (1915); George B. Wilson, *Nationalisation of the Liquor Traffic. Ought the Churches to Advocate It?* (n.d. but c.1915) James Samuelson, *Drink and the War* (Sidmouth, 1916); Arthur Mee and J. Stuart Holden, *Defeat or Victory? The Strength of Britain Book* (1917); Arthur Mee, *The Parasite* (1917) and *The Fiddlers* (1917); and a bound volume of *The Prohibitionist* covering the period. The recent information on the state management schemes came from the Home Office. The liability of teetotallers to V.D., and other anti-teetotal material, came from Ernest E. Williams, and the unrest caused by the beer shortage is described in *True Temperance Monographs*.

## CHAPTER TWENTY-FOUR

The source for most of the critical comments on the temperance movement, Mr. Pussyfoot's adventures and the failure of local option in Scotland was Ernest E. Williams. The prohibitionists' solitary success was described by Edwin Scrymgeour, *Britain's First Prohibition Bill* (Coatbridge, 1923). The

Fellowship of Freedom and Reform was exposed by Arthur B. Barker, the historian referred to, and was criticised by the *Report of the Royal Commission on Licensing* (*England and Wales*) (1932). Sir Arthur Quiller-Couch's heresies on drink are recorded by George B. Wilson, *Leif Jones* (U.K. Alliance, n.d.). The hostile description of 'improved' public houses is by H. Cecil Heath, *The Control of a Dangerous Trade* (1947) and the 'cathedral' comment, and the praise of drink, come from *True Temperance Monographs*. The temperance propagandist mentioned is the Rev. T. Arthur Williams, *Temperance and the Nation* (n.d. but a prize essay at the Royal National Eisteddfod 1930), an example of Welsh teetotalism at its most fanatical, and the source of information on the court cases, the speech about young people and beer and the Ancient Order of Frothblowers. Maud was discovered by Ernest Selley, *The English Public House As It Is* (Longmans, 1927) and the Mass Observation Report is *The Pub and the People* (Gollancz, 1943). On the recent history of the temperance movement I used *The Alliance News*, especially the January–February 1961 issue, figures supplied by various temperance organisations (the comparison with 1892 being based on *The Northern Temperance Yearbook for 1894*); an article in *The Sunday Telegraph* for 18th November 1962, which referred to the survey of Methodists and the decline of Temperance Sunday; and *The Guardian* for 4th February 1963, which referred to the 1961 campaign against licensing applications. The expert who estimated the number of teetotallers was the General Secretary of the National Temperance Federation.

# Index

Abbey, John, 193
Accrington, 39
Acts of Parliament: Licensing Act 1552, 5; Gin Act 1736, 11; Factories Act 1819, 37; Sale of Beer Bill (The Duke of Wellington's Beer Bill) 1830, 20–2, 23, 25–7; Beer Act 1834, 31; Metropolitan Police Act 1839, 159; Forbes-Mackenzie Act 1845, 159; Sale of Beer Act 1854, 162, 166; Sale of Beer Act 1855, 166; Refreshment Houses Act 1860, 228; Public House Closing Act 1864, 229–30; Wine and Beer-House Act 1869, 32; Education Act 1870, 130; Intoxicating Liquors (Licensing) Bill 1871, 230, 242; Intoxicating Liquor (Licensing) Act 1872, 231; Lawson's Resolution 1880, 223; Local Government Bill 1888, 225, 242; Anti-Sipping Act 1901, 239; Licensing Bill 1904, 246; Children's Act 1908, 239; Licensing Bill 1908, 249–56; Temperance (Scotland) Act 1913, 280; Sunday Closing Bill 1914, 168; Defence of the Realm Act 1914, 257; Intoxicating Liquor (Temporary Restrictions) Bill 1914, 257; Defence of the Realm (Amendment No. 3) Bill 1915, 267; Licensing Act 1921, 171, 277; Lady Astor's Act 1923, extended 1953, 239; Licensing Act 1961, 288
Afghanistan, 217
Albert, Prince Consort, 198, 199
Albert Hall, The, 253
Alcohol: Alternatives to, 8, 125, 175–6, 193; and the Bible—*see* Bible Wine Controversy; and Children—*see* Children; as Alleged Cause of Spontaneous Combustion, 174–5; as 'Confederate of V.D.', 264–5; as Love Potion, 9; as Medicine, 172, 178; as Poison, 174; as Theme of Picture Postcards, 283; Attitude of the Churches to, 2–3, 28–9, 39, 53, 66–7, 82, 126, 182–91, 233, 250; Early History of, 1–12; Effect on Animals and Plants, 131, 178–9, on Athletes, 180–1, on Cruelty to Children, 279, on Female Virtue, 194, 290–1, on Mental Effort, 178, on the National Economy, 139, on Public Schoolboys, 132–3, 178; Grape-juice (Non-Alcoholic), 186, 190; in Food, 175; National Expenditure on, 278; Non-Beverage Uses for, 126, 274; Alcoholism, 202, 275, 288
Alliance, The, *see* United Kingdom Alliance
Althorp, Lord, 25
Amethyst Club, the, 290
Amulree, Lord, 281
Ancient Order of Frothblowers, 283
Anderton, David, 44
Anderton, Henry, 47–8, 51, 54, 55
Anglesey, 61
Annan, 270–1
Anti-Prohibition League, The, 276
Appleshaw, Hants, 246
Arundel, 26, 27
Aspatria, 80
Asquith, Herbert Henry, 248, 259
Association for the Suppression of Beershops, 32
Astor, Lady, 290n.
Athenaeum, The, 249
Athy, 112–13
Australia, 265
Austria, 266

Bailey, Captain, 53
Bailey, Nathaniel, 69–70
Baker, The Rev. W. R., 172–3
Balfour, A. J., 249, 253
Balfour, Mrs. Clara, 127
Balmoral, 139, 198
Band of Hope, The, 105, 122–33, 240–1, 279, 284, 287, 290, 291
Band of Hope Union, The, (later the United Kingdom Band of Hope Union), 124–5

Bangor, 266
Bannockburn, 16
Baptists, 39, 121, 136, 152, 183, 185, 190, 215n., 284, 285
Barnet, 84
Barnum, P. T., 196
Bass, Michael, 222, 224
Bath, 32, 66, 73, 105
Bayly, Mrs. Mary, 203–4, 210
Bedfordshire, 85
Beer-houses, *see* Public Houses
Belfast, 34, 35, 107
Belper, 48
Berkeley, Francis, 161, 165, 166, 217
Berkshire, 25, 26, 28, 193, 286
Bessbrook, 221–2
*Bible, The* (used in Temperance arguments), 52, 104, 148, 152, 183, 185, 186, 187, 190; Cana, Miracle at, 186–7; *Deuteronomy*, 185; Good Samaritan, The, 3; *Isaiah*, 187; Last Supper, The, 185; Passover, The, 186, 187; St. Paul, 52, 104, 186, 187, 188, 190; *Song of Solomon*, 187; Timothy, 104, 148, 186, 187, 188, 191; *Zechariah*, 187
Bible Christians, The, 33, 89
'Bible Wine Controversy', 185–91
Birmingham, 24, 35, 48, 57, 65, 118, 152, 161, 233, 245, 282
Bishopswearmouth, Sunderland, 79
Black, Sir Cyril, 285–6, 291
Blackburn, 40, 48, 77, 244; Temperance Society, 56–7
Blackheath, 170
Blomfield, Charles, 35, 59
Blondin, 180
Blue Ribbon movement, 216
Bodmin, 54, 67–8, 173
Bolton, 35, 40, 56, 138, 155, 283–4, 288
Bolton, Mrs. R. D., 178, 193
'Bona fide travellers', 163–7, 170–1
'Bootlegger', 135
Boston, 33, 144, 174, 196
Bottomley, Horatio, 253
Bournemouth, 246
Bradford, 35, 43, 57, 63, 65, 93, 115; Temperance Society, 35, 57
Bradlaugh, Charles, 190
Brampton, Cumberland, 80
Brewers' Society, 282
Brighton, 180
Bristol, 35, 65–70, 72, 86, 115, 161, 166, 194, 269, 289
British and Foreign Society for the Suppression of Intemperance ('Suppression Society'), 60
British and Foreign Temperance Society, 35, 50, 57–8, 96
British Association for the Promotion of Temperance, *see* British Temperance League
British League of Juvenile Abstainers, 121–5
British Medical Association, 176, 262
British Medical Temperance Association, 176
British National Temperance League, 60n., 289
British Teetotal Temperance Society, 51, 59
British Temperance Association (later British Temperance League, q.v.) 56, 58, 78, 241
British Temperance League, 56, 58, 60n., 138
British Temperance Society, 289
British Women's Temperance Association, 216, 240
British Women's Total Abstinence Union, 279, 280
Broadcasting: Radio, 281, 283; Television, 290
Brodbelt, John, 44, 51, 121
Brotherton, Joseph, 89, 92, 95, 136
Brougham, Lord, 116
Browne, Sir James Crichton, 180
Bruce, Henry, 230, 231, 242
Buckingham, James Silk, 59, 83, 89, 124, 134, 135, 136, 150, 168, 174, 291
Buckinghamshire, 25
Burnley, 49, 65
Burns, The Rev. James Dawson, 136, 147, 187, 193
Burton, Westmorland, 78
Burton-on-Trent, 249
Butler, R. A., 285

Cadbury, John, 57
Caernarvon, 61
Calcraft the younger, John, 20
Camborne, 71, 272
Cambridge, 180, 181
Cambridgeshire Public House Trust, 252
Campbell-Bannerman, Sir Henry, 248
Canada, 49, 174, 236, 264–5
Canterbury, 221
Canterbury, Archbishop of, 219, 243, 247, 255; Memorial to, 219–20
Canterbury, Convocation of, 189; Report of Convocation on Intemperance, 221
Card, Nathaniel, 136
Cardiff, 167, 286, 288
Carlile, Anne Jane, 122
Carlisle, 83, 217, 269, 270, 271, 272, 273, 281, 285, Bishop of, 272
Carlisle State Management District, 272, 277

Carlow, 112
Carlyle, Jane Welsh, 116
Carlyle, Thomas, 115
Cashel, Galway, 108
Cassell, John ('The Manchester Carpenter'), 62–3, 135–6
Catholic Total Abstinence Society, 183
Cecil, Lord Robert, 252
Central Association for Stopping the Sale of Intoxicating Liquors on Sunday, 168
Central Liquor Control Board, 267–71, 277
Chadwick, Edwin, 94
Chamberlain, Joseph, 233
Chandos, Marquess of, 27
Chartists, 45, 152
Chatsworth, 161
Cheltenham, 24
Cheshire, 55–6
Chester, Bishop of, 233, 235
Children: Anti-drink Literature for, 125–30; 'Child-messengers', 238–9; Essay competition for, 131; Given drink by parents, 38–40, 93, 129; *see also* Acts of Parliament, Children's Act; Band of Hope; Pledges, Children's
Chocolate and cocoa, 8, 180, 207, 209, 211, 259, 262, 278
Cholera, 104, 109, 173, 204; Blamed on Intemperance, 173, 179; Brandy as Cure for, 172; Feigning of to Obtain Brandy, 162
Church of England, The, 53, 149, 157, 184, 188, 189, 190, 205, 213, 220, 247
Church of England Temperance Society, 180, 189, 190, 218, 220, 240, 279, 288
Churchill, Lord Randolph, 225
Churchill, Winston, 253n., 254, 280
Church of Scotland Women's Section, 289
*Church Times, The*, 189
Cinema, 280
Cirencester, 70
Clarke, Ebenezer, 127
Clough, John ('Colin'), 87
Club and Institutes Union, 252
Clyde District, 265
Cobbett, William, 38, 92, 152
Coffee, 8, 43, 73, 74, 75, 94, 95, 149, 193, 197, 207, 210, 211, 222, 235, 237
Coffee Public House Association, 210
Coffee-houses, 8, 35, 195, 206–10
Coffee-stalls, 210–11
Collins, William, 34, 35, 63
Commercial Travellers' Temperance Society, 35
Committee on Public Breweries, 14
Congregationalists, 272
Consumers' Association, 272
Conway, 126
Cork, 108–10, 114, 115, 117, 120, 259
Cornwall, 60, 71, 90, 101,168, 226, 279
Cornwall Teetotal Association, 67
Cotton, Elizabeth (later Lady Hope), 206–8, 210, 212
Covent Garden, 93
Cowherdites, The (later known as The Bible Christians, q.v.), 33
Crewe, Lord, 255
Cromarty, 268, 269, 281
Cruikshank, George, 124, 125, 135, 197, 198
Crystal Palace, The, 123, 130, 155, 241
Cumberland, 80

D'Abernon, Lord, 268
Dartmoor, 212
Davidson, Dr., Archbishop of Canterbury, 247
Davies, Clement, 287
Davies, J. Glyn, 126
'Democritus', 103, 174
Denbighshire, 65
Denton, Paul, 150
Devonport, 244
Devonshire, 28, 65, 66, 69, 193, 235, 236, 253
Devonshire, Duke of, 161
Dewsbury, 253
Dickens, Charles, 105, 174
Dickinson, Edward, 44, 51
Dilke, Sir Charles, 217
*Discovery, The*, 180
'Disinterested management', 233–8, *see also* Carlisle State Management District, Gothenburg
Disraeli, Benjamin, 218
Donnybrook Fair, 15
Donovan, Father, 108
Doré, Gustave, 197
Dorking, 207, 210
Dorset, 279
Douglas, Aretas Akers, 246
Dow, Neal, 135, 151, 153
Driberg, Tom, 286
Drinking Customs: 'Ales', 3; 'Drinking for a Muzzle', 6; in churches, 182; Pin-drinking, 3; Drinking Usages, 17–20, 38
Drugs, 279, 290; Adulteration by, 14; Laudanum, 155
Drunken Committee', 'The, *see* Select Committee on Drunkenness
Drunkenness, 3, 6, 7, 12, 15, 16, 37, 53–4, 90–3, 94, 107, 114–15, 137, 149, 159, 167, 201, 219, 228, 232, 247, 260–1, 269–70, 275
Dublin, 10, 15, 18, 34, 109, 112, 122, 259
Dukes, Dr. Clement, 132

Dumfriesshire, 270
Dundee, 75
Dunfermline Association for the Promotion of Temperance, 35
Dunfermline Temperance Society, 34–5
Dunlop, John, 17–20, 34, 38, 59–60, 107
Dunse, 147
Durham (City), 105
Durham (County), 82–3
Durham, Bishop of, 140

East Ham, 199
East India Company, 91, 96
East Preston, Sussex, 177
Eaton, Joseph ('Old Iron Hoop'), 72
Eccles, 163
Ede, James Chuter, 284
Edgar, Dr. John, 34–5, 107
Edinburgh, 15, 121, 123, 125, 147, 149, 159, 190, 225; Lord Provost of, 159
Edwards, Jeffery, 34
Egham, 31
Enfield Lock, 269, 272
Essex, 24, 25, 29, 30, 84, 85
Esterbrooke, John, 123
Everlasting Club, The, 7
Exeter, 66–7, 72, 100, 194, 222; Archdeacon of, 132; Bishop of, 222
Exeter Hall, 51, 58–9, 83, 124, 135, 146, 149, 154, 156

Farnham Case', 'The, 245
Fellowship of Freedom and Reform, 277
Finch, John, 36, 37, 44, 45, 47, 53, 107
Flushing, nr. Falmouth, 90
Folkestone, 147
Forbes, Henry, 35, 43
Fowey, 74
Framlingham, Suffolk, 85
France, 34, 228, 261, 263, 264
Free Church Council, 267
Freedom Association, 279
Fry, Elizabeth, 122

Garibaldi, 215
Garnett, Samuel, 72
Garstang, 65
George V, King, 266
Germany, 266
Gin Palaces, *see* Public Houses
Gladstone, W. E., 113, 223, 225, 228, 230, 231
Glasgow, 34, 115, 153, 155, 159
Glasgow and West of Scotland Temperance Society, (later Scottish Temperance Society), 34
Gloucestershire, 70
Good Templars, The Independent Order of, 125, 214, 216, 224, 234, 240, 266, 279, 281, 289
Goodwood, 237
Goschen, George, 242
Gothenburg System, 232–3, 270
Gough, John B., 144–51, 153–6, 182, 184, 214, 240; *Autobiography*, 145, 155
Grace, W. G., 181
Gratrix, John, 44, 51
Gravesend, 163
Grayshott and District Refreshment Association, 236
Great Exhibition, 1851, The, 134
Great Pitmen's Strike, 105
Greenock, 17, 34
Greenwich, 84, 162
Greenwood, Arthur, 281
Gretna, 269–70, 272, 281
Grey, Earl, 236–7
Grindleton, 76
Grindrod, Dr. Ralph, 61–2, 172
Grossmith, George, 170
Grosvenor, Lord Robert, 164
Grubb, Edward, 48, 60, 155
Guardians of the Poor, 177
Guinness's Brewery, 240–1, 259

Haigh, William, 54
Halifax, 57, 115
Hampshire, 24, 28–9, 235, 245–6
Hampstead, 163, 170
Hampton Court, 162
Hampton Lucy, Warwickshire, 234
Hanley, 24
Hanway, Jonas, 8
Harcourt, Sir William, 225
Hardie, Keir, 247
Harlow, 85
Haslingden, 54
Hastings, 29, 253
Healy, Tim, 259
Hector, New York State, 33
Henderson, Arthur, 267
Henley, 180
Hereford, 253; Bishop of, 255
Hertfordshire, 245
Hertfordshire Trust, 237
Hicks, Bishop, of Lincoln, 189
Hitchin, Herts., 245
Hobbs, Jack, 181
Hockings, John ('The Birmingham Blacksmith'), 48–9, 118
Hole, Dr. S. R., 189
Holloway, 170
Hope, John, 121, 123, 125, 190
Horabites, The Independent Order of, 74
Horsham, 16–17
Horsley, Sir Victor, 176–9, 261
House of Commons, 14, 20, 24–5, 27, 91, 94, 96, 160–1, 216–18, 228–9, 231, 247, 251–2, 255, 267, 269

House of Lords, 11, 92, 218, 227, 235, 245, 247, 252, 256
Howarth, William ('Slender Billy'), 47, 50
Huddersfield, 115, 151; Temperance Society, 54
Hudson, Thomas, 69, 70, 71, 73, 74
Hull, 4, 131
Hume, Joseph, 92
Hunt, Henry, 38
Huntingdon, 249
Hurstbourne Tarrant, Hants, 246
Hyde Park, 88, 164–6, 187, 253–4

Icklesham, 25
India, 1, 9, 137
Industrial Revolution, 12, 37
Ingatestone, 24
Inn Signs, 4, 139–40
Insurance, Marine, 61
Inwards, Jabez, 139
Ipswich, 229
Ireland, 13, 15, 19, 34, 107, 166, 259
Isle of Man, The, 64–5
Isle of Wight, The, 168
Islington, 177
Italy, 9, 215, 264
Itchen Abbas, 28

Janson, William ('Barley Water Billy'), 61
Jellicoe, Admiral, 265
Jersey, 147
Jesuits, 183
Jews, 186
John, Servant to Fr. Mathew, 117
Johnson, W. E. ('Pussyfoot'), 276–8, 280
Jones, Leif (later Lord Rhayader), 268, 271–2, 278

Kellogg, F. W., 135, 144, 146
Kendal, 79, 245
Kennedy Judgment', 'The, 248
Kennington, 83
Kensington, 190
Kensington Potteries, The, 203
Kent, 65, 144, 163
Kerry, 110
Keswick, 79–80
Kettering, 82
Kidderminster, 249
Kilkenny, 108
Killarney, 115
King, John, 43–4, 51, 54, 241
Kingstown, 117
Kitchener, Lord, 260–1

Lamb, Thomas, 75
Lambeth, 30, 162, 264
Lancashire, 24, 33, 55–6, 60, 62, 65, 68–9, 163, 168, 209
Lancaster, 40, 61, 77, 78
Lansdowne, Lord, 255–6, 268
Law, Bonar, 267
Lawson, Sir Wilfrid (the elder), 80, 217n.
Lawson, Sir Wilfrid (the Younger), 80, 216–27, 229, 232, 247, 272
League of Juvenile Abstainers, 125
Leeds, 35, 121–3, 147, 160–1, 253; Music Hall, 152, 154, 209
Lees, Dr. Frederick ('Orator' Lees), 139, 151–7, 173, 184–6, 214, 239
Leicester, 83, 134; Total Abstinence Society, 48
Leigh, 48
Liberty and Property Defence League, 252
Licensed Trade, 3–8, 10–14, 20–32, 84, 92–4, 96, 99, 112, 114, 135–42, 158–71, 196, 209, 215–91; Attacks on, 93, 99–100, 128, 136–42, 200, 210–11, 215–16, 218, 240, 244–7, 282–3; Attempts at Self-defence, 116, 140–2, 160, 222, 230, 242, 249–54, 278–9; Compensation Controversy, 242–56; Proposal for State Purchase, 266–7, 272; *see also* 'Disinterested Management', Public Houses
Licensed Victuallers Protection Association, 141
Lichfield, 12
Liebig, Professor, 175
Limehouse, 93
Limerick, 110, 112, 115
Lincoln, 158, 260; Bishop of, 159, 184, 188–9
Liverpool, 18, 23, 32–3, 36, 44, 48, 53, 56, 64, 94, 96, 115, 129, 138, 147, 209, 269; Temperance Society, 33, 58
Livesey, Joseph, 37–46, 47, 49–54, 56–7, 59, 63–4, 66, 77–8, 83–4, 90, 136, 138, 152, 173, 175, 200, 222–3, 241, 281, 291
Livesey, Mrs., 39, 45, 74
Llandaff, Lord, 108
Llanfair, 63
Lloyd George, David, 251, 253n., 256, 258–9, 265–6, 267, 273, 275
Local Government Board, 177
Local Option, *see* Prohibition and The Permissive Bill
Lockhart's Cocoa Rooms, 209
London, 5–7, 26, 30, 35, 47–8, 50, 57, 59, 61–3, 65, 74, 83–4, 86, 93, 104, 115, 116, 123–5, 132, 153, 155, 160, 162–5, 174, 177, 180, 193, 195, 198, 203, 206, 213, 221, 228, 237, 253–4, 258, 279, 282, 286–7; Bishop of, 237,

247, 253; County Council, 282; Entertainment Society, 199; School Board, 130
London Temperance Hospital, The, 176
London Temperance League, 60, 134–5, 144, 146, 147
London Temperance Society, *see* British and Foreign Temperance Society
Loughborough, 134
Low Countries, The, 4, 6, 9, 261
Luton, 85, 177

Macnish, Robert, 172
Magee, Dr. William, Bishop of Peterborough, 219–20
Maguire, John Francis, 113, 117–19
Maine Law, *see* Prohibition
Malins, Joseph, 214, 234–6
Malvern Spa, 62
Manchester, 16, 35, 46, 49, 53, 55, 61–2, 65, 75, 80n., 83, 115, 136, 138, 155, 160, 163, 172, 190, 194, 197, 238, 253, 282
Manning, Cardinal, 139, 183, 231
Market Harborough, 83
Marlborough, Duke of, 164
Martin, William ('Billy'), 109–10
Marylebone, 160
Maryport, Cumberland, 80, 270
Mathew, Father Theobald, 108–20, 122, 136, 173, 183–4, 201, 240
Maynooth College, 108, 113
Mee, Arthur, 264, 273
Memorial Hall, The, Farringdon Street, 224
Mercier, Dr. C. A., 179–80
Mersey, The River, 18, 36, 209
Merthyr Tydfil, 27
Methodists, 46, 64, 67, 80, 98–101, 112, 145, 150, 283, 288
Metropolitan Free Drinking Fountain Association, 206
Mexico, 264
Michaelmas Fair, 3
Middle Classes Defence Organisation, 252
Miles Platting, 55
Minehead, 73n., 193
Mitchell, John, 123
Modbury, nr. Plymouth, 70
Mohammedans, 186
Moore', 'Father, 74
'Moral Suasionists', 135, 137, 153, 253
Moreau, New York State, 33
Morpeth, Lord, 11
Morrell, The Rev. J. M., 168, 170, 229, 279
Mortehoe, 193
Mothers' Society, 204
Mudge, Henry, 54, 67, 173

National British Women's Temperance Association, 235
National British Women's Total Abstinence Union, 289–90
National Commercial Temperance League, 280
National Efficiency Committee, 273
National Society for the Prevention of Cruelty to Children, 279
National Temperance Federation, 266, 289
National Temperance League, 60, 96, 153, 241
National Temperance Publications Depot, 200
National Temperance Society, 60
Neath, 66
New British and Foreign Temperance Society for the Suppression of Intemperance, 59, 103
New York, 144, 148
Newark, 82
Newburyport, 145
Newcastle, 35, 80, 82, 275
Newcastle Programme, 225
Newhaven, 268
Nightingale, Florence, 139
Norfolk, 24, 26, 28–9
Norfolk, Duke of, 116
North of England Temperance League, 289
North Wales Temperance Association, 75
Northampton, 183, 185
Northamptonshire, 82, 183, 185
Northamptonshire Chamber of Agriculture, 193
Northumberland, 50, 82, 217
Norwich, Bishop of, 175
Nottinghamshire, 153, 180
Nunney, nr. Frome, 72

O'Brien, William, 259
O'Connell, Daniel, 95, 114
Okell, George ('The Rector of the Obelisk'), 48
Old Cockpit, The, Preston, 43, 45–6, 49, 64–5, 67
Orkney Islands, The, 156
Osborne, Sir Cyril, 286
Osgoldcross, Yorkshire, By-election, 226
Oswestry, 103
Oxford, 132, 147, 272
Oxfordshire, 208

Page, The Rev. Thomas, 31–2
Paisley Juvenile Temperance Association, 121
Palmerston, Lord, 217

Palmerston Mission Working Men's Choir, 199
Parsonstown, 112
Pasteur, Louis, 180
Paxton, Sir Joseph, 161
Peckham, 251, 253
Peel, John, 217
Peel, Lord, 243, 247
Peel, Sir Robert, 116
Pennsylvania, 196n.
Penrhyn, 71
Penrith Temperance Society, 79
Penzance, 74, 102, 147, 168, 213
People's Café Company, 210
People's Refreshment Houses Association, 235
Permissive Bill, The, 216, 218–22, 223–4, 226
Perth, 260
Peterborough, 219; Bishop of, *see* Magee, Dr. William
Philadelphia, 33
Phiz, 103
Piccadilly, 163
Pilkington, Lancs., 24
Place, Francis, 94, 96
Pledges: 'American', 59–60; Chastity, 290; Children's, 61, 121–3, 129–30, 184; 'Extreme Necessity', 56; 'Long' and 'Short', 59; 'Moderation', 33–5, 55–60; Religious Significance of, 184; St. Ives Teetotallers, 100; Spinsters' and Widows', 63; Teetotal, 33–5, 43–4, 46, 53, 55–60, 184, 190, 208; 'War of the Pledges', 59
Plymouth, 70, 86, 194
Political Parties: Conservatives, 224, 231–2, 242, 246, 249, 255, 266–8, 285; Labour, 224, 247, 267–8, 281, 284–7; Liberals, 222–4, 227, 229–30, 232, 247, 249, 251–5, 285; Radicals, 27, 38, 45, 88, 89, 92, 96, 152, 216, 218, 221, 226; Tories, 20; Whigs, 20
Polk, President, 120
Pollard, William, 80n.
Pope, The Rev. George, 193
Portland, Maine, U.S.A., 135
Port Sunlight, Cheshire, 221
Portsmouth, 138
Presbyterians, 122, 182, 188, 190
Preston, 36–40, 42, 44–5, 47–9, 51–2, 56–7, 60–1, 64–8, 74, 76, 78, 81, 83, 98, 107, 241, 253, 281, 291
Preston Temperance Society, 42–3, 56, 65
Preston Total Abstinence Society for Boys and Girls, 121
Primitive Methodists, 72, 98, 99, 183
Prince of Wales, The (later Edward VII), 124, 199, 255
Prohibition: in Britain, 216, 220, 223, 248, 253, 280, 281; in the United States, 127n., 194, 214, 264, 276, 278, 280, 281; Maine, 130, 136, 218, 282; Maine Law, 135, 136, 150, 153, 159, 196; National Prohibition Party, 224, 272; Prohibitionists, 95, 135–43, 151, 153, 168, 192, 216, 225, 263, 267, 268, 272–3, 275; Scottish Prohibition Party, 224; *see also* United Kingdom Alliance
Public Houses, 2–5, 7–8, 10–11, 13–14, 16, 20, 23–31, 37, 71, 74, 78, 84, 92–4, 96, 138, 141, 150, 161, 196, 208, 221, 229–30, 233–9, 243–4, 248, 254, 267, 274, 281–3; *Boar's Head, The*, Hampton Lucy, 234; *Gretna Tavern, The*, 271; *Waggon and Horses, The*, Ridge Hill, 237; Opening Hours, 229–30, 243, 257–8, 268, 275, 277
Public House Trusts, *see* 'Disinterested Management'
Publicans' Parliament', 'The, 231
Pudsey, 253
'Pussyfoot', 276

Quakers, 33, 71, 109, 115, 136, 182, 221
Quiller-Couch, Sir Arthur, 278–9

Reading, 13, 26, 245; Temperance Council, 245
Rechabites, The Independent Order of, 65–6, 104–5, 240, 279, 289
Reigate, 177
Rhondda, The, 288
Rhyl Temperance Society, 61
Richardson, Dr. Benjamin Ward, 126
Richmond, 162
Ringmer, 25
Ringwood, 29
Robinson, Miss Sarah, 212
Rochdale, 46
Rochester, Dean of, *see* Hole, Dr. S. R.
Roebuck, John, 27, 168, 218
Roman Catholics, 53, 108, 113, 183–4, 219, 284
Rosebery, Lord, 225, 255
Rouse the Nation Council, 281
Royal Commission on Licensing, 1860, 159, 226, 234; 1896, 170 243, 245; 1929, 278, 281
Royal Commission on Sunday Closing in Wales, 167
Royal Naval Temperance Society, 244
Rugby School, 132, 178
Rum Ration in the Armed Forces, 212, 261–2, 268n.
Rumney, 167
Rural Labourers League, 252
Russell, G. W. E., 137

Russell, Lord John, 95, 119
Russia, 263, 264, 274
Russom, J., 32
Rutland, Duchess of, 208

St. Ives, 67, 98–101, 152, 185, 226
St. Just, 100
Salford, 33, 65, 89, 163, 229, 250
Salisbury Infirmary, 177
Salisbury, Lord, 224, 229, 243, 255
Salvation Army, The, 290
San Francisco, 174
Sandgate, 144
Sandringham, 199
Scarborough, 87–8
Scotch Baptists, 39
Scotland, 9, 15, 17–18, 34, 107, 137, 153, 159, 166, 168, 227
Scottish Licensing Committee, 227
Scottish Temperance League, 137, 195, 222
Scrymgeour, Edwin, 280
Sebastopol, 136–7
Select Committees: on Beerhouses, 27, 31; on the Control of Places of Public Entertainment, 1853, 160–1; on Drunkenness, 37, 92, 94–5; on Intemperance, 219; on Sunday Closing, 165–6
Shaftesbury, Lord, 210
Shaftesbury Park Estate, 221
Shapcott, John, 72
Sharp *v.* Wakefield, The Case of, 245
Sharpe, Dr. William, 178
Sheffield, 56, 60n., 91, 96, 138, 154, 161, 168, 260, 289
Shildon, nr. Bishop Auckland, 83
Shirley, Stephen, 124–5
Shoreditch, 162
Shotley Bridge, nr. Newcastle, 80–1
Shrewsbury, 8, 99, 139, 205–6
Shropshire, 103
Sicily, 186
Skibbereen, 34
Skye, 15
Slaney, R. A., 206
Sly', 'Sam, 73, 105
Smeeton, Thomas, 103–4, 174, 190
Smith, F. E., 249
Smith, George, ('Bosun'), 213
Smith, Harold, 250
Smith, John, 37, 44, 51
Smith, The Rev. Sydney, 25
Smollett, Tobias, 10
Snow, Dr. John, 173
Snowden, Philip, 247, 249, 279
Somerset, 65–6, 69, 72, 87
Songs and Verses: Anti-Temperance, 68, 276–7; Drinking, 4–5, 18
Sons of Temperance, 240, 289
Soskice, Sir Frank, 286
South Africa, 217, 265
South Shields, 183
Southampton, 162; Temperance Society, 57
Southwark, 183
Spurgeon, The Rev. Charles, 241
Staffordshire, 24, 168, 215
Stanhope, Earl, 59–60
Stewart, Mrs. Eliza ('Mother'), 216
Stirling, 16
Stockport, 46, 76
Stockton-on-Tees, 250
Stockwell Asylum, 177
Street, nr. Glastonbury, 66, 70, 87
Strength of Britain movement, 273
Sturge, Dr. Mary, 178–9
Suffolk, 85
Sunday Closing, 4–5, 31, 94, 96, 158, 171, 230, 243, 249, 268, 277, 286–7
Sunderland, 79, 81–2, 215
Surrey, 30–1, 206, 245
Sussex, 16, 25–6, 28, 177, 235
Swansea, 66
Sweden, 232–3
Swindlehurst, Thomas, 36, 45, 47, 56

Tait, Dr., Archbishop of Canterbury, 255
Tara, 114
Taunton, 66, 86
Tavistock, 194
Taxation: of Drink, 9–11, 21, 30, 220, 242, 258–9, 278; of Tea, Chocolate and Coffee, 8, 95, 259
Tea, 8, 43, 73, 95, 103, 143, 149, 155, 175, 193, 207, 210, 211, 212, 222, 235, 237, 259, 262–3; alleged ill effects of, 279
Teare, James, 42, 45, 64–8, 71, 76, 78, 86, 98, 139
'Teetotal' (the word), 33, 46–7
Teetotal Wesleyan Methodists of St. Ives, 100
Temperance Council of Christian Churches, 280, 290
Temperance Lifeboat Crews, 215
Temperance Movement: and the Army, 212, 260; Attitude of Medical Profession to, 61, 172–3, 176–8, 278; Bands, 72, 118; Boarding Houses and Hotels, 61, 74–5, 149, 221, 243; Captured by Teetotallers, 54; Conferences, 55–6, 59–60, 132; Connection with Evangelicals, 53; with Improving Conditions of Rural Life, 208–9, with Radical Politicians, 106, 247; with Sanitary Movement, 206; with Social Reform, 203; Effect of American

Prohibition on, 276, 280; of Crimean War, 136–7, 165; of Economic Depression, 280; of First World War, 275; of Great Pitmen's Strike, 105–6; of Indian Mutiny, 137; of Irish Famine, 119; Excursions, 134, 206–8; Halls, 65; Libraries and Reading Rooms, 118–19; Mechanics' Institution, 61; Medals, 118–19; and the Navy, 212–13; Nicknames for Moderation Men, 54; for Teetotallers, 73, 222; Origins in United States, 33; in Great Britain, 33–5; Paid Agents, 64, 121; Periodicals, 50, 192; Prejudice against, 103; Processions, Fetes, etc., 56, 73, 114, 134, 147; Pseudo-Temperance Societies, 277; Significance of 'Teetotal Pig', 69; of Stuffed Birds, 63; Strength of, 34, 60–1, 239–40, 288–90; in Parliament, 291; Violence against, 48, 56, 66, 70–1, 77, 80, 82, 84–7, 116, 138–9, 164–6, 222, 276–8; *see also* under names of individuals and places
Temperance Pills, 201–2
Temperance Placards, 200
Temperance Propaganda: Almanacks, 200; Alphabets, 127–8; Drawings and Paintings, 109–10, 198; Lantern Slides, 197–8, 238; Lozenges, 201; Mugs, 201; Picture Books, 128; Plays, 195–7; Recitations, 200; Songs and Verses, 48, 122–3, 125–8, 150, 169, 196–200, 216; Wafers, 201; Wallpaper, 201
Templar and Temperance Orphanage, The, 214
Temple, Dr., Bishop of Exeter, 222
Tenniel, John, 197
Texas, 150
Thomas, George, 286
Thomas, Iowerth, 288
Tied-house System, 13–14, 248, 252
*Times, The*, 96, 116, 137, 142, 147, 159, 162–3, 164, 218, 251, 254, 262–3, 271, 276
Tipperary, 110
Tiverton, 72
Todd, Dr. Robert, 172
Tottenham, 84
True Temperance Association, 278, 281–2
Trust Houses Ltd., 237
Tunnicliff, The Rev. Jabez, 121–3
Turner, The Rev. Jonathan, 99–102, 152, 226
Turner, Richard ('Dicky'), 46–7, 56

United Free Church of Scotland, The, 289
United Kingdom Alliance, The, 136–43, 151, 153, 216, 223–5, 231, 253, 266–7, 272, 276, 282, 289
United States, The, 33, 75, 96, 120, 127n., 144, 153, 156, 159, 194–6, 214, 216, 264, 276
United Temperance Councils, 240, 244–5
Ulster Temperance Society, 34
University College Hospital, 176
Uxbridge, 84

Victoria, Queen, 12, 119, 139, 178, 198–9, 217, 239, 241

Wakefield, 81, 115
Wakley, Thomas, 165–6
Wales, 14, 23, 60, 63, 159, 166, 168, 227
Walton, 38
Wantage, 26
Wapping, 94
Warrington Temperance Society, 35, 52, 55–6
Washington, 279
Washingtonians, The, 145
Water, 109, 126, 150, 186, 220
Water-treatment, (Hydropathy), 201
Waterford, 110, 112
Watford, 250
Wellington, Duke of, 22, 32, 116
Wesley, John, 67, 98
Wesleyans, 66, 71, 80, 98, 99, 157, 183, 188, 215, 269
Western Temperance League, 240, 277, 289
Westminster, 93, 123, 180, 218, 233, 253
Westminster, Duke of, 210
Westmorland, 78, 245
Weston, Miss Agnes, 212–13
Weston, E. P., 180
Weymouth, 283
Whitbread, Samuel, 249
Whitby Lifeboat, The Loss of the, 87
Whittaker, Thomas, 76–88, 118, 136, 175, 182
Whittaker, Sir Thomas P., 243, 247, 249, 254, 267
Wigan, 40
Wightman, Mr. and Mrs. Charles, 205
Wilsden, nr. Bradford, 63
Wilson, The Rev. T. P., 129
Wilson, William, 153–4
Wiltshire, 203
Wimbledon, 291
Winchester, 28, 246
Windsor, 162
Windsor Castle, 198
Winskill, Peter, 215–16
Wolverhampton Workhouse, 177
Wood, Mrs. Henry, 195

Woodstock, 208
Worcester, 253
Wordsworth, Dr. Christopher, Bishop of Lincoln, 158, 188
Workhouse Drink Reform League, 177
World Temperance Convention, 47, 96
World War, First, 257–74
World War, Second, 284
Wright, Frank, 190–1, 241

Yates's Wine Lodges, 209
Yeovil, 182, 276
York, 115; Archbishop of, 164–5, 219; Convocation of, 189
Yorkshire, 56, 65, 76, 168
Young Abstainer's Union, 132